LITERARY/CULTURAL THEORY

NATIONS AND NATIONAL ISMS

Literary/Cultural Theory provides concise and lucid introductions to a range of key concepts and theorists in contemporary literary and cultural theory. Original and contemporary in presentation, and eschewing jargon, each book in the series presents students of humanities and social sciences exhaustive overviews of theories and theorists, while also introducing them to the mechanics of reading literary/cultural texts using critical tools. Each book also carries glossaries of key terms and ideas, and pointers for further reading and research. Written by scholar-teachers who have taught critical theory for years, and vetted by some of the foremost experts in the field, the series Literary/Cultural Theory is indispensable to students and teachers.

Also in the series

Psychoanalytic Theory and Criticism
Feminisms
Jacques Lacan
Dalit Literature and Criticism
Ecocriticism
Postcolonialism Now
Modernisms
Marxist Literary and Cultural Theory
Postmodernisms
Mikhail Bakhtin
Popular Culture
Queer Studies
Frantz Fanon

LITERARY/CULTURAL THEORY

NATIONS AND NATIONAL ISMS

A SHORT INTRODUCTION

KAUSTAV CHAKRABORTY
Southfield College, Darjeeling, West Bengal

Edited by
KRISHNA SEN
University of Calcutta

Orient BlackSwan

NATIONS AND NATIONALISMS: A SHORT INTRODUCTION

ORIENT BLACKSWAN PRIVATE LIMITED

Registered Office
3-6-752 Himayatnagar, Hyderabad 500 029, Telangana, India
Email: centraloffice@orientblackswan.com

Other Offices
Bengaluru, Chennai, Guwahati, Hyderabad, Kolkata, Mumbai, New Delhi, Noida, Patna, Visakhapatnam

First published 2021

ISBN 978 93 5442 056 6

Typeset in Aldine 401 BT 10.5/13 *by*
Akhil Offset Printers
Hyderabad 500 020

033316

Printed at
Graphica Printers and Binders,
Hyderabad 500 013

Published by
Orient Blackswan Private Limited
3-6-752, Himayatnagar,
Hyderabad 500 029, Telangana, India
Email: info@orientblackswan.com

Contents

Editor's Preface

The idea of the nation is in jeopardy today. From India to Africa to Eastern Europe and the Americas religious and ethnic minorities, subnational factions and a variety of neo-liberal interest groups are vociferously contesting the paradigm of the homogeneous nation and its emblems, the national flag and the national anthem. Simultaneously, neocolonial market capitalism, global cultural hegemonies, cross-border pandemics and ecological disasters, the worldwide tentacles of social media and the digital revolution, and the scourge of international terrorism, all threaten to destabilise the integrity of the bounded nation. Nationalism, which Rabindranath Tagore had championed in 1917 as the elixir to reinvigorate his enslaved homeland, is all too often denounced nowadays as archaic or right-wing or even dangerously fascist. Tagore's brief, in his *Nationalism*, had of course been for adherence to India's ancient civilisational values together with a cosmopolitanism based on liberal ideals, and not to a chauvinistic patriotism. However, in this era of transnational nomadism, when even sections of the 'middle class' own homes and businesses on more than one continent, and the world has transited to what might be called 'soft' national borders being criss-crossed with ease by 'globizens' (global citizens), the whole issue of cultural allegiance to a specific civilisation may well be interrogated. Indeed, with several diasporic communities now legally holding dual passports, the very notion of nationality has become ambivalent. Clearly, the time is ripe for a critical review of monologic formulations and overarching imaginaries of the nation.

Kaustav Chakraborty's monograph, *Nations and Nationalisms* (the plurals in the title tell their own story), published as part of Orient BlackSwan's *Literary/Cultural Theory* series, addresses precisely these dichotomies and dilemmas. It does this by tracking the many contending manifestations of nationhood that exist today – ideological, identitarian, isolationist, expansionist, internationalist – and contextualising them within actual historical circumstances, as well as cultural formations articulating these concerns. As the editor of this interdisciplinary study, I note its relevance for diverse academic fields, from the social sciences to the liberal arts – political science, history, sociology, area studies, cultural studies, philosophy and literature. This book will also appeal to the general reader in its lucid analysis of major theoretical and empirical issues, with a special focus on the Indian subcontinent and apposite illustrations from contemporary situations ranging from populist politics to tribal econationalisms and the social repercussions of the Covid-19 catastrophes. The short but up-to-date bibliography for further reading and the handy glossary will be useful for both categories of readers.

The concept of the modern nation evolved in early modern Europe following the Peace of Westphalia (1648) that concluded the Thirty Years' War. That long combat was putatively a religious conflict between entrenched Roman Catholicism and emerging Protestantism, but actually a political struggle by Western European countries for cultural and linguistic autonomy from the feudal shackles of the Holy Roman Empire. The Westphalian premise of sociolinguistic singularity permeates the standard Eurocentric definition of the nation, which came to be equated with the sovereign nation-state in Western political theory. Thus the *Concise Oxford Dictionary* says, 'Nation: A large group of people united by common descent, culture or language', while the *Merriam-Webster* dictionary goes, 'A nation is a group of people who share culture, ethnic origin and language'. Neither of these definitions applies to present-day United States or India, or to countries with ex-colonial citizenry such as the United Kingdom or France, or to white settler countries with large indigenous populations like Australia and Canada. A further complexity was indicated by Tagore in *Nationalism* when he noted the disjunction between the political/militaristic connotations of the Western term 'nation' and the emotional aura surrounding the Indian word *desh* (or homeland), for which he coined the neologism 'No-Nation'. Following Tagore, we can see that even today, for every Indian expatriate with an overseas passport, no matter how long the sojourn, the 'home' state back in India remains forever and always his or her *desh*. The configurations of nationhood have transited through many phases, inflected by memory, culture, political will, the desire for self-government or the contingencies of history.

Nations and Nationalisms meticulously charts these permutations and transformations in the conceptual space of the nation.

The study begins with a concise coverage of theories of the nation from the classical theorists such as Marx and Max Weber to contemporary intellectuals like Foucault and Habermas, and liberal nationalists like Rawls and Yael Tamir. While exploring classifications of nationalism by thinkers like Hechter, Wirth, Plamenatz and others, this opening section also focuses on the 'primordialism versus modernism' debate, the duality of civic and political nationalism, and the fraught relationship between the nation-state and its component minority communities. In the second chapter our gaze swivels to a completely different perspective – the postcolonial nation with India as the prime example. While engaging critically with the main tropes and debates on nation-building in India, and the contribution of stalwarts like Nehru and Sardar Patel, the author foregrounds the continuing legacy of the colonial past that still haunts this post-colony, 'Partition and the (Alie)Nation'. Chapter Three traces the extended parameters, but also the limitations, imposed on the modern nation by globalisation and the impact of national diasporas, as well as by affiliation to collectivities of nations concerned with trade regimes or climate change or international terror. Chapter Four, 'The Nation and its Discontents', examines the rise of conservative neo-nationalism in many countries, prompted by divisive religious or ethnic opposition to perceived majoritarianism, or the influx of refugees from war zones. This chapter also highlights the recent problematic phenomenon of the dissident cyberstate in the digital space. The fifth chapter moves to a completely different plane – the connection between literature and the arts and the nation, with India as the focal point. It looks at certain productions in music, art and dance, but especially at literature. Taking both Indian English Writing and compositions in Indian languages, and their negotiations with the crucial moments in our national experience, the author critically assesses their contribution to the project of narrating the nation. The sixth and final chapter turns our attention to the future. With the norms of 'nation' and 'nationalism' either severely eroded today by a gamut of contentious forces, or in many cases (especially in Eastern Europe, Central Asia and Africa), being propped up either by jingoistic populism or xenophobia or a return to dictatorial tendencies, what remains? Could there be such a thing as the 'postnation'? The author discusses the political and philosophical options currently being suggested as possible ways forward.

Nations and Nationalisms is a book to make us think – of our roles as citizens of a particular country and as members of the world fraternity, and also of how we can shape either a meaningful or a harmful prototype for the nation of the future within our limited individual capacities. It is this dimension that adds immense value to this compact, cogent and comprehensive volume.

Krishna Sen

Chapter One

Nation, Nation-state and Nationalism

A CRITICAL SURVEY OF ORIGINS, DEFINITIONS, CLASSIFICATIONS AND THEORETICAL EXPLORATIONS

THE AMBIVALENT 'NATION'

'Nation', as a category of identification, is commonly used in discussions on constructs of peoplehood. But critics have pointed out a remarkable inconsistency in the way the term is deployed: 'Although the word "nation" is used all around the world every day . . . [s]cholars, too, are unable to come to an agreement about a working definition of the nation and often give up trying to define the term' (Hroch and Malečková 203). The word 'nation' has been used incongruously in varying contexts. In medieval universities, the term was used to denote students who had come from outside the university cities and 'were just as much foreigners as were once the immigrants into Roman centers of population' (Zernatto and Mistretta 353). These students, along with their professors, started participating in various debates and 'nation' as a term began to be used as a 'unit' of particular opinion (Greenfeld 252). '*Nationes*' was the term popular in Leipzig University to refer to the four associations of professors with ideological differences. *Nationes*, thus, seems to connote interest groups or unions. In 1731, when a bishop named John Innocent Mico demanded the Romanian people's (Walachian nation) right to have their representation in the Transylvanian Parliament, he was harangued: 'There is no Walachian nation, there is only a Walachian Plebs'. The word 'nation', in this context, was used to mean the aristocracy. Later on, it became a regular term for the people 'who had come into money and esteem' (Zernatto and Mistretta 364). Scholars, however, disagree vehemently on when or how the term came to mean 'people', although it has been established that the term was well-known in eighteenth-century Europe. According to Peter Alter, 'nationalism' first appeared in a text by the German philosopher Johann Gottfried Herder in 1774 (4), while in Walker Connor's opinion, the term first appeared in 1798 (98).

A nation is often seen as an innate identity, 'more or less immutable characteristics as common descent, territory, history, language, religion, way of life, or other attributes' into which one is born (Petersen 181). Opposed to this is the idea that a nation is an acquired identity that a group politically aspires to, 'a community of sentiment which would adequately manifest itself in a state of its own' (Weber 176). For some scholars, 'nation' stands for 'class': as Benjamin Disraeli remarked in *Sybil* , 'two nations . . . are ordered by different manners and are not governed by the same laws, the rich and the poor' (66). It is also believed that when a tribe – as 'the largest social group defined primarily in terms of kinship, and . . . normally an aggregate of clans, intermediate to nationality' (Coleman 423) – conceives a territory and a language exclusively as its own, the tribe turns into a nation. Nation allows a group to emerge as citizens based on equal rights from their position as subjects. 'Dalit nation' and 'queer nation', as choice-based trans-territorial bonds evolved from common experiences of marginality, are examples of the latest expansion in the connotational references of the term 'nation'.

These inconsistencies in defining 'nation', originating from its complex relationship with other forms of societal, territorial and kinship identities, provide ample evidence for the fact that the classification is not a constant primordial reality but a historical product of an ever-changing flow of unity and association. Despite the ambivalence related to its meaning and usage, the concept of nation, as an invention of the past, is instrumental in tracing the roots of the complexities implied in the interactions among peoples belonging to different races, nations and ethnic groups.

NATION AND COLLECTIVENESS

'Nation', 'race' and 'ethnicity' are related yet distinguishable concepts. A 'race' is a genetic group with discernible, and highly debatable, physiological attributes. A nation is supposed to be a sociopolitical construct, intimately associated with the boundaries of a confirmed or possibly sovereign domain. An ethnic group is perceived as a cultural category, without a specific state boundary, composed of people who follow certain traditional practices that are transferred from one generation to another. Although there is an ongoing debate on whether 'nation' is a category that is more political than cultural, Eley and Suny have rightly pointed to the fact that it involves the politicisation of culture along with the culturalisation of politics:

> If politics is the ground upon which the category of the nation was first proposed, culture was the terrain where it was elaborated, and in this sense nationality is best conceived as a complex, uneven, and unpredictable process, forged from an interaction of cultural coalescence and specific political intervention, which cannot be reduced to static criteria of language, territory, ethnicity or culture. (8)

From the standpoint of capitalist world economy, a nation that is transformed from the interstate order into a sovereign nation-state can be regarded as 'the political superstructure of this historical system', while race, as the outcome of an axial division of labour, can be understood in terms of 'the core–periphery antinomy' where an ethnic group develops as the centre of accumulating capital through 'the creation of household structures that permit the maintenance of large components of non-waged labour' (Balibar and Wallerstein 79).

The nation is one among various forms of kinship structures that have assisted humankind in asserting commonalities and maintaining differences. Like a family where members share a common past, language and cultural practices, the nation is a social relationship in which its people exhibit the 'collective self-consciousness' of having some common linguistic and sociocultural traditions which differentiate them from others. As the members of a family or a locality reveal an intimate attachment with their village/ region, the people who see themselves as a nation develop a strong 'national sentiment' and attachment with the soil of their perceived territory, which is thought to have accrued over a long time. The identity of being a nation surpasses all other sociopolitical identities, mostly during times of war and conflict when patriotism seems to dominate regional or familial attachments.

The notion of the nation as a territorial community assumes larger group formations where the criteria of membership is either birth within the territory or descendance from parents who are already recognised members of the territory. In this sense, 'nation' is the name that a territorial community assigns itself on the basis of having a uniform culture that is based on a common religion, language and set of laws, and a willingness to form institutions that can deal with issues related to self-determination, membership and territorial boundaries. This conviction is challenged by critics such as Ernest Gellner: 'The great, but valid, paradox is this: nations can be defined only in terms of the age of nationalism, rather than, as you might expect, the other way round' (*Nations and Nationalism* 55). In Gellner's opinion, the reason behind the projected wilful adherence to a broader national culture of a territory, by cutting across one's own micro-groupings, can only be understood when one sees the formulation of a nation in the context of the emergence of nationalism that transforms all erstwhile cultural proliferations. The cultural homogeneity imposed by the industrial society culminates in an 'inescapable imperative [that] eventually appears on the surface in the form of nationalism' (39). Nationalism, as an imposed high culture mediated through schools and academic institutions, is uniformly codified for easy bureaucratic and technological communications which destroys erstwhile local groups and folk cultures with a forced implantation of a 'nation', that eventually takes the form of a political legitimacy which is further promoted as a wilful fusion of the self, culture and polity.

There is a clear disjunction between the objective and subjective definitions of the nation. Some theorists feel that 'objective' markers like language, ethnicity, religion, and shared history and descent, which contribute to the formation of a common culture, promote a sense of responsibility and care among the people, prompting them in assembling as a nation: 'Hence, despite the fact that one cannot claim that a certain nation exists just because its members share certain objective features (or have the illusion that they share some), it is still plausible to claim that the fact that they share these features played a constitutive role in the formation of the nation' (Tamir, 'Reconstructing the Landscape of Imagination' 90). In defining the nation on the basis of 'subjective' components like self-consciousness, unity, loyalty and a collective will, thinkers like Ernest Renan describe it as 'a large-scale solidarity, constituted by the feeling of the sacrifices that one has made in the past and of those that one is prepared to make in the future' (19). Transcending the dichotomy of these objective and subjective elements, Calhoun has shown how a nation emerges out of a group formation based on common markers of belonging along with a political awareness, induced partly by the discourse of nationalism: '"Nation" is a particular way of thinking about what it means to be a people, and how the people thus defined might fit into a broader world-system. The nationalist way of thinking and speaking helps to make nations. There is no objective way to determine what is a nation. There are no indicators that are adequately independent of the claims made on behalf of putative nations' (99). More than the actual presence of commonalities, it is the claim of having things in common that seems to be the determining factor in the formation of a nation.

NATION AND THE STATE

Nation denotes a shared loyalty and sworn allegiance to a demarcated territory. Although a nation always remains alert about its territorial domain, it is not synonymous with 'state' which denotes the political power to enforce order for protecting a sovereign domain. A state is not even a logical corollary of the formation of a nation. Gellner has shown how the state, which was never a necessity for pre-agrarian hunting and food-gathering communities who did not practise division of labour, became an option during the agrarian stage, only to become a steady specialised institution of enforcing order in the industrial, post-agrarian phase: 'once none had the state, then some had it, and finally all have it' (*Nations and Nationalism* 5).

Even then, all states have not succeeded in surviving as strong nation-states. According to Rotberg, Indonesia, Colombia, Sri Lanka and Zimbabwe are early-twenty-first-century examples of weak nation-states that are on the verge of failing (16). Yemen, Chad, the Central African Republic and Sudan have been consistently assessed as 'failed' states. States like Somalia, Syria and South Sudan are declared as 'collapsed' states. Collapsed states, as extreme versions of 'failed states', are political domains where warlords have created quasi-states within the state, using their own armed forces, networks of terror and trade arrangements: 'As the decision making center of government, the state is paralyzed and inoperative: laws are not made, order is not preserved, and societal cohesion is not enhanced' (Zartman 5). The internationally unrecognised Islamic State in Syria or the Somaliland in northwestern Somalia are examples of a quasi-state created within a collapsed state.

The state helps in preserving the integrity of the national territory by its use of military force and a written standardised law of the land that specifies the codes of conduct that have to be followed consistently throughout the territory. General Meng Tian's plan to construct the Great Wall of China in 221 BCE or Charles Martel's victory in 732 CE in the Battle of Tours over Muslim warriors who were expanding their territory under the command of Amir Abdal-Rahman, are examples of how the state uses its force to secure the boundaries of a nation. Translating the Bible into various languages, and the writing of legal texts such as *Treatise on the Laws and Customs of England* (1187) by Ranulf de Glanvill, the *Treatise* (1260) by Henry de Bracton and the Magna Carta (1215), are examples of formulating legal codes of conduct, derived from religion and conventional customs, to be followed uniformly across the nation.

The urge to preserve the cultural commonality among the people within a bounded terrain with a common government and laws to protect the right to self-determination, gives birth to a 'nation-state'. However, there are many examples of those who consider themselves 'proto-nations' but do not have a nation-state: for example, East Turkestan, the Basque region in Spain, Quebec in Canada, the Taiwanese in China, and the supporters of independent Kashmir and Kurdistan.

THE NATION-STATE

Both 'nation' and 'nature' are etymologically derived from the Latin *nat*, meaning birth, while the Latin *natio* means 'the people' (of a particular tribe). Hence a nation-state can be comprehended as an association of people related by kinship ties and a political sense of belonging to their land. It can also denote the diverse peoples who share a sovereign landscape. 'America the Beautiful', the famous American patriotic song, celebrates 'purple mountain majesties, and fruited plains, from sea to shining sea', while India's national anthem sings of 'Vindhya Himachal Yamuna Ganga'. Thus a nation-state comes into existence when the people inhabiting a particular geography, 'see themselves as sharing a common destiny and view their individual success and well-being as closely dependent on the prosperity of the group as a whole. They think of their self-esteem and their accomplishments as related to the achievements of other group members, and take pride in the group's distinctive contributions' (Tamir, 'Reconstructing the Landscape of Imagination' 86), along with safeguarding the sovereignty of their land. A nation-state is not always based, with a few exceptions like Japan, on the principle of 'one-nation, one-state'. In the case of Switzerland, for instance, fractions of various nations have come together to form a nation-state. Again, various multilingual, multiracial and multi-religious nations together constitute most nation-states in southern Africa and South Asia.

Many modern thinkers have tried to understand the nation in relation to its mode of contriving the nation-state, which they feel is a modern phenomenon based on bureaucratisation, political and social emancipation, and communications (Tilly, *The Formation of National States in Western Europe*; Rokkan; Puhle; Giddens 83). According to Breuilly, the nation has to be studied 'in close association with the development of the modern state' (*Nationalism and the State* xii). 'What makes the nation integral to the nation-state', writes Giddens, '. . . is not the existence of sentiments of nationalism but the unification of an administrative apparatus over precisely defined territorial bounds' (172). Through Michel Foucault we have also learned how, with the rise of nation-states, there evolved a necessity for the production of national citizenship through governmentality, where the state increasingly began to perform as an administrative machinery aiming at making populations socially and economically productive (Foucault, 'Governmentality'). The most recent notion of nation as an 'imagined community' underscores the significance of the circulation of ideas through print, the rise of a bourgeois class, Enlightenment ideas of popular sovereignty, and an imagined peace between republican nations and/or industrialisation (Gellner, *Nations and Nationalism*; Anderson).

The identification of a nation centred around a nation-state has four major significances. First, it can be used in dividing the world between 'we' and 'they' – the acknowledgement by the nation-state becomes the criterion for labelling people as friends or enemies. Second, a complete loyalty before the nation-state becomes a hegemonic guideline that legitimates absolute power and dominance of the nation-state over the differences of opinion arising among the people of the nation, under the pretext of cohesion and adherence to the national ideologies. Third, the nation-state gradually gets projected as a natural and moral entity, which in turn propagates a 'national identity as a system of absolute values'. Such an advocacy can be easily popularised since 'the relativism of ethnic shifters has been transformed into a set of reified eternal verities' (Herzfeld 42). Finally, the nation-state becomes the rationale behind the formation of various institutions for its effective functioning which gradually get viewed not as impositions but as centres of manufacturing national sentiments by the citizens, who, in turn, are programmed to internalise the national idiom.

The term 'country', commonly used as a substitute for the nation-state, can specifically refer to the geographical expanse of a nation. The spatial attachment of the people of a nation to their country – the demarcated territory – can be best expressed by the term 'homeland'. Often, this attachment is enhanced by the notion of an organic belonging through the rendering of the territory as a 'motherland' or a 'fatherland' – for instances, in the poem 'Vande Mataram' (1870) by Bankim Chandra Chatterjee (1838–94) where the nation is addressed as the mother; the painting by Abanindranath Tagore (1871–1951) where the nation is portrayed as 'Bharat Mata' (1905), a mother figure in a saffron sari; or the Latin word *patria* meaning fatherland. In this sense, the territorial boundaries of the nation are seen as an inheritance from one's ancestors and a site of possession and protection. This further demands that it be handed over only to one's own offspring in future, to ensure the continuation of an intergenerational transmission.

In order to keep the entire nation aware of the responsibilities towards the native land, as an indebted response to the land's maternal/paternal care, many nations celebrate a national day – such as the Great Union Day (1 December) in Romania, Araw ng Kalayaan (12 June) in the Philippines, Statehood Day (25 June) in Croatia and Dia da Independência (7 September) in Brazil. Imagining the country, by dismissing the public/private divide, as a motherland/fatherland also validates Hannah Arendt's observations: 'We see the body of peoples and political communities in the image of a family whose everyday affairs have to be taken care of by a gigantic, nation-wide administration of housekeeping. . . . the collective of families economically organized into the facsimile of one super-human family is what we call "society," and its political form of organisation is called "nation"' (*The Human Condition* 28–29).

In opposition to the kingdoms and princely states of earlier times, the nation-state is commonly considered to be a modern Western political construct. The principles laid down in the Treaty of Westphalia (1648; also known as the Peace of Westphalia) that ended the Thirty Years' War (1618–48) in Europe were traditionally held to be the basis of the modern idea of national sovereignty, although many contemporary political scientists dispute this view. Nevertheless, it was from the seventeenth century onwards that a considerable body of European political theory emerged on the nation, the state and the nature of sovereignty. Yet, there has never been a concrete answer to the question whether the contemporary idea of the nation is a natural development from the pre-modern political identifications. Approaching the emergence of the nation as an evolution from an early medieval Western experience, Hastings argues that any ethnic group may naturally transform into a nation the moment their unique vernacular shifts from the stage of orality to written usages and ultimately to the production of literature, specifically in translating the Bible (11–12). Patrick J. Geary opposes this idea of continuity, from early medieval times to the contemporary world, as a myth. According to him, the sociocultural conditions related to the names that were attached to the various ethnic groups in early-medieval Europe underwent a complete change due to mobility, exogamous marriages and recasting of alliances, but the names themselves remained intact, and 'they held the potential to convince people of continuity, even if radical discontinuity was the lived reality' (118). By appropriating those names and constructing a national identity that is triumphant over all other individual or group identities, the martial bands mobilised people and framed them into a nation:

> . . . with victory and territorialization, bold claims created the reality that they asserted and, in a matter of generations, social and political groups with widely differing pasts, values and cultures accepted the victor's right to articulate for them a common past. Myths of common descent and shared history, myths molded less by indigenous oral tradition than by classical ideas of peoplehood, masked the radical discontinuity and heterogeneity that characterized Late Antiquity. (Geary 156).

If this is true, what binds the people designated as a nation together? One of the perplexing answers is their wish to perform a self-sacrifice in expressing patriotism – an ideology that is internalised through the retelling of legends and stories. As Marvin and Ingle observe,

> The creation of sentiments strong enough to hold the group together periodically requires the willing deaths of a significant portion of its members. The lifeblood of these members is shed by means of a ritual in which designated victims become outsiders and cross the boundary of the living group into death. The most powerful enactment of this ritual is war. (5)

Appadurai has shown us how the modern nation-state sometimes provokes a 'needful violence' to forge a communitarian sense that might have otherwise failed to emerge from other commonalities like a shared religion or/and language: 'violence (internal violence associated with ethnic cleansing; more capillary techniques of surveillance and schooling; or external violence associated with expansion, empire and colonialism) produces full attachment, rather than the reverse' (132). Another reason why the people unite as a nation is the demand for an 'other' that is fulfilled by the creation of categories of 'enemies': 'The positing of an other is what allows for the closure which facilitates the individuation of a certain identity' (Norval 65). Thus, barbed-wire barricades concretise the frontier around which, as we have learnt from Duara, communities consolidate themselves as nations.

NATION AND THE CLASSICAL THINKERS

The classical thinkers on the ideas of the nation, state and nationalism – such as Thomas Hobbes (1588–1679), John Locke (1632–1704), David Hume (1711–76), Jean-Jacques Rousseau (1712–78) and Immanuel Kant (1724–1804) – have mainly tried to address 'nation' on the basis of territorial sovereignty and parameters of state power. Hobbes provided the 'first organizational and juristic model of a state, equated with coercion and authority' (Warner 68). According to Hobbes, human beings, by nature, are in a continual fight with one another, and the only way to overcome war and insecurity is to establish a 'social contract' that gives birth to the formation of a sovereign state, where 'sovereignty meant absolute power above the law, and states therefore were actually outside the law' (Molesworth 46). Hobbes contributed greatly in fortifying the absolute authority of the ruler: 'The sovereign may,without injustice, inflict any harm whatsoever on "innocent" foreign persons in the pursuit of state interests, also in peacetime' (Nardin and Mapel 77). The *Leviathan*, who defines justice, is beyond the framework of just/unjust (187). Since the *Leviathan* is portrayed as a 'mortal god', no one has the right to rebel against him (187).

Responding to Hobbes's ideas in *Leviathan* (1651) of a civil state centred round a ruler vested with supreme authority through a social contract, Locke highlighted the issue of the consent of the people in obeying the laws of the state: 'no one can be put out of this estate and subjected to the political power of another without his own consent' (*Second Treatise on Civil Government* 52). The recommendation – 'I easily grant, that civil government is the proper remedy for the inconveniences of the state of nature' ('Economic Writings and Two Treatises of Government' 221) – illustrates aptly that for Locke, the civil society formed by a social contract was 'a state also of equality, wherein all the power and jurisdiction is reciprocal, no one having more than another . . .' (218). For Locke, 'a common language is the prerequisite for men to live together as a nation in a self-sustaining political system which has its form and government and its governors determined by consent' (Seliger 22).

David Hume in his celebrated essay 'Of National Characters' (1748) defined 'nation' as 'a collection of individuals' having national affiliations, whose manners 'are frequently determined by moral causes' (198). Hume differentiated physical causes – like 'those qualities of the air and climate, which are supposed to work insensibly on the temper, by altering the tone and habit of the body, and giving a particular complexion' – from moral causes of

> all circumstances, which are fitted to work on the mind as motives or reasons, and which render a peculiar set of manners habitual to us. Of this kind are, the nature of the government, the revolutions of public affairs, or penury in which the people live, the situation of the nation with regard to its neighbours, and such like circumstances. (199)

An ideal state, according to Rousseau, is the protector of individual property, life and liberty, created through a contract where the people decide that '[e]ach one puts into the community his person and all his power under the supreme direction of the general will; and as a body, we incorporate every member as an indivisible part of the whole' (61). Once the sovereign power of the state is firmly established, the people, as its citizens, require a government as

> an agent of its own to bind it together and set it to work under the direction of the "general will", to serve as a means of communication between the State and the Sovereign, and to do for the collective person more or less what the union of soul and body does for man! Here we have what is, in the state, the basis of government, often wrongly confused with the sovereign, whose minister it is. (102).

Rousseau had an idealistic expectation that governmental mechanisms function under equitable conditions as means of augmenting tolerance, democracy and welfare. However, in the opening chapter of his *The Social Contract* (1762), he framed the critique that although every human being has the right to liberty of thought and action, the civil state and its laws turn every person into a slave – 'Man is born free, and everywhere he is in chains'. This observation proves that Rousseau was aware of the fact that the submission to the 'general will' as the basis of 'citizenship' was not always unforced.

Kant has never been considered as a nationalist, but his *Perpetual Peace* (1795) has time and again been read as anticipating a 'league of nations'. According to Sharon Byrd and Joachim Hruschka, even Kant's *Doctrine of Right* (1797) can be interpreted as a plea for a 'state of nation-states'. For Kant, the establishment of the state is 'in itself an end (*that each ought to have*)' (*Practical Philosophy* 289; italics in original), and the first step towards the 'ethical commonwealth' (*Perpetual Peace* 376). The 'freedom of every member of the state as a human being', the 'equality of each with every other as a subject' and the 'independence of every member of a commonwealth as a citizen' are the three major and underlying principles that form the foundation of a state (*Königlichen preußischen* 290). Like Hobbes, Kant also believes in the social contract that gives birth to the state.

For Hegel (1770–1831), as Richard Kroner has observed, '[t]he nation embodies the spirit of the world. It is God who appears in it. The state is the organization of the nation; it is, therefore, the reality of the moral idea, or the divine idea, as it exists on earth' (196). In a pantheistic linking of the world and nations with God, Hegel believed that every nation has been created by God to accomplish His mission. Thus, from Hegel's standpoint, a nation does not only serve the interests of a territory but becomes an integral part of the interests of the entire humanity; and, accordingly, a state is seen to be intimately related to the concerns of the world through mutual cooperation.

Linking the notion of self-government with a well-organised and effective government for political stability, J. S. Mill (1806–73) defined the nation from the liberal notion of a non-invasive government:

> A portion of mankind may be said to constitute a Nationality if they are united among themselves by common sympathies which do not exist between them and any others – which

> make them cooperate with each other more willingly than with other people, desire to be under the same government, and desire it should be government by themselves or a portion of themselves exclusively. (361)

However, Mill never believed in the equality of the nations; rather he supported a hegemony where nations of 'civilised and highly cultured people' should be able to enjoy a privileged position over 'inferior and backward' nations (Varouxakis 19–20). Moreover, by stating that, 'Where the sentiment of nationality exists in any force, there is a *prima facie* case for uniting all the members of the nationality under the same government' (362), Mill seems to have bestowed on the state and governmental machineries supreme legitimacy as apparatuses of political inclusion, at the cost of denying the people the liberty to raise their voice in dissent and demand for a separate statehood of the minoritised in a multi-nation state.

Marxism offers another stringent critique of the nation-state and nationalism. Karl Marx (1818–83) and Friedrich Engels (1820–95) considered the nation-state to be a problematic political entity managed by the capitalist bourgeoisie with the ulterior motive of amassing property and power by controlling the means of production. Nationalism, in this view, is thus no more than a self-serving capitalist ideology. Marx says that with the formation of the nation-state, '[i]ndependent, or loosely connected provinces, with separate interests, laws, governments and systems of taxation, became lumped together into one nation, with one government, one code of laws, one national class interest, one frontier and one customs tariff' (71–72). Lenin (1870–1924) states that '[i]n place of all forms of nationalism, Marxism advances internationalism, the amalgamation of all nations in the higher unity' (34). He further explains how Marxist ideology, nevertheless, always supports the right to self-determination of the oppressed nations in their struggle against capitalist imperialism and subjugation: 'Insofar as the bourgeoisie of the oppressed nation fights the oppressor, we are always, in every case, and more strongly than anyone else, in favour, for we are the staunchest and the most consistent enemies of oppression' (411–12). Despite this apparent concession to minority aspirations (and their problematic realisation under the erstwhile Soviet Union), it is the famous definition of the nation, and by implication the nation-state, provided by Stalin (1878–1953) that foregrounds the absolute homogeneity demanded by the Marxist perspective: the definition delineates the nation as 'a historically constituted, stable community of people, formed on the basis of a common language, territory, economic life, and psychological make-up manifested in a common culture. . . . It is only when all these characteristics are present together that we have a nation' (13–14).

Kant was a pioneer of an inclusive cosmopolitanism that accommodated both intranational and international diversity – this broader concept was later adapted by John Bordley Rawls (1921–2002), Jürgen Habermas (b. 1929), Brian Barry (1936–2009), Onora O'Neill (b. 1941), Martha Nussbaum (b. 1947) and Thomas Pogge (b. 1953). By contrast, there are mainly two schools of nationalist philosophers who are exclusivist. On the one hand, we have the German school of extreme pro-nationalist thinkers like Johann Gottfried Herder (1744–1803) for whom culture is essentially national; Johann Gottlieb Fichte (1762–1814) who felt that though each community has its distinct attributes, one must inculcate the patriotic sense that one's nation is superior to all others; and Novalis (Georg Philipp Friedrich Freiherr von Hardenberg, 1772–1801) and Karl Wilhelm Friedrich Schlegel (1772–1829) who together propagated a totalitarian nationalism. On the other hand, philosophers like John Stuart Mill (1806–73) of England and Ernest Renan (1823–92) of France contended that a nation should comprise those whose solidarity is based on common traits in their heritage. The debate continues to this day.

ETHNIC AND CIVIC NATIONS

The close relationship between nation and ethnicity has raised controversy between the two models of nationhood: ethnic nationhood and civic nationhood. An ethnic nation, as a community of people who share a common culture, is believed to be a product of nature: 'politics create states, nature creates nations' (Herder, qtd. in Delannoi 25). The Germans believed that the nation (*Volk*), as an organic unit of people, with a distinct origin as revealed in the common religious, linguistic and cultural practices, predated the political unit of the state: 'Despite the emphasis placed on the state, the Romantic understanding of nationhood is fundamentally ethnocultural. The *Volksgeist* is constitutive, the state merely expressive of nationhood' (Brubaker, *Citizenship and Nationhood in France and Germany* 9). An ethnic nation is more a product of birth ties and blood relationships, than personal preferences. The theory of the social contract, the *nation-contrat*, which was dominant in France, popularised the notion that one is not born into a nation, rather one becomes a nation by voluntarily subscribing to the social contract. In contrast to the ethnic nation, based on common beliefs and customs, a civic nation emerges out of a shared commitment of people, regardless of race, creed, colour, language, gender or ethnicity, who reckon themselves rationally 'as a community of equal, rights-bearing citizens, united in patriotic attachment to a shared set of political practices and values' and are abiding by a common law (Ignatieff 4). Overcoming genealogical differences, a group of individuals develop a territorial bond that is not 'pre-political' but 'national', in order to assemble as a civic nation of mutual legal and political recognition. The individuals, irrespective of regional, religious or linguistic differences, when voluntarily engaged as law abiding citizens aspiring for justice, collectively construct a civic nation as 'an artifice, a product of will, dictated by rationality, to integrate everyone into a single political space, even those with whom one feels no natural solidarity' (Putte 62).

The ethnic idea of nationhood perceives the nation as a 'rational attachment' with the land/social boundaries that one inherits as a 'national belonging', while a civic nation can evolve out of an appropriated nationalism in which people choose to identify their nationhood with a preferred sovereign domain. In an ethnic nation, the individuals can only be defined in relation to the community, but in a civic nation it is the individuals who define the national community. Countries like Estonia and Latvia, with their strict laws on language and citizenship, are examples of ethnic nations, as opposed to Ukraine and Kazakhstan, where these post-independent states have consciously used the rhetoric of civic nationhood, such as tolerance and inclusiveness, before the global audience. Nira Yuval-Davis' emphasis on the three dimensions of the nation is relevant in this context: 'volknation' (the creation of a 'genealogical nation' following the blood lines), 'staatnation' (the civic nation) and 'kulturnation' (imagining a nation based on shared ideology, culture and language).

Even if a nation is formed on cultural lines of common ancestry, it has to be bestowed with civic ties (Seymour). The moral purpose behind the differentiation between civic and ethnic nationhood is supposedly to negate the rigidity and exclusiveness of ethnic nations. However, it is often forgotten how the so-called unity of a civic nation is fortified through the brutal use of violence, like the killings and mob violence against the Huguenots during St. Bartholomew's Day massacre (23–24 August 1572) in France, or the slaughtering of Native Americans in the American civil war: 'After all, American citizens have been denounced and persecuted for clinging to unAmerican political principles as well as for their backgrounds. And as George Mosse reminds us, it was the decidedly civic nation of the French Jacobins that invented many of the techniques of persecution and mass paranoia exploited by twentieth-century fascists and xenophobic nationalists' (Yack, 'The Myth of the Civic Nation' 115–16). Moreover, the acultural notion of the civic nation as a purely political enterprise, contrary to the ethnic nation formed by an ascriptive culture, is also misleading. Keating, in his definition of a civic nation as an identity of 'adaptation', has also emphasised that it is based on 'common values and institutions, and pattern of social interaction. . . . There need to be a structured set of political and social interactions guided by common values and a sense of common identity' (Keating 5–6). This definition, ironically, proves that just like an ethnic nation, even a civic nation produces and operates on a cultural index. Scholars like Lind (1995) and Hollinger (1995) have shown how even in a civic nation like 'America', there is an 'American' culture.

THE NEED FOR ENVISAGING THE NATION

The world polity theory, derived from the diffusion theory of Meyer et al. (1997), assumed that the rise of the nation-state across the globe in the course of the last two hundred years, was prompted not by the internal reforms initiated by the people of the domain but by imitating the external model provided through the rapid diffusion of the formation of nation-states in the neighbouring areas. But citing examples of manifold routes to the rise of nation-states – the 'reform from above as in Japan; gradual transition into nation-statehood as in Sweden and Thailand; the overthrow of an *ancien régime* through revolution as in Russia or through civil war as in the United States; nationalist secession as in Yugoslavia and Mexico; and unification movements such as in Germany and Yemen' (785) – Wimmer and Feinstein have concluded that the worldwide rise of the nation-state was mainly the result of internal events. Inspired by the rise of nation-states in the neighbourhood or within the colonial empire, the nationalists painstakingly mobilised movements that delegitimised the colonial authorities in order to overthrow the established order, or the old regimes of power gradually grew weak through recurrent wars and, thereby, provided opportunities for the nationalists' efforts to foster the nation-state.

The positive perspective on the nation is mostly derived from the premise that it fosters the communitarian attachment that helps in establishing an individual's sociocultural identity. It is argued that the nation, as an affinity based on a level of cultural uniformity, increases each member's sense of obligation towards one another, which subsequently, transforms the networked community into a moral bond. People who become a nation seem to believe that the decision to come together would do good to them, particularly in the context of 'calculations of interest, feelings of social friendship and beliefs about justice' (Yack, *Nationalism and the Moral Psychology of Community* 221). Max Weber too stated that 'nation' has always been seen as a 'value-concept': 'There is no nation without national consciousness, i.e. an awareness of membership in the nation, coupled with a view that this membership is an inherently valuable quality' (qtd. in Hroch 12). A stable and mature personal identity is believed to be dependent upon a strong communitarian existence, and it is the nation that seems to be capable of providing a sustained notion of a secured communal life:

> We are, to put it crudely, lost if we cannot identify ourselves with some part of an objective social reality: a nation, though not necessarily a state, with its distinctive traditions. What

> we find in people—and as deeply embedded as the need to develop their talents—is the need not only to be able to say what they can do but to say who they are. This is found, not created, and is found in the identification with others in a shared culture based on nationality. (Nielsen 32)

A nation as an 'inclusive identity, accessible to members of all cultural groups' (Miller, *Justice for Earthlings* 91) is a metaphor for a multicultural collaboration – for example, the British national identity that includes the English, the Scottish and other ethnic identities. The unique cultures that each of these 'nations' represent demonstrate the various 'forms of life' which ultimately contribute to the growth of a composite culture based on cultural pluralism.

Formation of a distinct nation is often viewed as the utmost mode of establishing minority rights. By providing safeguards and institutional autonomy to the minorities, the nation-state also becomes a crucial agency of delivering differential rights and promoting equality. As David Miller argues in *On Nationality*, people decide to unite as a nation on the basis of a shared identity in order to enjoy greater social justice. According to Kymlicka, the realisation that 'individual choice is dependent on the presence of a societal culture, defined by language and history' (8) underlies the formation of nations. However, Kymlicka goes on to problematise this concept by showing how the nation-state of today is very different from the homogeneous Stalinist definition: present-day nation-states are defined by their multiculturalism, characterised by their diversity in terms of race, ethnicity, gender, religion and sexual orientation, and multinationalism where people from diverse ancestries aspire for self-governance.

Critics of nationalism, shifting their focus from the nation to the subnational and the supranational, have argued that nations can often become tools for enhancing power and exploitation. According to Canovan, 'the advantage that nations have over alternative sources of collective power is that they can lie dormant without being defunct' (73). Once nationhood is entrenched, it can be deployed, occasionally, as a powerful resource. However, according to Brubaker, 'the strength, salience and centrality of national feeling, national identity and nationalist politics tend to be overestimated'

('Myths and Misconceptions in the Study of Nationalism' 283), since in reality people are often more attached to their immediate community bonds – such as the family and the ethnic group to which they belong – rather than the nation. A relevant case in point is the debate around Indian nationhood in North East India where the people feel more comfortable associating themselves with their tribalhood than with the rest of India which they call the 'mainland' (Tunyi and Wouters 7). The state, by propagating an institutionalised nationhood, and contriving rigid 'national' and 'non-national' indicators, seeks to retain unity among those it endorses as 'nationals': 'States selectively confirm, co-opt, reinforce, or even create identity-bestowing social networks within which people organize work, sociability and collective action; to some degree, all such networks come to depend on the state's backing, or at least its toleration' (Tilly, 'A Bridge Halfway' 18). In this context, the stand taken by the Indian government regarding the National Register of Citizens (NRC) and Citizenship Amendment Act (CAA) are interesting instances to reveal how the state can selectively define citizenry by turning select sections of refugees into nationals, while paving the way to recasting other sections of the inhabitants as non-citizens. India's Citizenship Amendment Act 2019, as per the explanation provided by the government, attempts to grant Indian citizenship to the Hindu, Buddhist, Sikh, Christian and Zoroastrian communities who, having faced religious persecution, had come to India before 31 December 2014 from Bangladesh, Pakistan and Afghanistan. This process excludes members of the Muslim community who might also have faced oppression and, therefore, have come to India from the other neighbouring countries like Myanmar, Bhutan, Nepal and Sri Lanka.

Duara has remarked that with the structuring of the nation, '[w]hat occurs, then, is a hardening of boundaries' (168–69). From Marvin and Ingle we have also learnt that '[w]e cannot remove ourselves from a system of totem violence. . . . Wherever we are, killing rules are in effect' (313). It can thus be asserted that nations need to send their men to wars for strengthening their boundaries. In this context of war and violence, Anne McClintock's observation that '[a]ll nationalisms are gendered, all are invented and all are dangerous – dangerous . . . in the sense that they represent relations to political power and to the technologies of violence' (260), is highly significant.

Hans Kohn sees two main factors in the formation of nations – a nation is either established by 'a rational and universal concept of political liberty' or it is 'basically founded on history' (574). It is now mostly accepted that 'nation' is formed in and by time and through people's inventing of a common past. Since all 'present identities are built out of the materials that are handed down, not started from scratch' (Miller, *On Nationality* 175), the nations formed in recent times are transformed products of an ancient assemblage. From the standpoint of the pro-nationalist, 'the pattern of life in a society is similar to that of a biological organism' (Berlin 341). Hence, the nations of the present-day must be interpreted as the aftermath of an organic metamorphosis. According to Hegel, 'Nations may have had a long history before they finally reach their destination – that of forming themselves into states' (qtd. in Herb and Kaplan 48). Modern Israel, conceived as a nation-state emerging out of the memories of Moses leading the exodus of the Israelites out of Egypt because they were God's chosen people, is a case in point. In Ernest Renan's view, a nation 'presupposes a past' (19), while for Hobsbawm, 'nations without a past are contradictions in terms' (255).

Situating the rise of the nation in modern times, some modernist thinkers of nationalism have considered the nation as a construct crafted by certain historians to propagate nationalist ideologies through their projection that all history is in fact histories of potential or emerging or existing nation-states. In this sense, the contemporary nation is believed to have emerged out of the historian's endeavour to construct a national history. There are also historians who have denounced nationalism by apprehending that it often seems to provide foundation for Nazism and Fascism (Smith, 'Nationalism and the Historians' 45; Breuilly, 'Historians and the Nation' 62–68). Other historians like Ernest Gellner (*Nations and Nationalism*, 1983) and Benedict Anderson (*Imagined Communities*, 1991) have been critical of nation and nationalism, and yet have upheld them as necessary myths on the basis of their functionality.

Perceptions about the nation and nationalism have a close association with literary articulations, and especially with narrative forms. A prime example is Jawaharlal Nehru's *The Discovery of India* (1946). In this book, Nehru created an 'idea of India' and of a shared Indian civilisation even before India came into existence as a sovereign nation-state. Likewise, the American psyche was shaped by the didactic writings of the seventeenth-century Pilgrim Fathers, and later by Frederick Jackson Turner's 'Frontier Thesis' (1892), Israel Zangwill's play *The Melting Pot* (1908), and James Truslow Adams' enunciation of the American Dream in *The Epic of America* (1931). Another instance would be the anti-West agenda of Slavophilism and pan-Slavism in nineteenth-century Russian literature, art and architecture. This discursive notion of nation and nationalism can be explained by Bourdieu's concept of *habitus* in 'Rethinking the State' – based not only upon *homo nationalis*, but very significantly on the linguistic markers of a *national corpus*. Other significant work in this field (Martin and Wodak; Anthonissen and Blommaert; and Wodak) offer interdisciplinary discourse analyses of discursive nation-building strategies in Hong Kong, Poland, Australia, South Africa, Germany and Austria. On the other hand, Žižek, arguing against this discursive notion of nation and nationalism, has underscored that 'national identification is by definition sustained by a relationship toward the Nation qua Thing' (201). Drawing from Lacanian psychoanalysis, Žižek has argued that every community develops a shared belongingness towards a 'Nation-Thing' which, more than a symbolic identification, 'exists as long as the members of the community believe in it' (202). The 'Nation-Thing' is an entity through which a community '*organises its enjoyment*' (201, original emphasis), and gets treated as 'accessible only to us' by the community members, out of the apprehension that others want to 'steal our enjoyment' (203).

PRIMORDIALISTS AND MODERNISTS

The question of whether nations had existed in the form of national consciousness even before the evolution of the modern nation-state has spurred disputes between the primordialists and the modernists.

According to the primordialists, a nation as a category of human bonding had existed all through antiquity. Johann Gottfried Herder (1744–1803), as one of the pioneering primordialists (also known as the perennialists), considered the nation as natural and organic, unlike the state which is artificially created (Evrigenis and Pellerin xxxv–xxxix). The primordial attachment to the nation is regarded as a given and, therefore, a timeless phenomenon. For Shils, the nation as 'a necessity of human existence in society', 'has repeatedly happened in world history' (109). Adrian Hastings has shown how 'nation-formation and nationalism have in themselves almost nothing to do with modernity', but have emerged out of 'a typical medieval and early modern experience of the multiplication of vernacular literatures and of state systems around them, a multiplication largely dependent upon the Church, its scriptures and its clergy' (205).

The modernists, on the other hand, seem to be convinced that '[n]ationalism is a doctrine invented in Europe at the beginning of the nineteenth century' (Kedourie, *Nationalism* 9). Gellner elucidated how industrialisation, modernisation and a new education system, moulded regional differences 'of the pre-existent cultures, generally transforming them in the process' (*Nations and Nationalism* 48), and created a community of a homogenised culture where the people of that community began to interact with one another through a standardised mode of communication as co-nationals: 'Nationalism is not the awakening of nations to self-consciousness: it invents nations where they do not exist' (Gellner, *Thought and Change* 168). Other modernists like Charles Tilly (*The Formation of National States in Western Europe*), John Breuilly (*Nationalism and the State*) and Michael Mann tend to argue that 'nations and nationalism have primarily developed in response to the development of the modern state' (Mann 45), where the state gradually obtained the utmost attention from military, administrative and governmental machineries. Modernity, apart from bringing economic and cultural transformations, also induced notions of national self-determination, sovereignty, democracy and citizenship among the people who were politically inspired for 'seeking or exercising state power' (Breuilly, *Nationalism and the State* 2).

Citing Massimo d'Azeglio's (1798–1866) famous utterance after the unification of Italy in the 1860s – 'We have made Italy, now we have to make Italians' (qtd. in Hobsbawm 256–57) – Hobsbawm has affirmed that nationalism as a political agenda is 'in historic terms a fairly recent one', which further proves that 'groups defined as "nations" have a right to, and therefore ought to, form territorial states of the kind that have become standard since the French Revolution' (256–57).

Anderson charted the three stages of transition through which premodern societies were transformed into modern ones, while proclaiming the advent of nationalism: first, the communities shifted their loyalty from religion to what they thought of as a 'nation'; secondly, in a 'homogenous, empty time' (Anderson 24) the individuals found themselves in an open space where they began to relate themselves with unknown masses as co-nationals and thereby became part of an imagined community; and thirdly, with the onset of 'print-capitalism', the newspapers, appreciated as 'one-day best-sellers', standardised the vernacular and promoted an image of the world 'visibly rooted in everyday life' (36) that finally induced the inception of a nation as 'an imagined political community – and imagined as both inherently limited and sovereign' (6).

Moving beyond the perennialist–modernist polemics, Aviel Roshwald has put forward the view that

> . . . nationalism is at once ancient and very modern; it employs twin conceptions of time, cyclical and linear; it seeks self-determination while manifesting a sense of victimhood; it insists on the nation's particularity of chosenness while claiming a universal mission; and finally, it reveals a symbiosis of kindred and mingled blood, of ethnic and civic nationhood. Through these antinomies, nationalism is constantly able to renew itself and adapt to different situations'. (638)

NATIONALISM AND ITS VARIATIONS

Considering 'nationality' as a sociocultural entity that may not have any corresponding politico-geographic territoriality (state) which ultimately fulfils the criteria of regarding a collective of ethnic groups – who have come together based on a 'political integration' which can be termed as 'nationism' – as a 'nation', Jashua A. Fishman has stated that the organising spirit in the transition of 'nationality-into-nation' can be regarded as nationalism. Ashis Nandy's distinguishing of patriotism from nationalism is important for arriving at a less confused conjecture about nationalism. First, nationalism's sole concern is the people's obsession with the state, while patriotism 'presumes the existence of communities other than the country and gives them due recognition, sometimes even priority' (6). Second, patriotism can choose to be or not to be statist, while in case of nationalism, some degree of statism is unavoidable. Third, unlike nationalism, patriotism does not demand the pre-eminence of national identity over other subnational loyalties that one may share with one's village, city, religion, etc. Fourth, nationalism is believed to be an adjunct of modernity, while patriotism thrived even among pre-modern communities. Fifth, a nationalist carries and is defined by certain markers of her/his national identity, but patriotism is more fluid and does not rigidly define a patriot. Sixth, 'nationalism, being an ideology, has to have not merely an identifiable content but also a theoretical frame, however coarse and repetitive', and this 'theoretical frame of nationalism strengthens its homogenising role in society and turns it into a housebroken version of patriotism in a modern state' (Evera 8). Lastly, patriotism as a sentiment is more engaged with the real lives of the people, while nationalism as an ideology keeps the nationalists always worried regarding the honour of the abstract nation which they feel is never adequately promulgated, and as a consequence, 'the more the nationalists come to love the abstract entity called the nation, the more they dislike the real-life persons and communities that constitute the nation' (Evera 9).

Michel Seymour, in his endeavour to define the contemporary nation, has delineated it as a political community with a national majority, along with national minorities and ethnic communities, who develop a national consciousness around a demarcated territory (427). For Hechter, nationalism as the direct consequence of the modern state emerges out of the political activities that a distinct collectivity undertakes towards self-governance through strengthening the boundaries of its state (7). Deriving from Seymour and Hechter, nationalism can be seen as concerns that are shared by the people of a nation-state, despite the possibilities of tension between the national majority and the rest, which incite them to formulate governmental mechanisms in order to maintain the well-being and dignity of its citizens while safeguarding the sovereignty of its state. Reconsidering nationalism under the lens of modernity and governmentality, it can be seen as the 'political utilisation of the symbol of nation through discourse and political activity, as well as the sentiment that draws people into responding to this symbol's use' (Verdery 38) through the inconspicuous practices of power, also known as 'micro-physics' in Foucauldian diction.

Hechter has classified nationalism on the basis of territorial governance into four different types. The first variety, 'state-building nationalism', is marked by 'efforts at cultural homogenization' (56) where multicultural communities are assimilated into a homogenous national culture (Nepal, for instance, with the imposition of Khas-kura as lingua franca) and culturally incongruous people are sometimes expelled (like in the case of the expulsion of the Bhupalese from Bhutan). The second variety is 'peripheral nationalism' in which either the people of a discrete territory resists assimilating with people whom they perceive as representing an alien culture (like Xinjiang in China), or attempt to secede and form a separate government (for example, Scotland and Catalonia). The call for an *Akhanda Bharat* through the unification of India, Pakistan and Bangladesh; or Venezuela's claim on the Guayana Esequiba that is under the Guyanese administration are instances of the third type of nationalism, the 'irredentist nationalism' where a state tries to increase its territory by merging surrounding states whose inhabitants are perceived by the expanding state as its co-nationals. The final variety is that of 'unification nationalism', demonstrated through the unification of East and West Germany, where people of a homogenised culture, formerly divided along political lines, decide to unite into a single state.

Max Handman has presented another classification of nationalism based on a different paradigm. The first type is what he calls 'oppression nationalism', arising out of a group of people within a state who find themselves under subjugation and multiple 'disabilities' – such as lack of economic resources, absence of administrative and political representation, lack of opportunities to promote their language – and suffering a sense of humiliation. The Romanians in Hungary and Russia, or the Croats in Hungary, have displayed oppression nationalism. The Bulgars and the Serbs have exemplified the second type of nationalism, 'irredentism', in which a community which perceives itself as a nation feels that a large number of their members are under foreign domination. Another variation of nationalism can be seen in 'precaution-nationalism' that 'responds to the stimulus presented by the competitive organization of the modern state-system as well as by the identification of commercial expansion with the interests of national security and of general national well-being. At a given point, this precaution-nationalism is difficult to distinguish from imperialism' (Handman 109). Handman's typology ends with 'prestige-nationalism' which is prevalent among nations who feel that they have not been given the recognition and esteem commensurate with their accomplishments. Black nationalism or Third World nationalism that inspired most of the countries in Asia, Africa and Latin America, are examples of prestige-nationalism.

Influenced by Handman's classifications of nationalism, Louis Wirth has also distinguished four types of nationalism. The first type, 'hegemony nationalism', denotes national movements – like the pan-Slavism of Czarist Russia and the pan-Germanism of the old German Empire – that audaciously seek to merge distinctive dynastic units into a common state through the identification of similarities in language and culture. Prevalent in countries such as Finland, Czechoslovakia and Lithuania, 'particularistic nationalism' gives birth to the demand for national autonomy and secession. National movements initiated by 'marginal people – i.e., a population in the frontier region between two states' (Wirth 733) with a mixed cultural, linguistic and racial context, as has been evident in Silesia, Alsace, Lorraine, the Territory of the Saar Basin, and the Rhineland – result in the formulation of the third type of nationalism, 'marginal nationalism'. The fourth type is the 'nationalism of the minorities' who continue to struggle to assert their own rights by emerging as proto-nations, for example, the Tamils of Sri Lanka.

Opposing Gellner's argument about the 'invented' nation which points to a 'falsity' that is historically deceptive, Anderson has shown that the 'coalition of Protestantism and print-capitalism' historically enabled people to 'think' the nation. Anderson elaborated on the idea of an 'official nationalism' where the government by its official programmes, in the form of 'compulsory state-controlled primary education, state-organized propaganda, official rewriting of history, militarism . . . and endless affirmations of the identity of . . . nation' (101), tries to impose a national sentiment on the citizens. The 'Czarist Russification', or what Paul Doornbo has called 'Sudanization' (Flint and de Waal 14–15), are key examples of official nationalism. Then, there is 'methodological nationalism' with its tendency to assert that all studies in social sciences on society and modernity treat the nation-state as a natural and indispensable unit. 'Scholars who share this intellectual orientation', as Wimmer and Schiller has rightly observed, 'assume that countries are the natural units for comparative studies, equate society with the nation-state, and conflate national interests with the purposes of social science' (576).

Nationalism has been divided into Western and Eastern nationalisms by John Plamenatz. According to him, nationalism originated in Western Europe, while the nations of Eastern and Central Europe, who suffer from 'a feeling of inferiority or inadequacy' (29) because of their belated modernisation, imitated their Western counterparts. After having '[d]rawn gradually into a civilisation alien to them . . . they have had, as it were, to make themselves anew, to create national identities for themselves' (30). Eastern nationalism, therefore, is 'both imitative and hostile to the models it imitates, and is apt to be illiberal' (34). Partha Chatterjee has shown how even postcolonial nations work with 'the same essentialist conception based on the distinction between "the East" and "the West", the same typology created by a transcendent studying subject, and hence the same "objectifying" procedures of knowledge constructed in the post-Enlightenment age of Western science' (38). Nationalism in non-Western countries is, thus, a 'derivative discourse' as they mostly fail to create identity categories that are free from Western influences. All anti-imperialist nationalist movements, as Chatterjee affirms, have ended up creating a coercive 'state-representing-the-nation' (168).

OPPOSITIONS AND CELEBRATIONS

Postnationalist scholars like Saskia Sassen, Yasemin Soysal and Damian Tambini, and the upholders of cosmopolitanism, such as Kwame Anthony Appiah and Jürgen Habermas, tend to consider nationalism as a hindrance to international imaginings. Rawls has put forward the argument that nations, as people organised around a bounded society and considered as citizens by their adherence to constitutionality, liberal rights and democracy, demonstrate differing 'conceptions of the good', but in their avidity for a global distributive justice, are 'ready to propose principles and standards as fair terms of co-operation and to abide by them willingly, given the assurance that others will likewise do so' (*Political Liberalism* 49). Barry has confirmed that '[t]here is no reason for civic nationalism to be opposed to this [global] redistribution' (60). Liberal nationalists like Yael Tamir have also supported the view that a country founded upon civic nationalism, where 'there is no common being, but there is being *in* common' (Nancy 4) amidst the plurality of opinions, is deeply intertwined with democratic principles, and hence, is in no way a hindrance to global distributive justice (Tamir, 'Reconstructing the Landscape of Imagination').

On the other hand, Ranciere has shown how a 'democratic' nation-state, centring around 'mass individualism, with its ever-increasing demands and emphasis on particularism and communitarianism' can degenerate into 'the reign of narcissistic "mass individualism"' (40). Consequently, the assumed 'will of the people', dreamt of by classical exponents of social contract, is replaced by the group-will of the select party elite. The allegations made by the central government in India against farmers protesting against new farm laws (2020–21), and the branding of protesters as 'anti-nationals', are a case in point. Paul Ricoeur too, in 'The Political Paradox' (1965), has detailed how the theoretical notion of an ideal legitimate authority deriving its legitimacy from the consent of the governed, is shattered by the political praxis where the authority functions through the subjugation of the governed.

Michael Billig has coined the term 'banal nationalism' to 'cover the ideological habits which enable the established nations of the West to be reproduced. . . . Daily, the nation is indicated, or 'flagged', in the lives of its citizenry. Nationalism, far from being an intermittent mood in established nations, is the endemic condition' (6). The frenzied nationalism emerging out of this banal nationalism can be best understood in terms of what Arendt has called the 'tribal nationalism' that postulates how the people of its own nation, 'incompatible with others', are surrounded by 'a world of enemies', 'one against all', and 'denies theoretically the very possibility of a common mankind' (*The Origins of Totalitarianism* 293).

Scholars have also pointed out how nation-states, far from operating as sovereignties free of any external interferences, are controlled by the international weapons trade and the mobility of the capital. For instance, Robert Pape's *Dying to Win* helps decipher the causes of suicide terrorism through the lens of nationalism. According to Hutchinson, 'nationalism, nations, nation-states, and collective violence are linked in several way' (120). However, there are also others who argue that most of the wars since 1945 were the outcome of the weakening of nationalism, resulting in intra-state wars (Holsti 146), and that a strong national identity is needed to curb the 'new wars' aimed at weakening the integrity of the nation-state (Munkler).

Foucault has shown how the modern state, transformed into a 'surveillance society', is operative around the disciplining of bodies. The division between what must be defended in a society and what must be dead, as the enemies of the population determined through biopolitics, produces what Foucault calls 'state racism' (Foucault, *Society Must Be Defended*). This notion of state racism resulting in the denunciation of the 'other' of the citizens, just as nationalism's creation of (non/anti)nationals, makes nationalism one of the biopolitical totalitarian apparatuses. Steve Garner has revealed the interconnection between racism, nationalism and biopolitics by arguing that that the biopolitical state 'controls the definition of the nation through education, immigration and nationality/citizenship legislation; and carries out practices of enforcement' (72), and therefore, as a 'racializing machine' it banks on nationalism to produce its people and the non-nationals.

Hannah Arendt observed that with the emergence of nationalism in the nineteenth century, the state and the nation were consolidated in such a way that 'the state was partially transformed from an instrument of the law into an instrument of the nation' (*The Origins of Totalitarianism* 296). Her estimation that 'being French, Spanish or English is not a means of becoming a man, it is a manner of being a man' ('The Nation' 141) hints at her discomfort with nationalism's mandate to perceive one's identity solely as a territorio-political state-identity. Like Agamben, she perceives the nation's citizens as being subjugated by biopolitical mechanisms of the modern state which restrains the individuals' rights to the extent of rendering everyone as a possible *homo sacer* (Ek 368). The *homo sacer* is an outlaw who is unacceptable to both the Gods (unfit for sacrifice) and the law of the state (as not protected against homicide). The *homo sacer* represents the condition of a 'bare life' devoid of rights and recognitions. Agamben, while unmasking 'an inner solidarity between democracy and totalitarianism' (10), uses the figure of a *homo sacer* who experiences the law of the state in its most exclusionary form in the concentration camps. Agamben, emphasising the state's deploying of sovereignty as the totalitarian power over life and death, condemns the nation-state that functions on 'the production of a biopolitical biopolitics', where any person considered unwanted by the state can be treated as a biological unit that has to be erased out of the body politic using the label of an 'outlaw', there by rendering the subject 'stateless'.

Based on the analogy that 'features characteristic of a nation – language, history, culture, religion, geography – are among the most substantive components of individual identity' (Tamir, 'The Enigma of Nationalism' 427), Stuart Hampshire has argued that '[i]n the last analysis, a sane nationalism is to be justified by a utilitarian argument – that most men and women are happy only when their way of life prolongs customs and habits which are familiar to them' (qtd. in Gray 104). However, theorists like Kedourie are convinced that the nation is not a natural classification for humanity: 'to insist that the only legitimate type of government is national self-government . . . would be . . . both ruinous and futile' (*Nationalism in Asia and Africa* 28). According to contemporary critics of nationalism, a single nation-state or a coalition of states exhibits all markers of Gramscian hegemony.

Judith Butler, in her conversation with Spivak in *Who Sings the Nation-State?*, has criticised the nation-state by suggesting that 'the state presupposes modes of juridical belonging, at least minimally, but since the state can be precisely what expels and suspends modes of legal protection and obligation, the state can put us, some of us, in quite a state . . . of non-belonging, even produce that nonbelonging as a quasi-permanent state' (3–4). Spivak, on the other hand, suggests that it is important to free the nation-state from the delimiting 'prejudices' of nationalism: 'Nationalism is an assumption that the epistemic functioning of the national is more in keeping with the state's work and, therefore, more deserving of it. It is not an epistemic project, such as tolerance. The state . . . should be the instrument of redistribution. This definitive function has been curtailed in the global state' (97–98). It is not possible to overcome all the demerits of nationalism. They function as the bedrock of the modern nation, perceived by Arendt as a 'pseudocommunity' that can render anyone stateless. However, as Habermas has cautioned us, it is also not feasible to retreat into 'pre-political' communities. According to Habermas, any attempt to challenge nationalism by reviving a pre-political existence based on kinship and blood ties – thereby replacing modern forms of integration based on legitimate laws, political consciousness and communication – results in further repression. As he concludes, rather than reviving pre-modern organisations formed along cultural lines, the focus should be on developing a national culture based on the interpretations of constitutional principles: 'A "constitutional patriotism" based on these interpretations can take the place originally occupied by nationalism' (Habermas, *The Inclusion of the Other* 118).

REFERENCES

Agamben, Giorgio. *Homo Sacer: Sovereign Power and Bare Life*. Trans. D. Heller-Roazen. California: Stanford UP, 1998. Print.

Alter, Peter. *Nationalism*. London: Edward Arnold, 1989. Print.

Anderson, Benedict. *Imagined Communities: Reflections on the Origins and Spread of Nationalism*. London and New York: Verso, 1991. Print.

Anthonissen, Christine, and Jan Blommaert, eds. *Narratives of the Past*. Spec. issue of *Journal of Language and Politics* (2006). Print.

Appadurai, Arjun. 'The Grounds of the Nation-State: Identity, Violence and Territory'. *Nationalism and Internationalism in the Post-Cold War Era*. Ed. Ulf Hannerz, Charles Westin, and Kjell Goldmann. London: Routledge, 2000. 129–42. Print.

Appiah, Kwame Anthony. *Cosmopolitanism*. London: Penguin. 2007. Print.

Arendt, Hannah. *The Human Condition*. London: The U of Chicago P, 1998. Print.

---. 'The Nation'. *The Review of Politics* 8.1 (1946): 138–41. Print.

---. *The Origins of Totalitarianism*. New York: Schocken Books, 2004. Print.

Balibar, Etienne, and Immanuel Wallerstein. *Race, Nation, Class: Ambiguous Identities*. London: Verso, 1991. Print.

Barry, Brian. 'Self-Government Revisited'. *Theorizing Nationalism*. Ed. R. Beiner. New York: State U of New York P, 1999. 247–77. Print.

Berlin, Isaiah. 'Nationalism: Past Neglect and Present Power'. *I. Berlin: Against the Current: Essays in the History of Ideas*. New York: Penguin, 1979. 420–49. Print.

Billig, Michael. *Banal Nationalism*. London: Sage, 1995. Print.

Bourdieu, Pierre. 'Rethinking the State: Genesis and Structure of the Bureaucratic Field'. *Sociological Theory* 12.1 (1994): 1–18. Print.

Bracton, Henry De, and Portius Azo. *Select Passages from the Works of Bracton and Azo*. Whitefish: Kessinger Publishing, 2009. Print.

Breuilly, John. 'Historians and the Nation'. *History and Historians in the Twentieth Century*. Ed. P. Burke. Oxford: Oxford UP, 2002. 55–87. Print.

---. *Nationalism and the State*. Manchester: Manchester UP, 1993. Print.

Brubaker, Rogers. *Citizenship and Nationhood in France and Germany*. Cambridge: Harvard UP, 1992. Print.

---. 'Myths and Misconceptions in the Study of Nationalism'. *The State of the Nation: Ernest Gellner and the Theory of Nationalism*. Ed. J. A. Hall. Cambridge: Cambridge UP, 1998. 272–306. Print.

Butler, Judith, and Gayatri Chakravorty Spivak. *Who Sings the Nation-State?: Language, Politics, Belonging*. London: Seagull Books, 2007. Print.

Byrd, B. Sharon, and Joachim Hruschka. 'From the State of Nature to the Juridical State of States'. *Law and Philosophy* 27 (2008): 599–641. Print.

Calhoun, Craig J. *Nationalism*. Buckingham: Open UP, 1997. Print.

Canovan, Margaret. *Nationhood and Political Theory*. Cheltenham: Edward Elgar Publishing, 1996. Print.

Chatterjee, Partha. *Nationalist Thought and the Colonial World: A Derivative Discourse?* London: Zed Books, 1986. Print.

Coleman, James Samuel. *Nigeria: Background to Nationalism*. Berkeley and Los Angeles: U of California P, 1958. Print.

Connor, Walker. *Ethnonationalism: The Quest for Understanding*. Princeton: Princeton UP, 1994. Print.

Delannoi, Gil. *La theorie de la nation et ses ambivalences. Theories du nationalisme.* Paris: Kime, 1991. Print.

Disraeli, Benjamin. *Sybil*. London: John Lane, 1945. Print.

Duara, Prasenjit. 'Historicizing National Identity, or Who Imagines What and When'. *Becoming National*. Ed. G. Eley, and R. G. Suny. Oxford: Oxford UP, 1996. 151–77. Print.

Ek, Richard. *Giorgio Agamben and the Spatialities of the Camp: An Introduction*. *Geografiska Annaler* 88.4 (2006): 363–86. Print.

Eley, Geoff, and Ronald Grigor Suny, eds. *Becoming National*. Oxford and New York: Oxford UP, 1996. Print.

Evera, Stephen Van. 'Hypotheses on Nationalism and War'. *International Security* 18.4 (1994): 5–39. Print.

Evrigenis, Ioannis D., and Daniel Pellerin, trans. and eds. *Johann Gottfried Herder: Another Philosophy of History and Selected Political Writings*. Indianapolis: Hackett, 2004. Print.

Fishman, Joshua A. 'Nationality–Nationalism and Nation–Nationism'. *Language Problems in Developing Nations*. Ed. Fishman, J. A., C. A. Ferguson, and J. Das Gupta. New York: Wiley, 1968. 39–51. Print.

Flint, Julie, and Alex de Waal. *Darfur: A Short History of a Long War*. London: Zed, 2005. Print.

Foucault, Michel. 'Governmentality'. *The Foucault Effect: Studies in Governmentality: With Two Lectures by and an Interview with Michel Foucault*. Ed. G. Burchell, et al. Chicago: U of Chicago P, 1991. Print.

---. *Society Must Be Defended: Lectures at the Collège de France, 1975–1976*. London: Penguin Books, 2004. Print.

Garner, Steve. 'The European Union and the Racialization of Immigration, 1985–2006'. *Race/Ethnicity: Multidisciplinary Global Contexts* 1.1 (2007): 61–87. Print.

Geary, Patrick J. *The Myth of Nations: The Medieval Origins of Europe*. Princeton: Princeton UP, 2002. Print.

Gellner, Ernest. *Nations and Nationalism*. Oxford: Blackwell, 1983. Print.

---. *Thought and Change*. London: Weidenfeld and Nicolson, 1964. Print.

Giddens, Anthony. *The Nation-State and Violence*. Cambridge: Polity Press, 1985. Print.

Glanvill, Ranulf. *Treatise on the Laws and Customs of England*. Oxford: Clarendon Press, 1993. Print.

Gray, John. *Isaiah Berlin*. London: HarperCollins, 1995. Print.

Greenfeld, Liah. 'Etymology, Definitions, Types'. *Encyclopedia of Nationalism: Volume I*. Ed. A. J. Motyl. San Diego: Academic Press, 2001. 251–65. Print.

Habermas, Jürgen. *The Inclusion of the Other: Studies in Political Theory*. Ed. Ciaran Cronin, and Pablo De Greiff. Cambridge: Polity Press, 2005. Print.

---. *The Postnational Constellation*. Cambridge: Polity Press, 2001. Print.

Handman, Max Sylvius. 'The Sentiment of Nationalism'. *Political Science Quarterly* 36.1 (1921): 104–21. Print.

Hastings, Adrian. *The Construction of Nationhood: Ethnicity, Religion and Nationalism*. Cambridge: Cambridge UP, 1997. Print.

Hechter, Michael. *Containing Nationalism*. Oxford: Oxford UP, 2000. Print.

Herb, G. Henrik, and David Kaplan, eds. *Nations and Nationalism: A Global Historical Overview, Vol I*. Santa Barbara: ABC-CLIO, 2008. Print.

Herzfeld, Michael. *Cultural Intimacy: Social Poetics in the Nation-State*. New York and London: Routledge, 1997. Print.

Hobbes, Thomas. 'Leviathan'. *Hobbes: Leviathan*. Ed. R. Tuck. Cambridge: Cambridge UP, 1996. Print.

Hobsbawm, Eric. 'Ethnicity and Nationalism in Europe Today'. *Mapping the Nation*. Ed. G. Balakrishnan. London: Verso, 1996. 255–66. Print.

Hollinger, David A. *Postethnic America: Beyond Multiculturalism*. New York: Basic Books, 1995. Print.

Holsti, Kalevi J. 'From Khartoum to Quebec'. *Nationalism and Internationalism in the Post-Cold War Era*. Ed. K. Goldmann, U. Hannerz, and C. Westin. London: Routledge, 2000. Print.

Hroch, Miroslav. *Social Preconditions of National Revival in Europe: A Comparative Analysis of the Social Composition of Patriotic Groups among the Smaller European Nations*. Ed. and Trans. Ben Fowkes. New York: Columbia UP, 2000. Print.

Hroch, Miroslav, and Jitka Malečková. 'Nation: A survey of the Term in European Languages'. *Encyclopaedia of Nationalism*. Ed. A. S. Leoussi. New Brunswick-London: Transactions Publishers, 2001. Print.

Hume, David. 'Of National Characters'. *Essays Moral, Political and Literary*. Indianapolis: Liberty Fund, 1987. Print.

Hutchinson, J. 'Nationalism and Violence'. *After the Nation? International Political Theory Series*. Ed. K. Breen, and S. O'Neill. London: Palgrave Macmillan, 2010. 120–38. Print.

Ignatieff, Michael. *Blood and Belonging: Journeys into the New Nationalism*. London: Vintage, 1994. Print.

Kant, Immanuel. *Königlichen preußischen*. Vol 8. Ed. Akademie der Wissenschaften. Kants gesammelte schriften, Berlin: Georg Reimer (later Walter De Gruyter), 1922. Print.

---. *Perpetual Peace: A Philosophical Essay*. Trans. M. Campbell Smith. London: George Allen & Unwin Ltd., 1903. Print.

---. *Practical Philosophy*. Ed. Mary J. Gregor. Cambridge: Cambridge UP, 1999. Print.

---. *The Doctrine of Right*. Ed. Mary J. Gregor. Cambridge: Cambridge UP, 1999. Print.

Keating, Michael. *Nations Against the State: The New Politics of Nationalism in Quebec, Catalonia and Scotland*. New York: St. Martin's Press, 1996. Print.

Kedourie, Elie. *Nationalism*. London: Hutchinson, 1960. Print.

---, ed. *Nationalism in Asia and Africa*. London: Weidenfeld & Nicolson, 1971. Print.

Kohn, Hans. *The Idea of Nationalism: A Study of Its Origins and Background*. New York: Macmillan, 1944. Print.

Kroner, Richard. 'God, Nation, and Individual in the Philosophy of Hegel'. *Philosophy and Phenomenological Research* 2.2 (1941): 188–98. Print.

Kymlicka, Will. *Multicultural Citizenship: A Liberal Theory of Minority Rights*. Oxford: Oxford UP, 1995. Print.

Lenin, Vladimir I. *Collected Works. Vol 20.* Moscow: Progress Publishers, 1972. Print.

Lind, Michael. *The Next American Nation*. New York: Free Press, 1995. Print.

Locke, John. 'Economic Writings and Two Treatises of Government' [1691]. *The Works of John Locke in Nine Volumes*. Vol. 4. London: Rivington, 1824. Print.

---. *Second Treatise on Civil Government.* Ed. C. B. MacPherson. Indianapolis: Hackett, 1980. Print.

Mann, Michael. 'A Political Theory of Nationalism and Its Excesses'. *Notions of Nationalism*. Ed. S. Periwal. Budapest: Central European UP, 1995. 44–64. Print.

Martin, J. R., and Ruth Wodak, eds. *Re/reading the Past: Critical and Functional Perspectives on Time and Value*. Amsterdam/Philadelphia: Benjamins, 2003. Print.

Marvin, Carolyn, and David W. Ingle. *Blood Sacrifice and the Nation*. Cambridge: Cambridge UP, 1999. Print.

Marx, Karl. *The Revolutions of 1848*. Harmondsworth: Penguin Books, 1973. Print.

McClintock, Anne. '"No Longer in a Future Heaven": Nationalism, Gender and Race'. *Becoming National.* Ed. G. Eley, and R. G. Suny. Oxford: Oxford UP, 1996. 260–84. Print.

Meyer, John, John Boli, George M. Thomas, and Francisco O. Ramirez. 'World Society and the Nation-State'. *American Journal of Sociology* 103 (1997): 144–81. Print.

Mill, John Stuart. *Utilitarianism, Liberty and Representative Government* [1861]. Maryland: Wildside Press, 2007. Print.

Miller, David. *Justice for Earthlings: Essays in Political Philosophy*. Cambridge: Cambridge UP, 2013. Print.

---. *On Nationality*. Oxford: Clarendon Press, 1995. Print.

Molesworth, William, ed. *The English Works of Thomas Hobbes*. Volume 4. London: John Bohn, 1845. Print.

Munkler, Herfried. *The New Wars*. Cambridge: Polity, 2005. Print.

Nancy, Jean-Luc. 'Of Being-in-Common'. *Community at Loose Ends*. Ed. Miami Theory Collective. Minneapolis: U of Minnesota P, 1991. 1–12. Print.

Nandy, Ashis. 'Nationalism, Genuine and Spurious: A Very Late Obituary of Two Early Postnationalist Strains in India'. *Occasion: Interdisciplinary Studies in the Humanities* 3 (2012). Web. 10 December 2019. <http://occasion.stanford.edu/node/105>.

Nardin, Terry, and David R. Mapel. eds. *Traditions of International Ethics*. Cambridge: The Press Syndicate of the U of Cambridge, 1992. Print.

Nehru, Jawahar Lal. *The Discovery of India*. New York: Meridian Books, 1946. Print.

Nielsen, Kai. 'Secession: The Case of Quebec'. *Journal of Applied Philosophy* 10.1 (1993): 29–44. Print.

Norval, Aletta J. 'Thinking Identities: Against a Theory of Ethnicity'. *The Politics of Difference: Ethnic Premises in a World of Power*. Ed. E. N. Wilmsen, and P. McAllister. Chicago: U of Chicago P, 1996. 59–70. Print.

Ozkmmh, Umut. *Contemporary Debates on Nationalism: A Critical Engagement*. New York: Palgrave Macmillan. 2005. Print.

Pape, Robert A. *Dying to Win: The Logic of Suicide Terrorism*. New York: Random House, 2006. Print.

Petersen, William. 'On the Sub-nations of Western Europe'. *Ethnicity: Theory and Experience*. Ed. N. Glazer and D. P. Moynihan. Cambridge: Harvard UP, 1975. Print.

Plamenatz, John, 'Two Types of Nationalism'. *Nationalism*. Ed. Eugene Kamenka. Canberra: Australian National UP, 1973. 22–37. Print.

Puhle, H-J. 'Nation States, Nations and Nationalisms in Western and Southern Europe'. *Nationalism in Europe: Past and Present II*. Ed. J. G. Beramendi, et al. Galicia: University of Santiago de Compostela, 1994. Print.

Putte, Andre Van De. 'The Nation State and Multicultural Society'. *Whither Multiculturalism? A Political Dissensus*. Ed. Barbara Saunders, and David Haljan. Leuven: Leuven UP, 2003. 61–80. Print.

Ranciere, Jacques. *Dissensus, On Politics and Aesthetics*. Ed. and Trans. Steven Corcoran. London: Continuum, 2010. Print.

Rawls, John. *Political Liberalism*. New York: Columbia UP, 1993. Print.

---. *The Law of Peoples*. Cambridge: Harvard UP, 1999. Print.

Renan, Ernest. 'What is a Nation?'. *Nation and Narration*. Ed. H. K. Bhabha. London: Routledge, 1990. 8–22. Print.

Ricoeur, Paul. 'The Political Paradox'. *History and Truth*. Evanston: Northwestern UP, 1965. 247–70. Print.

Rokkan, Stein. 'Dimensions of State Formation'. *The Formation of National States in Western Europe*. Ed. C. Tilly. Princeton: Princeton UP, 1975. Print.

Roshwald, Aviel. *The Endurance of Nationalism: Ancient Roots and Modern Dilemmas*. New York: Cambridge UP, 2006. Print.

Rotberg, Robert I, ed. *State Failure and State Weakness in a Time of Terror*. Washington DC: Brookings Institution Press, 2003. Print.

Rousseau, Jean-Jacques. *The Social Contract*. Ed. Maurice Cranston. Middlesex: Penguin Books, 1968. Print.

Sassen, Saskia. 'Towards Post-National and Denationalized Citizenship'. *Handbook of Citizenship Studies*. Ed. E. F. Isin, and B. S. Turner. London: Sage, 2002. 277–91. Print.

Seliger, M. 'Locke, Liberalism and Nationalism'. *John Locke: Problems and Perspectives. A Collection of Essays*. Ed. John W. Yolton. Cambridge: Cambridge UP, 1969. 19–33. Print.

Seymour, Michel. 'On Redefining the Nation'. *The Monist* 82.3 (1999): 411–45. Print.

Shils, Edward. 'Nation, Nationality, Nationalism'. *British Journal of Sociology* 1.1 (1995): 93–118. Print.

Smith, Anthony D. 'Nationalism and the Historians'. *Myths and Memories of the Nation*. Oxford: Oxford UP, 1999. 29–55. Print.

---. 'Opening Remarks'. *Nations and Nationalism* 14.4 (2008): 637–63. Print.

Stalin, Joseph. *Marxism and the National Question*. Moscow: Foreign Languages Publishing House, 1980. Print.

Soysal, Yasemin Nuhoglu. *Limits of Citizenship, Migrants and Postnational Membership in Europe*. Chicago: Chicago UP, 1994. Print.

Tambini, Damian. 'Post-National Citizenship'. *Ethnic and Racial Studies* 24.2 (2001): 195–217. Print.

Tamir, Yael. 'Reconstructing the Landscape of Imagination'. *National Rights, International Obligations*. Ed. S. Caney, D. George, and P. Jones. Boulder: Westview Press, 1996. 85–101. Print.

---. 'The Enigma of Nationalism'. *World Politics* 47 (1995): 418–40. Print.

Tilly, Charles. 'A Bridge Halfway: Responding to Brubaker'. *Contention* 4.1 (1994): 15–19. Print.

---, ed. *The Formation of National States in Western Europe*. Princeton: Princeton UP, 1975. Print.

Tunyi, Zhoto, and Jelle J. P. Wouters. 'India's Northeast as an Internal Borderland: Domestic Borders, Regimes of Taxation, and Legal Landscapes'. *The NEHU Journal* XIV.1 (2016): 1–17. Print.

Varouxakis, Georgios. *Mill on Nationality*. New York: Routledge, 2002. Print.

Verdery, Katherine. 'Whither "Nation" and "Nationalism"?' *Daedalus* 122.3 (1993): 37–46. Print.

Warner, Daniel. *An Ethic of Responsibility in International Relations*. Colorado: Lynne Rienner Publishers Inc., 1991. Print.

Weber, Max. *From Max Weber: Essays in Sociology*. Ed. Hans Gerth, and C. Wright Mills. London: Routledge and Kegan Paul, 1948. Print.

Wimmer, Andreas, and Nina Glick Schiller. 'Methodological Nationalism, the Social Sciences, and the Study of Migration: An Essay in Historical Epistemology'. *The International Migration Review* 37.3 (2003): 576–610. Print.

Wimmer, Andreas, and Yuval Feinstein. 'The Rise of the Nation-State across the World, 1816 to 2001'. *American Sociological Review* 75.5 (2010): 764–90. Print.

Wirth, Louis. 'Types of Nationalism'. *American Journal of Sociology* 41.6 (1936): 723–37. Print.

Wodak, Ruth. 'National and Trans-national Identities: European and Other Identities Oriented to in Interviews with EU Officials'. *Transnational Identities: Becoming European in the EU*. Ed. R. Hermann et al. New York: Rowman and Littlefield, 2004. 97–128. Print.

Yack, Bernard. *Nationalism and the Moral Psychology of Community*. Chicago: U of Chicago P, 2012. Print.

---. 'The Myth of the Civic Nation'. *Theorizing Nationalism*. Ed. R. Beiner. New York: State U of New York P, 1999. 103–18. Print.

Yuval-Davis, Nira. *Gender and Nation*. London: Sage, 1997. Print.

Zartman, William I., ed. *Collapsed States: The Disintegration and Restoration of Legitimate Authority*. London: Lynne Rienner Publishers, 1995. Print.

Zernatto, Guido, and Alfonso G. Mistretta. 'Nation: The History of a Word'. *The Review of Politics* 6.3 (1944): 351–66. Print.

Žižek, Slavoj. *Tarrying with the Negative: Kant, Hegel, and the Critique of Ideology*. Durham: Duke UP, 1993. Print.

Chapter Two

Anticolonial Nationalism and the Postcolonial Nation

THEMES FROM POST-COLONIES, AND A CRITICAL SURVEY OF TROPES AND DEBATES IN INDIAN NATIONALISM

COLONIAL DOMINATION AND NATIONAL STRUGGLES FOR INDEPENDENCE: THEMES, MODES AND CHARACTERISTICS

It is unfortunate that liberal nationalism, which had inspired the Europeans to demand their own states, ultimately gave birth to imperialism. European empire-building followed two major trajectories. On the one hand, liberal political nationalism and the humanist ideology of internationalism advocated by Kant, Rousseau and Jeremy Bentham (1748–1832) were narrowed down by the rising political aspirations of smaller European communities – such as the Poles, Czechs, Danes, Germans, Hungarians, Romanians, Serbs, Italians and Bulgarians – revolting for their own nation-states (Kohn 15). On the other hand, the economic nationalism generated by the Industrial Revolution, with the subsequent transformation from liberalism to capitalist expansion, resulted in the search for new markets that spurred the acquisition of overseas colonies. By the First World War, ninety per cent of the territories were already under the domination of imperialists like Portugal, Spain, the United States, the Soviet Union, France, Belgium, Netherlands, Australia, Denmark, New Zealand, and chiefly Britain which had colonised a quarter of the world's population. 'Third world' and

'Tricontinentalism' (comprising Asia, Africa and Latin America) are labels that are commonly attached to countries, mostly from the Global South, which have a history of anticolonial struggle, and provide evidence of the exploitation of these nations by those of the Global North.

Colonialism was primarily motivated by commercial interests, rather than the need for creating foreign settlements or extensive proselytisation, which constitute the prime agendas of imperialism (Singh). Yet, in the course of time, colonies became a part of the imperialist policy of hegemonic expansion of the state power of the colonising nation through the constant regulation of the socio-cultural practices of the colonised and imposition of the cultural norms of the coloniser. The link between the commercial intent of colonisation, which ultimately led to acquisition, and the agenda of conquest implied in imperialism, is clear in Seeley's statement: 'Our acquisition of India was made blindly. Nothing great that has ever been done by Englishmen was done so unintentionally, so accidently, as the conquest of India. . . . [I]n India we meant one thing, and did another' (143). Unlike the imperial settlements in British North America, Portuguese Brazil or French Algeria, British India, Japanese Taiwan, Dutch East Indies or German Togo had lesser number of foreign settlements, saw fewer attempts at proselytisation into Christianity, and suffered greater economic exploitation as the indigenous society was transformed into a capitalist economy. But critics of colonial regimes, like Edward Said and Frantz Fanon, seem to have used 'imperialism' and 'colonialism' quite interchangeably on the basis of the similarities in anticolonial and anti-imperialist movements against foreign subjugation.

In *Nations and Nationalism*, Gellner demonstrates the strong link between industrialisation and the rise of nationalism. Developments that were promoted as markers of a scientific and advanced society – such as the use of mosquito nets, quinine and machine guns – encouraged imperialists in their mission of encroaching on subject territories under the pretext of 'civilising' those who were categorised as 'savage'. The *mission civilisatrice* was crucial in rationalising French imperialism as a 'noble mission' of spreading a 'noble' culture, religion and education among the 'unenlightened' people of sub-

Saharan Africa, Syria, Lebanon and Polynesia. The British imperial ideology also functioned on the basis of a paradoxical logic of exploiting the wealth of the 'niggers' for the benefit of the 'civilised nations', and striving for the uplift of the dominated 'barbarians' by spreading among them the 'civilised notions' of the colonisers: 'while on the one hand the abounding wealth of the tropical regions of the earth must be developed and used for the benefit of mankind, on the other hand an obligation rests on the controlling power not only to safeguard the material rights of the natives, but to promote their moral and educational progress' (Lugard 18). The 'economic nationalism/colonialism' binary not only propagated notions about the non-European and the non-Christian as the 'other' or the 'outsider' (or even as the 'outsider within' in the case of Jews during the Holocaust), but gradually instigated resistance movements among oppressed indigenes. This first took the form of 'emotionalisation', towards the generation of a cultural nationalism, through the revival of myths, legends, popular indigenous icons, art and music, native festivals, and so on. The next stage was direct confrontation. Anticolonialism as a conscious effort to put an end to the 'era of western domination over the rest of mankind' (Emerson 5) resulted in giving birth to several people's movements – for instance, the Herero Wars (1904–08) by the people of present-day Namibia (German South West Africa) against the German empire; Maji Maji rebellion (1905–06) against German colonial rule in contemporary Tanzania (German East Africa); Bambatha rebellion (1906) by the Zulu people in Natal against the British rule in South Africa; Kaocen revolt (1916–17) by the Tuareg people against French colonial rule in Northern Niger; Forest Brothers rebellion (1944–65) by Estonian, Latvian and Lithuanian partisans against the Soviet invasion of the three Baltic states; Mau Mau uprising (1952–60) in British Kenya, etc.

There were fierce critics of colonisation within colonising nations, such as William Ewart Gladstone (1809–98), John Morley (1838–1923), Henry Mayers Hyndman (1842–1921), Voltaire (1694–1778) and Montesquieu (1689–1755), among many others. *A Short Account of the Destruction of the Indies* (1542) by Bartolomé de las Casas is regarded as a pioneering work about anticolonialism and anti-slavery, with an earnest plea for defending human rights and right to equality. Edmund Burke (1729–97), through his impeachment of Warren Hastings (1732–1818), has to 'be credited for being one of the first voices to articulate the possibility that India comprised cultures and societies as yet unread by the West' (Suleri 46). Maximilien Robespierre's (1758–94) famous statement – 'Let the colonies perish, if they must cost you your honour, your glory, your liberty' (qtd. in Merle 162) – was a significant condemnation of imperialism, slavery and the exploitation of the Black people. The objection against the economic utility of colonies came from economists like Adam Smith: 'Great Britain should voluntarily give up all authority over her colonies' (172). Jeremy Bentham argued vehemently against colonisation by focusing on the rights of the 'natives' to self-determination: 'You choose your own government: why are not other people to choose theirs? So you seriously mean to govern the world, and do you call that *liberty*? What is become of the rights of men? Are you the only men who have rights? Alas! my fellow citizens, have you two measures?' (408). J. A. Hobson revealed how through its dependence on '[w]ar, militarism and "a spirited foreign policy"' (106), colonisation is 'irrational from the standpoint of the whole (colonised) nation' (47). Defending the native's resistance against imperialism, Diderot rightly remarked that European traders had validated themselves 'dangerous as guests' (qtd. in Muthu 75).

Japan's triumph over Russia in 1905 inspired the rest of Asia in their nationalist struggles. As Lenin noted, 'Following the 1905 movement in Russia, the democratic revolution spread to the whole of Asia – to Turkey, Persia, China. Ferment is growing in British India. A significant development is the spread of the revolutionary democratic movement to the Dutch East Indies, to Java, and the other Dutch colonies' (59). The Canadian and Irish Home Rule movements also provided impetus for anti-imperialist movements across the colonised nations. By the time of the Russian Revolution of 1917, a close alliance was established between revolutionary socialism and anticolonial struggles for self-determination. In the Fourth Communist International of 1922, an appeal was made, on the basis of the proposal made by M. N. Roy (1887–1954), for an anti-imperialist united front that will assemble all accessible revolutionary forces against imperialism. This was affirmed by delegates from nine non-Soviet Asian, five Latin American and three African countries.

There was a fundamental difference in the way the colonies developed their sense of nationhood. In England, the nation as a mode of belonging emerged out of the aspirations of the lower gentry who used nationalism for upward mobility under the Tudors. In France or Latin America, the ideology around the nation was deployed as a tool generated by the aristocracy to retain its privileged position. In Germany, non-aristocratic intellectuals (like Kant, Fichte, Herder or Hegel) combined with the nobles to propagate German nationalism. Unlike these examples, in the colonies, the concepts of 'official nationalism' and a unified nation (or national unification through the structuring of state machineries) developed through the intervention of colonial regimes. However, in time, these countries modified these inherited notions of nationhood. For instance, the United States of America threw off the British yoke in 1776 to create an egalitarian democratic nation with no monarchy or aristocracy, but with a strong leader like George Washington who rose from among the people.

It was Napoleon's victory over Prussia at Jena in 1806 that made Hegel propose that advanced countries should prioritise a strong state administration under a strong leader over the idea of a liberal nation, in order to be able to defend themselves from both external and internal forces of disintegration. Hegel's maxim seems to have influenced most independence movements since each of them had a powerful leader. In Latin America, strong leaders such as Francisco de Miranda (1750–1816), José Gervasio Artigas (1764–1850), Simón Bolívar (1783–1830), José de San Martín (1778–1850), Bernardo O'Higgins (1778–1842), Agustín de Iturbide (1783–1824), José Antonio Páez (1790–1873), Antonio José de Sucre Alcalá (1795–1830), Miguel Hidalgo y Costilla (1753–1811) and José María Morelos y Pavón (1765–1815) played crucial roles in combating colonial regimes; while Africa had prominent leaders like Jomo Kenyatta (1891–1978), Habib Bourguiba (1903–2000), Nnamdi Azikiwe (1904–96), Félix Houphouët-Boigny (1905–93) and Léopold Sédar Senghor (1906–2001) who came to lead the movements for independence. In Africa, anticolonial leaders like Kwame Nkrumah (1909–72), Julius Nyerere (1922–99), Ahmed Sékou Touré (1922–84) and Muammar Gaddafi (1942–2011) began their anti-imperialist campaigns by indigenising leftist doctrines as a route to return to a pre-colonial past that, according to them, was based on communalism. However, in most of the postcolonial southern African countries, it soon became clear that tribalism dominated the outlook of the people who 'concentrate upon its heroes, its historical successes, and its unsullied cultural purity, and are decked out with the mythic "rediscovered" social values of the past' (Vail 14).

Anticolonial resistance in Asia succeeded in giving birth to a series of independent nation-states after the Second World War – Vietnam, Indonesia, South Korea and North Korea in 1945; the Philippines in 1946; India and Pakistan in 1947; Burma (now Myanmar), Palestine and Ceylon (now Sri Lanka) in 1948; Cambodia and Laos in 1953; and many other countries. The list ends with the Democratic Republic of Timor-Leste which became a sovereign state in 2002. The leaders from twenty-nine newly independent 'postcolonial' Asian and African countries, including Sukarno (1901–70) of Indonesia, Gamal Abdel Nasser (1918–70) of Egypt, Jawaharlal Nehru (1889–1964), and Nkrumah, who were 'non-aligned' with both the Soviet and the Western blocs, assembled at the Bandung Conference (1955) to advocate the 'Third World' perspective on global affairs. After eleven years, in 1966, in the Tricontinental Conference in Havana, the Latin American and the Caribbean countries also joined the Asian and African countries to provide a more militant resistance of the united world of the exploited against Western imperialism. Che Guevara spelt out the agenda of this resistance:

> The contribution that falls to us, the exploited and backward of the world, is to eliminate the foundations sustaining imperialism: our oppressed nations, from which capital, raw materials and cheap labor (both workers and technicians) are extracted, and to which new capital (tools of domination), arms and all kinds of goods are exported, sinking us into absolute

> dependence. The fundamental element of that strategic objective, then, will be the real liberation of the peoples. . . . ('Message to the Tricontinental')

One of the striking features of the Asian anticolonial resistance was that, while on the one hand the communist influence was prominent in many of the nationalist endeavours for decolonisation – for example, the communist leanings of the Malay Nationalist Party of Malaya (Parti Kebangsaan Melayu Malaya, PKMM) or the Việt Minh led by Hồ Chí Minh, the Marxist-Leninist revolutionary – on the other hand, many of the anticolonial Asian leaders, to a great extent, maintained an intimate link with religion. For instance, Mahatma Gandhi (1869–1948), the father of the Indian nation, was greatly influenced by the ideals of the *Bhagavad Gita*; Saya San (1876–1931) initiated the Saya San Rebellion (1930–32) in British Burma as a Buddhist proto-nationalist movement; the Philippine Revolution launched by Andrés Bonifacio (1863–97) represented a Christian nationalism; and in Java, Diponegoro's (1785–1855) rebellion alluded to Islamic ideas. While an ardent spirit of nationalism drove the anti-imperialist movements in most cases in South Asia and Africa, in Latin America, the anti-imperialist resistance often combined with the struggle against feudalism that had already existed within the countries (Mariategui 131).

According to Robert J. C. Young, the various modes of political, military and ideological resistance to colonialism can be classified as follows (165–66):

1. Objection by Europeans from within on moral and humanitarian grounds
2. Objection by European liberal economists like Smith
3. Rivalry between European and non-European imperialists (for example USA–Japan–Russia)
4. The assertion of the right to self-determination in settler colonies (for example, Canada, USA, Bolivia)
5. Cultural/Religious/Bourgeois nationalism in the colonies (for example, Ireland, Poland, Kenya, Egypt, India)
6. Anticolonial internationalism (for example, pan-Arabism, pan-Africanism, the Negritude movement, the Khilafat movement)

7. Aggressive measures like strikes, protest-migration, peasant revolts, agitation over reforms, communalism, etc.
8. Armed national liberation movements and Marxist internationalism (for example, Vietnam, Angola, China, Mozambique, Cuba)

The 'Declaration on the Granting of Independence to Colonial Countries and Peoples', adopted by the United Nations, was a milestone in the process of bringing colonisation to an end. It recognised 'the passionate yearning for freedom in all dependent peoples and the decisive role of such peoples in the attainment of their independence', and resolved that '[a]ll armed action or repressive measures of all kinds directed against dependent peoples shall cease in order to enable them to exercise peacefully and freely their right to complete independence, and the integrity of their national territory shall be respected' (UN, General Assembly resolution 1514 (XV) of 14 December 1960).

While colonial regimes have been overthrown and national self-determination has been asserted by the colonised all over the world, various modes of colonial practices continue to persist even in the post–Cold-War era. A 'redecorated colonialism', as suggested by Father Miguel d'Escoto Brockmann (1933–2017) of Nicaragua, seems to be operational till date through the misuse of the doctrine of the 'Responsibility to Protect' (RtoP) by powerful First World nations, by which they justify their 'arbitrary and selective interventions against weaker states' (Knight and Egerton 260). Mahmood Mamdani has also argued that the end of the Cold War was succeeded by a new 'systematic shift' in international politics that, in theory, was supposed to be based on 'an international humanitarian order that promises to hold state sovereignty accountable to an international "human rights" standards' (273), but in practice entirely '[drew]on the history of modern western colonialism' (276). For instance, in Afghanistan, on the pretext of resisting the resurgence of the Taliban, US President George Bush installed Hamid Karzai as the head of the state, without making any attempts to rebuild the Afghan social infrastructure. For the majority of the Afghans, Karzai functioned merely as 'the mayor of Kabul' and represented an 'ineffective', 'corrupt' and 'illegitimate' government (Beaumont). Likewise, France, Russia and the United

States continued to support Saddam Hussein of Iraq despite his war with Iran and his own people, until the Halabja genocide of March 1988 where five thousand Kurds were killed. Thereafter, the sanctions, imposed mainly by Britain and the United States, resulted in the death of around 227,000 Iraqi children under the age of five (Cortright and Lopez 46), and destroyed the Iraqi civil society and middle class who could have transformed the country from within. Despite strong disapproval from the UN Security Council, Iraq was invaded by the United States in 2003 on the basis of unfounded allegations. According to the 'Iraq Body Count' (IBC) database, between January 2003 and December 2016, 'the documented civilian deaths from violence' were around 188751 ('Iraq Body Count: Documented Civilian Deaths from Violence', *Iraq Body Count*, at https://www.iraqbodycount.org/database/). The United Nations High Commissioner for Refugees (UNHCR), in December 2008, estimated that 'more than 4.7 million Iraqis have left their homes, many in dire humanitarian care. Of these, more than 2.7 million Iraqis are displaced internally, while more than 2 million have fled to neighboring states, particularly Syria and Jordan. . . . In 2006, Iraqis became the leading nationality seeking asylum in Europe' ('The Iraq Situation', at http://www.unhcr.org/iraq.html). There are many more instances – such as the implementation of RtoP in Libya but not in Bahrain since the latter was an American ally in the region, or the United States vetoing the UNSC proposal to condemn Israel's illegal invasions, aggravating the Gaza crisis – that prove how colonisation by the 'big powers' continue even in an era that is supposed to have marked the end of colonialism.

POSTCOLONIAL NATIONALISM

Whether nationalism is a 'political doctrine' or an 'idea' and a 'state of mind' is a topic of debate among scholars of nationalism. Postcolonial nationalism, as the basis of a political and organised attempt to establish a nation's right to self-determination by forming an independent nation-state which is perceived as the 'homeland', through a designed nationalist anticolonial encounter, can undoubtedly be regarded as 'a political movement by definition' (Brass 48). However, as scholars have pointed out, postcolonial nationalism, as an engagement initiated by the nationalist elite, often provides the privileged with the best of opportunities at the cost of the deprived masses, in the post-independence national scenario. Aijaz Ahmad observes that the postcolonial nationalism of the 'so-called Third World is generated mostly in the metropolises' and 'continues to be assembled within metropolitan institutes' (79).

Postcolonial nationalism's fallibility can be seen 'in murderous ethnic conflict, continued inequalities among societies, classes, and genders' (Dirlik 347). In order to enjoy power and sustain their influence, nationalist leaders of postcolonial nations often emulate their former colonisers. For example,

1. Postcolonial national leaders strive to expand the territorial boundaries of the nation-state by trespassing into neighbouring countries.

2. They often wish to sustain their influence by maintaining the gulf between majority and minority communities within the nation-state.

3. Using 'national integration' as a pretext to nation-building, the postcolonial nationalist plays a regressive role in the internal ethno-nationalist aspirations.

The ratification of a postcolonial nation is often based on various ethnic groups within the territory agreeing upon a civic alliance for the sake of defeating the coloniser, and the post-independent nation, in such cases, are often threatened by latent internal nationalist movements. Moreover, the issues that are highlighted by postcolonial nationalism as 'nation-protecting' – such as education, health, and language – are often viewed as privileging the majority community. A further paradox in postcolonial nationalism lies in the fact that the antagonistic ethno-nationalist groups fighting within the postcolonial nation often are 'co-ethnics' and co-operative 'co-nationals' outside the territory of the nation-state. In short, postcolonial nationalism seems to operate through 'external-territory-claiming', 'co-national protecting' and 'independence-protecting' (Barrington 22) strategies, which are used by the post-independent nationalist elite to propagate the idea of nationalism among the masses for the sake of forging a nationalist unity.

Strengthening a new, *formulated* notion of national solidarity seems to be the central motif of postcolonial nationalism, which it tries to attain by popularising certain 'nation symbols' – symbols that are recently constructed as well as those that are revived and revisioned from ancient myths and legends. For instance, in the post–9/11 era in the United States, the Twin Towers became almost a national symbol that denoted the economic prowess of the nation which was constantly threatened from outside. In India, the character of Sita is often revisited by the Hindutva nationalist to project an ideal *Bharatiya* womanhood, while the figure of Ravana has been revisioned by Dalits as a real indigenous hero who resisted a colonial invasion symbolised by the conquest of Lanka by Rama (Richman). The rise of sinophobic rap music in Mongolia, popularising a distinct Mongolian postcolonial nationalist identity, is an example of fabricating new modes of opposing colonisation.

Examples like Namibia, Bosnia and Mauritius show that it is possible for the nationalist elite of a postcolonial nation to create inclusive polyarchical regimes where multi-ethnic groups are accommodated through cross-ethnic negotiation and consensus. Although cases like Rwanda and Somalia provide examples of the degeneration of civic postcolonial unity caused by 'ethnic-nation-protecting' political claims, examples like Malaysia provide a model for creating a consociational nationalism by cooperative ethnic elites. Internal ethno-nationalist movements within India – for example, movements demanding a separate Telangana, Jharkhand, or Chhattisgarh – show how a dual nationalism based on both ethnic and civic collaboration operates on overlapping territorial spaces. Hence, postcolonial nationalism as a post-formulation of the post-coloniality is based also on intimacies and identities prior to colonisation, where the elites while certainly influential, are, nevertheless, compelled to follow certain traditional norms that are echoed by the masses. Thus, trying to blend the ethnic and civic loyalties of the citizens, postcolonial nationalism as a campaign appears to be both constructivist and constantly shifting.

Postcolonial nationalism is celebrated as 'popular nationalism' in Frantz Fanon's 'ontotheological' approach where the 'nation-people', regarded as the organic embodiment of the homeland, are perceived as the epitomes of the national 'spirit', for whom the only motto is the corporeal manifestation of a nation-state: 'the national cause goes on progressing, and becomes the cause of each and all. . . . Everywhere . . . we find a national authority. Each man or woman brings the nation to life by his or her action' (131–32). Edward Said, on the contrary, highlights the perils of postcolonial nationalism through derivation: 'Nationality, nationalism, nativism: the progression is, I believe, more and more constraining. In countries like Algeria and Kenya one can watch the heroic resistance of a community partly formed out of colonial degradations, leading to a protracted armed and cultural conflict with the imperial powers, in turn giving way to a one-party state with dictatorial rule' (277). Partha Chatterjee, influenced by Gramsci's theory of passive revolution, explains that, in the Third World in general and India in particular, when the anticolonial cultural nationalism is transformed into postcolonial nationalism, it becomes a capitalist instrument of the indigenous bourgeoisie. Analysing how marginal groups in India – such as the tribals and the lower castes – need to be positioned outside the political society, since '[p]olitical society and electoral democracy have not given these groups the means to make effective claims on governmentality' (61), Chatterjee argues that the major emphasis in a postcolonial nation should be on an effective welfare government that serves the marginal sections of the population. There is, thus, a hope that the postcolonial nation would not merely function as a comprador regime but would transform into a popular nation-state by focusing more on the 'people-nation', especially the 'subaltern'. Labelling the postcolonial nation as 'a condition of pessimism' where postcolonial nationalism is better understood as 'neocolonialism', Appiah also pleads for a transformation so that post-independent nations can get rid of not only the 'Western imperium but also the nationalist project of the postcolonial national bourgeoisie' (353).

This hope of transformation is dented when one recalls Derrida's assertion that the 'nation-people' attains freedom from colonial rule only by entering into a postcolonial bourgeois state that will finally associate the 'nation-people' with global capitalist interests: 'Like those of the blood, nationalisms of the native soil not only sow hatred, not only commit crimes, they have no future, they promise nothing even if, like stupidity or the unconscious, they hold fast to life' (169).

In recent times, there has been a tendency to treat the postcommunist condition as a postcolonial state (Barrington 281). However, one also needs to acknowledge that postcolonial nationalism has paved way for indigenous studies due to which one can now be exposed to a wide range of knowledge systems and cultural notions that are completely different from perspectives acquired through Eurocentrism. Dipesh Chakrabarty, in *Provincializing Europe*, studies how distinctively European concepts have been mistakenly treated as universal, and when applied in the non-European context, have resulted in providing an erroneous notion about the non-Western culture. Challenging Bhabha's liberal acceptance of 'in-betweenness' that facilitates the understanding of the 'self-as-other' and the 'other-as-self' in postcolonial condition, postcolonial nationalism seems to have created an extreme standpoint of 'nativism' that urges for a complete detachment from the 'cultural bomb' of the colonisers by a 'deliberate dissociation' even from the coloniser's language (waThiong'o 28).

Postcolonial nationalism has accelerated the struggle of the newly independent states to overcome external economic dependency because of the strong conviction that, '[i]f a country does not have its own economy, if it is penetrated by foreign capital, then it cannot be free from the tutelage of the country it is dependent on' (Guevara, *Che Guevara and the Cuban Revolution* 85). As Castro once stated, 'Colonies are not known until they have the opportunity to express themselves' (28). Postcolonial nationalism has been instigating an epoch of reversals where the 'toiling humanity, inhumanly exploited, these paupers, controlled by the whip and overseers' have 'decided to begin writing history for themselves for all time' (Castro 165–66).

INDIAN NATIONALISTS AND IDEAS OF NATIONHOOD

The territory that comprises present-day India has been described using many different terms in ancient texts – 'Meluhha' in ancient

Mesopotamian texts, 'Sapta Sindhava' in the *Rigveda*, the 'Sixteen Mahajanapadas' during the time of the Buddha, 'Jambudipa' in Ashokan inscriptions, 'Aryavarta' in *Manusmriti,* and 'Bharadvasa' in Kharavela's Hathigumpha inscription in Odisha, or 'Bharat-varsha' in the *Mahabharata*. Then 'came the name "India" by the Greeks, and the Chinese "Yun-tu" representing "Indu"', to be followed by the Iranian 'Hindustan' to denote the people by the Sindhu river – the claim that 'Hindustan' is 'a Sanskrit word meaning "land of the Hindus" is a modern invention' (Habib 4–5). Amir Khusrau's *Nuhsipihr* (1318) listed regional languages like Kashmiri, Tamil, Telugu and Sindhi, which he called 'Hindwi', along with Sanskrit, the language of the educated class. The Mughal empire, providing 'a political uniformity and a sense of larger allegiance' (Chand 141) essential for generating a concept of India as a country with a uniquely synthesised cultural domain, promoted the composition of India's earliest full-length history in the form of *Tabaqat-i-Akbari* (1592) by Nizamuddin Ahmad. The great saint-singers of India such as Kabir and Dadu Dayal also had a role in crystallising the idea of Indian nationhood. Evaluating the songs and sermons of these sages as the 'society's memory of its own past' (Raghavan 15) that are pervaded 'with an idea of nationality in a manner unknown in other parts of the world' (49), V. Raghavan insisted: 'The role of the saints, was then one of great social integration which went on for five or six centuries and which formed a stage in the evolution of the society towards an increasing sense of equality and nobility' (54).

The development and evolution of the idea of Indian nationhood and nationalism was mediated through a number of social, religious, reformist and political movements, and by several nationalist leaders. Beginning with Henry Derozio's (1809–31) Young Bengal movement and the Revolt of 1857, Indian nationalism as a political consciousness developed out of the anticolonial engagement. The liberal Indian nationalists launched movements of social reform to remove the social evils that had hindered India's progress to nationhood. Raja Ram Mohan Roy (1772–1833), the pioneering reformer of India's 'colonial modernity', perceived how the custom of child marriage, often resulting in early widowhood, along with discriminations based on caste and religion, have created 'divisions and subdivisions' among Indians and 'deprived them of patriotic feelings' (Ghose 929). Roy established the Brahmo Samaj in 1828 to interfuse the Upanishadic philosophy with the humanist doctrines of Islam and Christianity. Pandita Ramabai (1858–1922), an erudite scholar of Hindu shastras who converted to Christianity, established the Arya Mahila Samaj to eradicate the religious and cultural taboos that had caused immense suffering to Indian women. Annie Besant (1847–1933), associated with the Theosophical Society and Home Rule movement, maintained that 'it is religion which has ever bound individuals into a tribe and tribes into a nation' (300). According to her, Indian nationhood could be fortified through an education that had its roots in Indian doctrines and not overshadowed by Western cultural tenets. Jyotirao Govindrao Phule (1827–90) and his wife Savitribai Phule (1831–97) dedicated themselves to uplifting the wretched of the caste-ridden 'varnasramic' society – shudras and ati-shudras. The Phule couple, founders of the Satya Shodhak Samaj (Society of the Seekers of Truth), worked to liberate the lower castes and the poorest, the bahujans, from brahminical exploitation, through initiatives like conducting wedding ceremonies with minimum expenses and without priests or dowry. The Phules set up India's first indigenously run school for girls for students from all castes. Savitribai Phule is regarded as the first Indian woman teacher. Mahadev Govind Ranade (1842–1901), prominent spokesman of Prarthana Samaj and an enthusiastic promoter of Bhakti poets, argued that Christian virtues like 'power of organization, active hatred of sin', 'active philanthropy and a feeling of fraternity', 'have to be incorporated into the national character' of India (Ranade, *Religious and Social Reform* 23), so that the nation rears up 'its head – absorbing all that is best in the alien civilisation and polity and religions' (Ranade, 'Social Evolution', n. p.). Gopal Krishna Gokhale (1866–1915), founder of the Servants of India Society, believed that 'a feeling of common nationality, based upon common tradition, common disabilities and common hopes and aspirations' should inspire every Indian with a 'fervent patriotism which rejoices at every opportunity of sacrifice for the motherland' (qtd. in Natesan 915), so that 'the idea of a united and renovated India' (914) is actualised. Gokhale believed that this new India should be organised 'on a democratic basis' with 'the average strength of the mass of the people' raised through a compulsive elementary education instead of relying upon 'a few towering individuals' (qtd. in Karve and Ambekar 244). Moderate nationalists like W. C. Banerjee (1844–1906), Surendranath Banerjee (1848–1925), Pherozeshah Mehta (1845–1915), Madan Mohan Malaviya (1861–1946) and Badruddin Tyabji (1844–1906), through 'petition, prayer and protest', tried 'to promote by constitutional means the interests and well-being of the people of the Indian Empire' following 'the lines of general appreciation of British rule and of constitutional action for the removal of its defects' (Zaidi and Zaidi 479). The moderate nationalists' criticism of the British rule was centred around the perils of economic exploitation. Dadabhai Naoroji's (1825–1917) anxiety about India's poverty due to the drain of wealth from India to England provoked a series of critical enquiries – for example, *The Poverty Problem in India* (1895) by P. C. Ray, *Economic History of India* (in two volumes) (1901–03) by Romesh Chandra Dutt, and *Some Economic Aspects of British Rule in India* (1903) by Subramania Iyer.

The formation of the Muslim League in 1906, and the Punjab Hindu Sabha in 1909, followed by the Hindu Mahasabha in 1915, made the undercurrent of religious subnationalism palpable beneath the Indian nationalists' struggle for independence. The Arya Samaj, founded by Swami Dayanand Saraswati (1824–83) in 1875, marked the transition of neo-Hinduism from 'reform to revivalism' (Jaffrelot 6). The literary works of Bankim Chandra Chatterjee, filled with 'violent Hindu agenda' and Hindu–Muslim antagonism, had envisaged the 'religious militancy' of a triumphant Hindu community 'as a resolution to the problem of colonisation' (Sarkar 2560). This extremist nationalism, believing in militancy and the martial character of the nation, had its foundation in religious sectarianism and non-assimilationist politics. Bipin Chandra Pal (1858–1932) argued that Bankim's '*Bande Mataram*', where the 'Mother' nation combined 'Kali, Durga, Lakshmi, [and] Saraswati' in 'a new synthesis' (Pal 13), had to be sung by 'Brahmin preachers and reciters . . . all over Hindu India' (19). Blending his patriotism with his preoccupation with the *Gita*, the *Ramayana* and the *Mahabharata*, Bal Gangadhar Tilak's (1856–1920) prime intention was to 'be able to consolidate all the different sects into a mighty Hindu nation.' He believed that 'this ought to be the ambition of every Hindu' (37). Tilak's nationalism, 'a combination of the Vedanta ideal of the spiritual unity of mankind and the Western notions of nationalism' (Inamdar 116), was based on a firm conviction that religious union is crucial for political unity, which eventually motivated him to popularise Hindu celebrations such as Ganeshotsav and Shiv Jayanti (the birth anniversary of Chhatrapati Shivaji) for uniting Hindus against the British for the attainment of 'swaraj' as one's birthright. Swami Vivekananda (1863–1902), who relentlessly preached harmony and equality between Hindus and Muslims, nevertheless assigned Hindu ideals as decisive principles for the functioning of the body politic of the nation: 'For our own motherland a junction of the two great systems, Hinduism and Islam – Vedanta brain and Islam body – is the only hope' (376). Aurobindo Ghosh (1872–1950) categorically declared, 'nationalism is not politics but a religion, . . . it is the Sanatana Dharma which for us is nationalism. This Hindu nation was born with the Sanatana Dharma, . . . [t]he Sanatana Dharma, that is nationalism' (Aurobindo 12). Deriving that 'India cannot be assumed today to be a unitarian and homogeneous nation, but on the contrary these are two nations in the main, the Hindus and the Muslims in India' (17), Vinayak Damodar Savarkar (1883–1966) affirmed, 'Swaraj to the Hindus must mean only that in which their "Swaraj," their "Hindutva" can assert itself without being overlorded by any non-Hindu people' (18). Lala Har Dayal, influenced by Savarkar's communal nationalism, argued that the dignity of Hindustan depended on Hindu organisation, Hindu rule, *shuddhi* (reconversion) of Muslims and a Hindu conquest of Afghanistan for validating a 'Greater India' (Menon 93). Savarkar's attempt to relate Hindi linguistic nationalism with Hindu cultural nationalism finds resonance in C. Rajagopalachari's (1878–1972) endeavour to make Hindi a compulsory subject in schools in Tamil Nadu. Against this intellectual backdrop of a brahminic, pro-Hindi, pro-North-India, pro-Aryan identity, a Dravidian, anti-Hindi and anti-brahminical 'Self-respect Movement' emerged under the leadership of Periyar E. V. Ramasamy (1879–1973). Unlike the cultural nationalists who aimed at reviving the pre-colonial 'glorious' past, this anti-caste movement attempted a radical and complete rupture with the past.

Sir Sayyid Ahmad Khan's (1817–98) move away from his initial submission that '[b]y the word *qawm* (nation), I mean both Hindus and Muslims' (qtd. in Ali, *Sayyid Ahmad Khan ka Safar Namah-i Punjab* 160), was based on his response to the Urdu–Hindi controversy and other campaigns which he thought to be anti-Muslim. He laid the foundation of a Muslim nationalism in India through the Aligarh Movement – founded in 1888 to enforce Western education among Muslims through loyalty to the British – in order to foster a pan-Indian Muslim communal solidarity and to transform 'the Muslims into a "nation" on the basis of . . . a separate ideology' (Jain 184). Muhammad Iqbal's (1877–1938) enduring faith that 'politics requires religion to survive and to play an active role in the Muslim society' (Ali, *Pakistan In Search of Identity* 93) did not allow him to support a country-specific nationhood since his religious conviction was that Muslims comprise an '*Ummah*', and that the bond among Muslims is based on religion and not region. Hence, in spite of treating Hindus and Muslims as two 'nations', he dreamt of 'the creation of a Muslim India within India', with 'Punjab, North-West Frontier Province, Sind and Baluchistan amalgamated into a single State. Self-government within the British Empire or without the British Empire, the formation of a consolidated North-West Indian Muslim State' (Vahid 170–71). Iqbal, on the one hand, strived for separate Muslim domains inside India for Muslims to 'live their own lives, and develop on their own cultural lines' (190), while on the other hand, his political realism was moderated by his faith in a pan-Islamic international brotherhood of the Islamic 'League of Nations'. Hence, from 'Our India is the best of all countries in the world' (*Sare jahan se acha, Hindostan hamara*), he expanded his vision towards

> fleeing from his fatherland,
> Resolved the knot of Muslim nationhood.
> His wisdom founded one community,
> The world its parish. (qtd. in Fazal 64)

In 1933, after the failure of the Third Round Table Conference that broadened the gulf between the Indian National Congress and the Muslim League, Chaudhry Rahmat Ali, founder of the Pakistan National Movement, started making open demands for a Muslim-majority sovereignty, and 'the name Pakistan . . . was given to these territories . . . with a view to preserving their historical, national, and political entity as distinct from Hindustan proper' (Krenkow 174). By 1940, arguing that '[t]he Hindus have made it impossible to live together' (Khairi 249), Muhammad Ali Jinnah (1876–1948) 'was able to say that the Muslims were a nation apart and demanded a separate homeland' (325) for the self-determination of the Muslim nationality. Syed Abul A'la Maududi (1903–73), who believed that imperialism could not be replaced with a secular Westernised nationalism, argued for the *Tahrik-i Hijrat* (Migration Movement), migration of all Indian Muslims to Afghanistan, since British India was no more a part of the *Dar al-Islam*. His Islamic nationalism was against a non-Muslim rule over the Muslims in India, and not against the foreigners in India.

Contrary to the exclusivist Muslim nationalism, Husain Ahmad Madani (1879–1957), president of the Jamiyat al-ulama, propounded his theory of a composite nationalism by distinguishing *qaum* (community) from *millat* (meaning a collectivity based on Islamic law or way of life). He argued that as in the case of modern nation-states like England where communities of people from diverse faiths share a nation as co-nationals, the Muslims in India should unite with the non-Muslim fellow-nationals to attain freedom from the British rule, which was essential to practice all Islamic duties. A composite nationalism achieved through Hindu–Muslim unity was in evidence between 1919 and 1922, when the Khilafat and the Non-cooperation movements were in complete and mutual alliance under the leadership of Mahatma Gandhi.

Deviating from the Western notion of nationalism, Gandhi's 'home-grown' nationalism was aimed at establishing 'Ramraj'. The term, as Gandhi clarifies, 'do[es] not mean Hindu Raj' but a democratic 'ethical state' 'in which the meanest citizen could be sure of swift justice without an elaborate and costly procedure' (*Young India*, 19 September 1929). For Gandhi, an ardent practitioner of *ahimsa* (non-violence), the Western concept of state represented 'violence in a concentrated and organised form. The individual has a soul but the state is a soulless machine, it can never be weaned from violence to which it owes its very existence' (*The Modern Review*, October 1935). Nationalism for Gandhi was a commitment towards self-government and complete freedom from slavery in general and British domination in particular, by following the path of *satyagraha* for the cultivation of the *swadeshi* spirit. According to classical Indian thought, every territorial unit which had a distinct way of life was called a *desh*. According to Gandhi, India is a *desh* constituted by smaller *pradeshas* with unique cultural and ecological ambiences but united by a common civilisational bond and shared territorial boundary. Hence, *swadeshi* for Gandhi had multiple implications – community, nationality, provinciality, patriotism – and he did not use it to imply state-centric Western nationalism. *Swadeshi* means to preserve all that belongs to one's own homeland (Parekh 56–57). Gandhi's spiritual nationalism represents the *tapas* (prayer) of a *satyagrahi*, a political sanyasi, for attaining the following goals as *moksha* in the service of the motherland (Iyer 88): communal unity, abolishing untouchability, prohibition of alcohol, familiarising khadi, promotion of rural industries, *Nai Talim* or education based on crafts, adult education, upliftment of women, education in hygiene and health based on indigenous systems of medicine, development of regional languages, integration through a national language, economic equality through trusteeship, uplifting the peasants and workers, mainstreaming of the tribal/adivasi communities, students' welfare through the creation of a code of conduct, lending a helping hand to lepers and beggars, and non-violence towards animals. Empathy lies at the core of Gandhian 'disciplined' nationalism, as best exemplified by *sarvodaya* – universal well-being. Gandhi asserted that 'patriotism is the same as humanity' (*Young India*, 16 March1921) and that '[i]t is impossible for one to be internationalist without being a nationalist. Internationalism is possible only when nationalism becomes a fact' (*Young India*, 18 June 1925): 'Our nationalism can be no peril to other nations in as much as we will exploit none, just as we will allow none to exploit us. Through Swaraj we will serve the whole world' (*Young India*, 16 April 1931).

The Gandhian notion of nationalism inspired many other Indian nationalists. Following Gandhi's notion of *sarvodaya*, Vinoba Bhave (1895–1982) aimed at transforming India into a stateless society: 'The power of government will be decentralized and distributed among the villages. Every village will be a State in itself; the centre will have only nominal authority over them. In this way, gradually, we will reach a stage when authority in every form will have become unnecessary and will, therefore, fade away giving rise to a perfectly free Society' (Ramabhai 2). Vinoba led the Bhoodan movement to urge landlords to distribute surplus land among the landless, as a step towards forming a *Sarvodaya Samaj*. The next stage was *Gramdan* whose prime objective was to build a new social order for minimising class and caste antagonism on the basis of fellow-feeling, non-possession, cooperation, rendering voluntary service, and shared possession. Sarojini Naidu (1879–1949), another follower of Gandhi, was a nationalist with an internationalist perspective. Her confession – 'I am a bad nationalist. I am a nationalist only by the compulsion and the tragedy of the circumstance of my country' ('Presidential Address to All India Women's Conference' 138) – clearly showed that Naidu's nationalism was an anticolonial Indian nationalism that would 'extend to the welfare of the world, and not be limited to the prosperity of India', since the prosperity of the nation is intimately related with the 'world's progress' and peace (Naidu, *Speeches and Writings* 21, 22). Moving beyond divisive identity politics, she pleaded that 'we must rise above nationalism, above religion, above sex. Our common humanity is the bond that cannot, that must not, be broken' (Naidu, 'Presidential Address' 139). Portraying herself as 'neither a Bengali, nor a Madrasi, nor a Hyderabadi' (*Speeches and Writings* 9), Naidu epitomised a cosmopolitan affinity to interconnectivity and exchange: 'modern civilization progresses, as the world becomes more and more international in giving and receiving enlightenment' (35). Premchand (Dhanpat Rai Shrivastava, 1880–1936), the well-known Hindi and Urdu writer, shared Gandhi's notion of communal harmony: 'Neither I am a Hindu nor a Muslim. In a religion in which one cannot drink the water touched by others, there is no room for me' (qtd. in Premchand 113). As an advocate of anticolonial and anti-feudal ideologies, and a socialist transformation for the autonomy of the subalterns in India, Premchand was equally attracted towards the Russian revolution: 'I am a communist, but my communism is limited only to the extent that the Zamindars, seths and others, the exploiters of the peasants, should cease to exist' (qtd. in Guru 101). Prafulla Chandra Ray (1861–1944), a nationalist scientist, was another admirer of Gandhian nationalism: 'in serving my favourite science, I have only one idea in my mind, namely, that through her I should serve my country' (233). Supporting the Non-cooperation movement in 1924, he asserted, 'Science can afford to wait but Swaraj cannot' (228).

While he admired Gandhi, Ray was also sympathetic towards the militant revolutionaries who fought the British: 'I have really high opinion of young men like Subhas, Sasmal, Prafulla Ghosh and those who have made sacrifices for their motherland following Tilak, Gandhi, Aurobindo, Deshbandhu and others' (qtd. in Anon 224). In colonial government records, Ray himself was described as a 'revolutionary in the garb of a scientist' (272). Bhagat Singh (1907–31), one of these prominent *krantikaris* (militant revolutionaries), believed in *shaheedi* (martyrdom) as the ultimate sacrifice for the motherland. He was committed to *inquilab* (revolution), which did not just crave for a political *azaadi* (freedom) from the British but a social revolution that would bring *azaadi* to all those who are victims of internal social divisions and abuses: 'the struggle in India would continue so long as a handful of exploiters go on exploiting the labour of the common people for their own ends. It matters little whether these exploiters are purely British capitalists, or British and Indians in alliance, or even purely Indians' (qtd. in Chandra et al. 271). Singh blended his militancy with his aspiration for a new socialist order; and his nationalism was framed as a struggle for an egalitarian society.

Subhas Chandra Bose (1897–1945), owing to his ideological differences with Gandhi, left the Congress to launch an armed struggle against the British. Influenced by Lenin, Stalin, Éamon de Valera, Kemal Atatürk, Hitler and Mussolini, Bose dreamt of a national liberation of India on the basis of a radical nationalism, and raised the Indian National Army (INA) to achieve this. The

INA was renamed as Azad Hind Fauj (Free India Army), out of Bose's certitude that '[f]or an enslaved people, there can be no greater pride, no higher honour, than to be the first soldier in the army of liberation' (Bose 245). Bose declared the Azad Hind Sarkar (Free Indian Government) at Singapore on 21 October 1943. Slogans like '*Chalo* Delhi' and 'Jai Hind' inspired his revolutionary brigade, which included an all-women unit called the Rani of Jhansi Regiment. The INA was inspired by 'a feeling of oneness, a feeling of belonging to one national family' (Werth and Harbich 125).

M. N. Roy (1887–1954), a fierce critic of spiritual patriotism, appraised Gandhi 'as a religious and cultural revivalist' who 'was bound to be reactionary socially, however revolutionary he might appear politically' (Roy, 'Disagreement with Lenin' 292). Roy considered the Congress as a counter-revolutionary forum of the nationalist bourgeoisie. He wanted to combine nationalism with socialist radicalism. Roy characterised spiritual patriotism as an ideology which maintained that 'if the masses will not be spiritualized, let them go to the devil, and we will console ourselves with bottles of whiskey or the Upanishads', and asserted that revolutionary patriotism by its consciousness 'that Nationalism is no moonshine' would strive for the freedom of the labouring masses who had been the victims of the exploitation of the British colonialism while 'upper classes live in comfort, even opulence, in spite of British rule' ('On Patriotism', Web, n. p.). In his later years, Roy dissociated himself from Marxism and formulated a cosmopolitan 'Radical Humanism', which focused on gaining freedom for the individual, to liberate the individual from the deceitfulness of the collective ego, such as class or nationhood, as manifested in the communist class-state and the democratic nation-state: 'The basic idea of a new revolutionary social philosophy must be that the individual is prior to society, and individual must have priority over social organization' (*Humanist Way to Democracy* 20–21).

Rabindranath Tagore (1861–1941) opposed 'chauvinistic nationalism' as a 'post-spiritual' invention of industrial-capitalism. Tagore argued that 'India has never had a real sense of nationalism' (Tagore 7), and had a 'dual' attitude to nationalism – he supported 'its emphasis on self-respect' but rejected 'its patriotism' (Sen). For him, nationalism is useful so long as it is 'defensive and intensive rather than of an aggressive and extensive nature', so that 'in regions of mixed nationality . . . [it] may serve as a unifying element for rival nationalities and also as a check on the development of a conscious and too ardent nationalism' (Boehm 234–35).

Rejecting 'the *a priori* assumption of nation in existence' (Nigam 177), it has been often suggested that 'nationalism does not mechanically engender the nation' (Aloysius 225) in most of the South Asian states like India which are to be considered as '*collectives of nations coexisting within federal states*' (Oommen 443; original emphasis). According to Aloysius, nationality as a 'social feeling' of oneness has failed to emerge among the 'backward' masses, since, in the name of nationhood, the elements of 'traditional dominance' have been transferred 'into state power without undergoing any substantial change' (227), and due to this disjunction, India as a nation-state 'remains ontologically and politically inaccessible to its own citizens' (Inden 197). Critics like Nigam, Partha Chatterjee and G. Aloysius have critiqued Indian nationalism as a project of the elite that has failed to mobilise or liberate the deprived with 'the becoming of a nation', and observed that a mere 'setting up of a state system' has created a 'nationalism without a nation' (Aloysius).

The All-India Women's Conference (AIWC), Women's Indian Association (WIA) and the National Council of Women in India (NCWI), the major organisations of Indian women, were established to resist colonial dominance as well as a nationalism based on 'protective masculinity' which infantilises women. Muthulakshmi Reddi (1886–1968), in a speech titled 'Government's Attitude towards the Women's Movement and Its Responsibility in Social Reform Movements', delivered at the annual meeting of the Indian National Social Reform Conference in Madras in December 1927, openly expressed her dissatisfaction with the reformist nationalism that worked for women's reforms under the colonial rule. Many feminist nationalists have tried to debunk the idea of a 'golden past' and rejected prescriptive *shastras* that saw women as inferior. Kamalabai Lakshman Rau, while campaigning for the Sarda Bill, argued for the necessity of forging 'new *shastras*' for women (Rau 178). According to Maya Devi Gangulee, 'There has not been one instance on record in which the women of any community have sought to disassociate themselves from being members of one great national sisterhood. The women of all communities, Hindus, Muslims, Sikhs, Depressed Classes and Untouchables, have been working hand in hand in the nationalist movement without the least hint of communal disaffection' (553). Demanding a joint electorate for women, Shareefah Hamid Ali maintained that it is 'degrading' to be elected 'as a "Muslim" only' and 'not as an "Indian"'. As Muthulakshmi Reddi pointed out, the feminist nationalists understood that

> the only way to bring the Brahmans, the women and the pariahs together on a common platform is by enfranchising the women and the depressed classes on equal terms with others. If the women and the depressed classes are given freedom, power and responsibility, I am sure that they would very soon learn how to rectify the present social evil. (qtd. in Pearson 56)

Nationalism as a tactical gambit for generating an integrated Indian identity seemed to be the main focus of post-independence Indian nationalists. For instance, Abul Kalam Azad (1888–1958) propagated unanimity through his theory of '*wahdat-e-adyan*' (unity of religions). Another important feature of postcolonial Indian nationalism is the rise of Gandhian Marxists who believed in revolutionary *sarvodaya* – socialism through non-violence. Jayaprakash Narayan (1902–79), for example, insisted on a democracy without political parties where the power of the state, which he called '*raj shakti*' and '*dandashakti*', would be replaced by '*panchayat raj*' or '*swaraj* from below', which he called '*janashakti*', for achieving a 'total revolution'.

NATION BUILDING IN POST-INDEPENDENCE INDIA

India, according to Salman Rushdie, 'that became independent had never previously existed, . . . [i]t was an invention of the nationalist movement'; and through that 'very successful invention', India was promoted as a state with no determinable 'nation' that was yet to be developed scrupulously, with the 'independent nation-states' like 'Oudh or Bengal or Maratha kingdoms' agreeing 'to collectivise themselves into the idea of the nation of India' (58).

Independent India, where each of the federal units was composed of heterogeneous cultural and linguistic communities, can be termed a 'state-nation' where political boundaries did not necessarily go along with cultural boundaries. Hence, a pan-Indian political community had to be developed strategically. Jawaharlal Nehru (1889–1964) was the chief architect of this process of nation-building. He was assisted by ingenious collaborators like Homi J. Bhabha, P. C. Mahalanobis, Vikram Sarabhai, V. R. Krishna Iyer, Sarvepalli Radhakrishnan, D. S. Kothari, and many others. The major aspects of the 'Nehruvian legacy', which laid the foundations for the modernisation and sustainability of democratic institutions in India, include the fostering of a law-abiding culture and a sense of security among minority communities, mitigation of communal tensions, engagement with the opposition through a politics of bipartisanship in resolving issues of national importance, expansion of the space for civil society, cultivation of a scientific and pro-industrial temperament, a principled position in foreign policy that included the Panchsheel Treaty with China and the policy of non-alignment in response to the Cold War, and charting plan-based policies for self-sustaining economic growth.

The credit for building a unified India by successfully integrating more than five hundred princely states into a nation-state goes to Nehru's home minister Sardar Vallabhbhai Patel (1875–1950), who cajoled reluctant states like Travancore, Jodhpur and Bhopal to accede to India, and deployed troops to take over some of the disinclined states like Hyderabad and Junagadh. While they prevented the disintegration of the newly independent nation-state along communal and ethnic lines, Nehru's and Patel's primary task was to translate the political independence into an 'interdependence' of the multifarious inhabitants of the nation. Nehru took up a number of initiatives to ensure the political integration of the nation-state – such as the setting up of the National Integration Council (NIC) in 1961 for forging harmony among the 'collection of communities'; reorganisation of the federal states on a linguistic basis propelled by the creation of Andhra Pradesh in 1953 to endorse the linguistic subnationalism of the Telugu-speaking people; and the approval of statehood for Nagaland in 1963. Nagaland was given statehood, even though it was 'completely unreal' for 'an area the size of a standard Indian district . . . to be converted into a state' (Gopal 178). The move was aimed at making Nagas who had 'never experienced a sensation of being in a country called India' and 'were hardly influenced by the struggle for freedom or other movements' (Horam 44), feel that they are 'a real part of India' (Palat 273). However, these initiatives could not curtail the suspicion that 'the commitment of the citizenry' might suffer from 'competition from diverse forms of subnational loyalties . . . based on race, ethnic identity, language, caste, religion, or region' which 'have in common the capability of evoking sentiments in men very similar to those described as nationalism' (Smith 276). Moreover, due to 'the tensions created by the centralizing drives of the Indian state in a society where the predominant long-term social, economic, and political tendencies are toward pluralism, regionalism, and decentralization' (Brass 212), it was uncertain whether India as a 'mosaic of humanity will survive unfractured for any length of time' (Palkhivala 7).

An 'emotional integration' through a shared sense of belonging among communities from diverse traditions, through occasional concords and discords, seems to be entrenched in Indian 'democratic multiculturalism': 'If America is a melting-pot, India is a *thali*, a selection of sumptuous dishes in different bowls. Each tastes different, and does not necessarily mix with the next, but they belong together on the same plate, and they complement each other in making the meal a satisfying repast' (Tharoor n. p.). However, the Indian nation-state has lived through many challenges and subnationalist trends in its history. One instance of this is its negotiations with 'nationality-based-units'. Such units, who were not prepared to merge themselves fully with the nation-state, were accommodated through the constitutional position of 'asymmetrical federalism' where special provisions were made for certain citizens like those of Jammu and Kashmir (Article 370) and the tribal communities (VI Schedule) of Northeast India which had remained 'excluded' and 'partially excluded' areas in British India. Inspite of these preferential provisions for autonomy, in Kashmir, Indian nationalism was often contested by demands for '*azadi*' (freedom) through the promised UN referendum, as per the UN resolution adopted on 13 August 1948, even though it had been argued that Hari Singh, the ruler of the people of Kashmir, had agreed to accede to India. Moreover, in 1958, the special provisions safeguarding the representation of the people of Kashmir in the civil services were terminated, and 'the state ceased to be financially autonomous'. In 1959, the permit system regulating the entry of non-citizens was abolished, and in 1961, the 'jurisdiction of the Supreme Court and the Central Election Commission was extended to the state. In 1964, Article 356 of the Indian Constitution, which allows for the take-over of the state by the central government, was made applicable to J and K, and a Delhi appointed governor replaced the *Sadar-i-Riyasat*' (Chandhoke, 'Of Broken Social Contracts and Ethnic Violence' 17). With the gradual violation of the provisos of autonomy by the central government, along with the suppression of political parties except the National Conference, the militant *jihad* against the Indian state escalated in Kashmir, with endeavours to undermine the central authority. Sheikh Abdullah (1905–82) too was arrested because of his open support for Kashmir's independence from both India and Pakistan. Ultimately, the special status of the state of Jammu and Kashmir was repealed when the Modi government officially announced on 5 August 2019 the abrogation of Article 370 and its Provision 35A, and divided the state into two union territories – Jammu and Kashmir, and Ladakh. Similarly, Manipur has also faced a contested nationalism since September 1949 when, despite its status as an independent constitutional monarchy, Bodhchandra Singh, the Maharaja of Manipur, was made to sign a Merger Agreement with the Indian Union without consulting the elected Legislative Assembly of Manipur, and the state was given a 'Part C' status in the Indian Union. The fact that the Manipuris, who had 'established a sophisticated kingdom at a time when state formation was unknown to most parts of the region', were 'granted the status of a fully-fledged state, twenty-three years after the merger and later than Meghalaya and Nagaland' has contributed to the rising 'rhetoric of grievances and secessionism against the central government' (Chandhoke, 'A State of One's Own' 26).

Drawing on Frantz Fanon's critique of comprador postcolonial nationalism, it has been often observed that post-independent Indian nation has been 'incapable of great ideas and inventiveness' (141), and that it ultimately failed to bring about transformation through social consciousness, beyond nationalism (165). Moreover, (as revealed by the Subaltern Studies Collective) by privileging nationalism over other prevalent stratifications of class, caste and gender as the normative framework for regulating social life and strengthening the newly independent nation-state, recourse to sociocultural amendments was often compromised. Challenging the 'mainstream' nationalism, B. R. Ambedkar (1891–1956) sought an internal freedom of the nation against Brahminical imperialism over the people of the 'untouchable' castes, designated as 'Harijans' by Gandhi, 'Scheduled Castes' by the Constitution and 'Dalits' in contemporary discourse. As the prime motivator of the Dalit–Bahujan nationalism, Ambedkar declared that 'without social union, political unity is difficult to be achieved'. He argued that to recast India into a nation from a mere political state – since 'a State, which is not a nation, has small prospects of survival in the struggle for existence' (185) – an anti-caste modernity based on egalitarian Western ideals along with the emancipatory tenets of Buddhism has to be evolved, in order to pave way for the annihilation of caste hierarchy and caste-based exploitation.

India's cultural nationalism, which has its roots in an average Indian's plural and shifting identities, proves the fallacy of the solitarist theory that tries to construct identity by associating a person with a single social group. This essential characteristic of Indian nationalism has time and again thwarted every leader or movement that has tried to impose a belligerent, singular national identity by undermining multi-[sub]national alignments in a country of plural monoculturalisms. Sub-nationalist expeditions for the preservation of the discrete cultural nation/nationality in a regional political space, like the Khalistan movement's demand for an independent state for the Sikhs based on a religio-cultural nationalism or Periyar's call for a separate Tamil/Dravidian state for the Tamils premised on a lingo-cultural nationalism, illustrate the irregular instances of confrontations with the normative conception of India as a homogenised entity.

PARTITION AND THE (ALIE)NATION

The Partition of India, heralding the end of the British Raj while giving birth to West and East Pakistan (Bangladesh as a sovereign state was formed later from East Pakistan), resulted in the emergence of a 'nation of the homeless' (or a nation of the *udvaastu* or refugee). The consequent 'nostalgic nationhood' has sustained itself through trans-generational Partition trauma. For instance, even today, generations of post-Partition Bengalis residing in the Indian state of West Bengal dolorously evoke their ancestral villages in present-day Bangladesh as their own *desh* (homeland), exactly as the Muhajirs of Pakistan agonisingly recall their original homes in India.

Older historians have mostly tried to re-read Partition in terms of the polemics between a religious nationalism – tacked on Mohammad Ali Jinnah and his Muslim League associates – and a secular nationalism attached to the Congress leadership (Tripathi; Chandra). New researchers, however, have pointed out a 'callous haste' that was shown in demarcating the borders, with least care for 'the human cost of cutting a border through the heart of populous provinces' (Bhattacharjea 8), that resulted from 'self-delusion' and fatigue among the nationalist leaders: '"We were tired men", admitted Nehru, "Few of us could stand the prospect of going to prison again. . . . The plan of partition offered a way out and we took it . . . . We expected that partition would be temporary, that Pakistan was bound to come back to us' (qtd. in Mosley 77). Apart from the immediate destruction of over a million lives, abduction and rape of about 75,000 women and rendition of ten million people as refugees, the cross-border as well as internal forced migrations created ghettoes, contributing to long-term 'un-mixing' of religious communities. The havoc of the riots that took place later – for example, in Delhi (1984 and 2020), Gujarat (2002) and Muzaffarnagar (2013) – can be understood as unremitting postscripts of the alienation and mistrust inseminated by the Partition.

Partition literature and cinema, now a major field of academic interest, bring out many of these concerns. However, many scholars have pointed out regional biases in such representations and research. A Punjab-centric representation dominates these retellings of the violence that assumed genocidal proportions. In Punjab, however, the state and the army promptly intervened to assist with the evacuation and to undertake rehabilitation, unlike in Bengal where the refugees, who were neither regulated or aided by the army or the state, 'prove to have been active agents shaping their own destinies, not merely passive victims of history as they have sometimes been portrayed' (Chatterji 216). But their voices seem to be muffled in most of Partition scholarship. Another case in point is that of the Sindhis in India who, despite being a 'subnation', do not have a provincial state in the post-Partition India.

REFERENCES

Ahmad, Aijaz. *In Theory: Nations, Classes, Literatures*. Delhi: Oxford UP, 1991. Print.

Ali, Mubarak. *Pakistan In Search of Identity*. New Delhi: Aakar Books, 2011. Print.

Ali, Syyid Iqbal. *Sayyid Ahmad Khan ka Safar Namah-i Punjab.* Aligarh: Aligarh Institute Gazette Press, 1884. Print.

Aloysius, G. *Nationalism without a Nation in India*. Oxford: Oxford UP, 1997. Print.

Ambedkar, B. R. *Pakistan or the Partition of India*. Bombay: Thacker and Co., 1940. Print.

Anon. *Acharya Prafulla Chandra Ray Birth Centenary Souvenir Volume*. Calcutta: Calcutta University, 1962. Print.

Appiah, Kwame Anthony. 'Is the Post- in Postmodernism the Post- in Postcolonial?'. *Critical Inquiry* 17.2 (1991): 336–57. Print.

Aurobindo, Sri. 'Karmayogin'. *The Complete Works of Sri Aurobindo: Vol 8*. Pondicherry: Sri Aurobindo Ashram Trust, 1997. Print.

Barrington, Lowell W., ed. *After Independence: Making and Protecting the Nation in Postcolonial and Postcommunist States*. Ann Arbor: The U of Michigan P, 2006. Print.

Beaumont, Peter. 'Former UN Envoy Blasts new Hamid Karzai Cabinet as "Ccorrupt"'. *The Guardian*. 20 December 2009. Web. 20 January 2020. <https://www.theguardian.com/world/2009/dec/20/un-envoy-galbraith-blasts-karzai>.

Bentham, Jeremy. *The Works of Jeremy Bentham*. 11 Vols. Ed. J. Bowring. Edinburgh: William Tait, 1843. Print.

Besant, Annie. *India*. London: The Theosophical Publishing Society, 1913. Print.

Bhattacharjea, Ajit. 'Cyril's Scalpel', *Outlook*, 23 July 1997. Web. 10 November 2020. <https://www.outlookindia.com/magazine/story/cyrils-scalpel/203888.>.

Boehm, Max Hildebert. 'Nationalism'. *Encyclopaedia of the Social Sciences: Vol. XI*. Ed. R. A. Edwin et al. New York: The Macmillan Company, 1963. 231–40. Print.

Bose, Sugata. *His Majesty's Opponent: Subhas Chandra Bose and India's Struggle Against Empire*. New Delhi: Penguin, 2011. Print.

Brass, Paul. *Ethnicity and Nationalism*. London: Sage, 1991. Print.

Castro, Fidel. *Fidel Castro Speaks*. Ed. M. Kenner, and J. Petros. Harmondsworth: Penguin, 1972. Print.

Chand, Tara. *Influence of Islam on Indian Culture*. Allahabad: The Indian Press Ltd., 1963. Print.

Chandhoke, Neera. 'A State of One's Own: Secessionism and Federalism in India'. *Crisis States Research Centre Working Papers Series* 1.80. London: Crisis States Research Centre, London School of Economics and Political Science, 2006. Print.

---. 'Of Broken Social Contracts and Ethnic Violence: The case of Kashmir'. *Crisis States Research Centre Working Papers Series* 1.75. London: Crisis States Research Centre, London School of Economics and Political Science, 2005. Print.

Chandra, Bipan. *History of Modern India*. New Delhi: Orient BlackSwan. 2009. Print.

Chandra, Bipan, Mridula Mukherjee, Aditya Mukherjee, Sucheta Mahajan, and K. N. Panikkar. *India's Struggle for Independence*, 1857–1947. New Delhi: Penguin, 1989. Print.

Chatterjee, Partha. 'Democracy and Economic Transformation in India'. *Economic and Political Weekly* XLII.16 (2008): 53–62. Print.

Chatterji, Joya. 'New Directions in Partition Studies'. *History Workshop Journal* 67 (2009): 213–20. Print.

Cortright, David, and George A. Lopez. *The Sanctions Decade: Assessing UN Strategies in the 1990s*. Boulder, CO: Lynne Rienner, 2000. Print.

Derrida, Jacques. *Specters of Marx: The State of the Debt, the Work of Mourning, and the New International*. Trans. Peggy Kamuf. New York: Routledge, 1994. Print.

Dirlik, Arif. 'The Postcolonial Aura: Third World Capitalism in the Age of Global Capitalism'. *Critical Inquiry* 20 (1994): 328–56. Print.

Emerson, Rupert. *From Empire to Nation*. Cambridge, MA: Harvard UP, 1960. Print.

Fanon, Frantz. *The Wretched of the Earth*. Trans. Constance Farrington. New York: Grove Weidenfeld, 1963. Print.

Fazal, Tanweer. *'Nation-State' and Minority Rights in India: Comparative Perspectives on Muslim and Sikh Identities*. London: Routledge, 2015. Print.

Gangulee, Maya Devi. *Stri Dharma* 16.1 (September 1933). Print.

Ghose, Jogendra Chunder, ed. *The English Works of Raja Rammohan Roy: Vol IV*. New Delhi: Cosmo Publications, 1906. Print.

Gopal, S. *Jawaharlal Nehru: A Biography*: *Vol. 2, 1947–56*. New Delhi: Oxford UP, 1983. Print.

Guevara, Ernesto Che. *Che Guevara and the Cuban Revolution: Writings and Speeches of Ernesto Che Guevara*. Ed. David Deutschmann. Sydney: Pathfinder, 1987. Print.

---. 'Message to the Tricontinental'. April 1967. Web. 31 January 2020. <https://faculty.chass.ncsu.edu/slatta/hi216/documents/chetricontinent.htm>.

Guru, Rajeshwar. *Premchand ekadhyan*. Delhi: S. Chand and Co., 1964. Print.

Habib, Irfan, ed. *India-Studies in the History of an Idea*. New Delhi: Munshiram Manoharlal Publishers, 2005. Print.

Hobson, J. A. *Imperialism: A Study*. London: George Allen and Unwin, 1938. Print.

Horam, M. *Thirty Years of Naga Insurgency*. New Delhi: Cosmo, 1990. Print.

Inamdar, N. R. 'The Political Ideas of Lokmanya Tilak'. *Political Thought in Modern India*. Ed. Thomas Pantham, and Kenneth L. Deutsch. New Delhi: Sage, 1986. Print.

Inden, Ronald. *Imagining India*. Oxford: Blackwell, 1990. Print.

Iyer, Raghavan. *The Moral and Political Writings of Mahatma Gandhi: Vol. I*. Oxford: Clarendon Press, 1987. Print.

Jaffrelot, Christopher, ed. *Hindu Nationalism: A Reader*. Princeton: Princeton UP, 2007. Print.

Jain, M. S. *The Aligarh Movement: Its Origin and Development, 1858–1906*. Agra: Sri Ram Mehra and Co., 1965. Print.

Karve, D. G., and D. V. Ambekar, ed. 'Speech on the Education Bill addressed by Gokhale in the Calcutta Town Hall on the 2nd September 1911'. *Speeches and Writings of Gopal Krishna Gokhale: Volume 3*. Poona: Asia Publishing House, 1967. Print.

Khairi, Saad R. *Jinnah Reinterpreted: The Journey from Indian Nationalism to Muslim Statehood*. Oxford: Oxford UP, 1995. Print.

Knight, W. Andy, and Frazer Egerton, ed. *The Routledge Handbook of the Responsibility to Protect*. London and NY: Routledge, 2012. Print.

Kohn, Hans. *Prophets and Peoples: Studies in Nineteenth-Century Nationalisms*. London: Collier Books, 1969. Print.

Krenkow, F. 'Pakistan'. *Encyclopedia of Islam*. Muslim India Information Centre, 1937. Print.

Lenin, V. I. *The National-Liberation Movement in the East*. London: Lawrence and Wishart, 1962. Print.

Lugard, Frederick John D. *The Dual Mandate in British Tropical Africa*. Edinburgh: Blackwood, 1922. Print.

Mamdani, Mahmood. *Saviors and Survivors: Darfur, Politics, and the War on Terror*. NY, London: Doubleday, 2009. Print.

Mariategui, Jose Carlos. *The Heroic and Creative Meaning of Socialism*. Trans. Michael Pearlman. Atlantic Highlands: Humanities Press, 1996. Print.

Menon, Kalyani Devaki. *Everyday Nationalism: Women of the Hindu Right in India*. Philadelphia: U of Pennsylvania P, 2010. Print.

Merle, Mercel. *L' anticolonialisme Europeen, de Las Casas a Marx*. Paris: Colin, 1969. Print.

Mosley, Leonard. *The Last Days of the British Raj*. London: Weidenfeld and Nicolson, 1961. Print.

Muthu, Sankar. *Enlightenment Against Empire*. Princeton: Princeton UP, 2003. Print.

Naidu, Sarojini. 'Presidential Address to All India Women's Conference'. *Stri Dharma*, February 1930. Print.

---. *Speeches and Writings*. Madras: G. A. Natesan, 1924. Print.

Natesan, G. A., ed. *Speeches of Gopal Krishna Gokhale*. Madras: Natesan, 1920. Print.

Nigam, A. *The Insurrection of Little Selves*. New Delhi: Oxford UP, 2006. Print.

Oommen, T. 'Nation and Nationalism in South Asia'. *The Sage Handbook of Nations and Nationalism.* Ed. G. Delanty, and K. Kumar. London: Sage, 2006. 438–49. Print.

Pal, Bipin Chandra. *The Spirit of Indian Nationalism*. London: The Hind Nationalist Agency, 1910. Print.

Palat, Madhavan K., ed. *Selected Works of Jawaharlal Nehru: Second Series: Vol. 61.* New Delhi: Jawaharlal Nehru Memorial Fund, 2015. Print.

Palkhivala, Nani. 'A State without a Nation?'. *Statesman*, 30 May 1996. Print.

Parekh, Bhikhu. *Gandhi's Political Philosophy*. Indiana: U of Notre Dame P, 1989. Print.

Pearson, Gail. 'Reserved Seats: Women and the Vote in Bombay'. *Indian Economic and Social History Review* 20.1 (1983): 47–65. Print.

Premchand, Shivrani Devi. *Premchand gharmein*. Banaras: Saraswati Press, 1956. Print.

Raghavan, V. *The Great Integrators: The Saint-Singers of India*. Delhi: Publications Division, Ministry of Information and Broadcasting, 1966. Print.

Ramabhai, Suresh. *Vinoba and His Mission.* Sevagram: Akhil Bharat Sarv Seva Sangh, 1954. Print.

Ranade, Mahadev Govind. *Religious and Social Reform: A collection of Speeches*. Collected and Compiled by M. B. Kolasker. Bombay: Gopal Narayan and Co, 1902. Print.

---. 'Social Evolution'. *Sudharak*, 16 October 1893. Print.

Rau, Kamalabai Lakshman. quoted in *Stri Dharma* 14, no. 5 (March 1931). Cited in Mrinalini Sinha, 'Refashioning Mother India: Feminism and Nationalism in Late-Colonial India'. *Feminist Studies* 26.3 (2000): 623–44. Print.

Ray, Prafulla Chandra. *Life and Experiences of a Bengali Chemist: Vol. 1.* Calcutta: The Asiatic Society, 1996. Print.

Richman, Paula, ed. *Many Ramayanas: The Diversity of a Narrative Tradition in South Asia.* Berkeley: U of California P, 1991. Print.

Roy, M. N. 'Disagreement with Lenin'. *The Radical Humanist* XVI.25 (1952). Cited in John P. Haithcox. 'The Roy–Lenin Debate on Colonial Policy: A New Interpretation'. *The Journal of Asian Studies* 23.1 (1963): 93–101. Print.

---. *Humanist Way to Democracy.* New Delhi: Pamposh Publication Press, 1977. Print.

---. 'On Patriotism'. *Marxists Internet Archive.* Web. 29 January 2020. <https://www.marxists.org/archive/roy/1923/06/12.htm>.

Rushdie, Salman. 'A Fantasy Called India'. *India Today*, Special Issue, 1947–1997, 18 August, 1997. 58–61. Print.

Said, Edward W. *Culture and Imperialism.* London: Chatto and Windus, 1993. Print.

Sarkar, Tanika. 'Imagining a Hindu Nation: Hindu and Muslim in Bankimchandra's Later Writings'. *Economic and Political Weekly* 29.39 (1994): 2553–61.

Savarkar, Vinayak Damodar. *Hindu Rashtra Darshan*. Veer Savarkar Prakashan, 1984. Print.

Seeley, John Robert. *The Expansion of England*. Ed. John Gross. Chicago: U of Chicago P, 1971. Print.

Sen, Amartya. 'Foreword'. *Selected Letters of Rabindranath Tagore*. Ed. Krishna Dutta, and Andrew Robinson. Cambridge: Cambridge UP, 1997. Print.

Singh, Amardeep. 'Colonialism/Imperialism'. Web. 30 January 2020. <http://www.lehigh.edu/~amsp/eng-11-globalization.htm>.

Smith, Adam. *The Wealth of Nations*. 2 vols. Ed. E. R. A. Seligman. London: Dent, 1910. Print.

Smith, B. C. *Understanding Third World Politics*. Bloomington: Indiana UP, 2003. Print.

Suleri, Sara. *The Rhetoric of English India*. Chicago: Chicago UP, 1992. Print.

Tagore, Rabindranath. 'Nationalism in India'. *Nationalism*. Ed. Ramachandra Guha. New Delhi: Penguin, 2009. Print.

Tharoor, Shashi. 'An Adventure Called India', *The Hindu*, New Delhi, 5 August 2007. Print.

Tilak, Bal Gangadhar. *Bal Gangadhar Tilak, His Writings and Speeches.* Appreciation by Babu Aurobindo Ghose. Madras: Ganesh and Co., 1919. Print.

Tripathi, Amales. *Indian National Congress and the Struggle for Freedom: 1885–1947*. Tran. Amitava Tripathi. New Delhi: Oxford UP, 2014. Print.

Vahid, S. A., ed. *Thoughts and Reflections of Iqbal*. Lahore: Sh. Muhammad Ashraf, 1964. Print.

Vail, Leroy, ed. *The Creation of Tribalism in Southern Africa*. London: James Currey, 1989. Print.

Vivekananda, Swami. *The Complete Works of Swami Vivekananda.* vols. VI. Calcutta: Advaita Ashrama, 1999. Print.

waThiong'o, Ngugi. *Decolonising the Mind: The Politics of Language in African Literature*. New Hampshire: Heinemann, 1986. Print.

Werth, Alexander, and Walter Harbich. *An Eye-witness Account of Indian Freedom Struggle in Europe during World War II*. Calcutta: NRB, 1970. Print.

Young, Robert J. C. *Postcolonialism: An Historical Introduction*. Oxford: Blackwell, 2001. Print.

Zaidi, A. Moin, and Shaheeda Zaidi, eds. *The Encyclopaedia of the Indian National Congress: Vol. 3*. New Delhi: S. Chand, 1977. Print.

Chapter Three

Nationalism and Internationalism

GLOBALISATION, TRANSNATIONAL NOMADISM AND THE FUTURE OF INTERNATIONAL SOLIDARITY

Global conflicts like the Seven Years' War (1756–63), Paraguayan War (1864–70) and Ten Years' War (1868–78) led to a realisation that the 'pandemonium of nations' (Laitin 1) needs to be put to rest. However, the journey from a 'national patriotism' towards a 'world patriotism' (Durkheim 72) went through the violent and traumatic experiences of the two World Wars. The bullet shot by Gavrilo Princip, a Serbian extreme nationalist, triggered a chain of events leading to the First World War. Adolf Hitler's notion of achieving national honour and a purified nation by sending the non-Aryans to death camps led to the Second World War. Learning its lessons from the perversions of an otherised notion of exclusive nationhood, the same Germany later included non-German-origin players in its national football team. This gradual transformation of the traditional paradigm of a nation-state that is bounded territorially, culturally and economically, was largely influenced by two major forces of the twentieth century – globalisation and diaspora.

Wolfgang Welsch's 'Transculturality – the Puzzling Form of Cultures Today', Bill Ashcroft's 'Globalization, the Transnation and Utopia', and Arjun Appadurai's *Modernity at Large: Cultural Dimensions of Globalization,* are significant in the study of globalisation and diaspora. As shown by new scholarship on nationalisms, such as Thomas L. Friedman's *The World is Flat*, rigid notions of nationalism and bounded nations have been destabilised into a networked internationalism, by a number of factors – labour migrations and 'professional diasporas'; the emergence of soft borders within nation groupings; dual citizenship or near-dual citizenship (like in the case of India's Overseas Citizenship of India [OCI] card); the effects of supra-national organisations such as the UNO, World Bank and Nuclear Control treaties, and large MNCs (Hardt and Negri xii); the impact of global communications systems such as the World Wide Web and social media platforms; easier transportation; ease of international access to cultural productions like books, music and cinema; and the growth of cybercommunities, and of international human rights and minoritarian movements.

GLOBALISATION/GLOBALITY VS NATIONALISM

With the Korean War (1950–53), the Chinese realised that the Soviet Union was an unreliable ally. This and the American defeat in Vietnam (1975) were landmark events that forced leaders of the First World to strategise in terms of a balanced world order: 'All nations, adversaries and friends alike, must have a stake in preserving the international system' (Nixon 517). Globalisation, a term that emerged in the 1960s, can be defined as a set of social processes aimed at 'globality'. This denotes an interactional situation where, with the worldwide expansion of communication, transportation and liberal rules of marketing, inter-state borders and boundaries would become less rigid. In such a situation people across the world may gradually consider themselves as communities of exchange and interdependencies through environmental, economic, political and cultural interconnections, and eventually generate a multidimensional consciousness – such as 'supraterritoriality', 'planetarity' and 'glocality' – on the basis of deterritorialised and networked intimacies. The global dimension of the Novel Coronavirus (COVID-19) outbreak in 2020 confirmed that we like it or not, 'we need to learn to live in a world that is interconnected not only ethereally or ideally . . . but also materially, via direct embodied contact' (Marder, Web n. p.).

The ongoing debate between 'globalisation sceptics' and 'hyperglobalisers' has focused on issues of equality and uniformity related to the process of globalisation. It appears that countries of the Global North have achieved more economic benefits and interdependence, compared to those of the Global South, through 'financial or capital globalisation', 'telecommunication or media globalisation' and 'cultural globalisation'. The transformationalist view of globalisation views the phenomenon as partially profitable and partly unfavorable, and also as, at once, hybridising and homogenising.

There are a number of evidences that prove that the exchange of commodities, cultures and technologies across borders is not at all a modern phenomenon – for example, the spread of religions like Buddhism, the expansion of empires such as the Macedonian empire and the Islamic Caliphates, and cross-border commerce conducted by companies such as the British East India Company. However, the global interconnectedness was intensified by the initiatives of the rising European bourgeoisie and transatlantic communication corporations who were hugely benefited by the nineteenth-century developments in science and technology such as the invention of the telegraph and wireless radio communication. The process was accelerated by the twentieth-century explosion in population, and circulation of print media and television. While the population growth paved way for immigration to countries such as Canada, the United States of America and Australia, the boost in industrial output aggravated colonial endeavours by imperialists, resulting in the reinforcement of nationalism through anticolonial struggles. The hostilities did not come to an end with the end of the Second World War. Instead, the Cold War between a liberal–capitalist camp headed by the United States and an authoritarian–socialist camp led by the Soviet Union continued to divide nation-states.

Amidst such polarity, in 1944, towards the end of the Second World War, invoking globalisation through the 'liberation' of world economies, the economically powerful countries from the Global North assembled at Bretton Woods for an economic conference. The attendees wanted to repeal their protectionist economic policies for the sake of expanding international trade on the basis of unanimously approved rules and regulations, and thereby, pave way for what was termed as the 'golden age of controlled capitalism'.

The US dollar became a global currency under the Bretton Woods arrangement and by the early 1970s, the amount of gold stocked by the Federal Reserve Bank was of lesser value compared to the amount of dollar bills circulating outside the USA. This conference laid the institutional foundations of three international organisations – the International Monetary Fund (IMF), the International Bank for Reconstruction and Development (later known as the World Bank), and the General Agreement on Tariffs and Trade (GATT, the predecessor of the World Trade Organisation [WTO]). Neoliberalism was a step towards a single global market shaped out of the initiatives for privatisation by ushering in foreign institutional investments (FII) and discarding the controls on foreign direct investments (FDI) to ensure a steady global financial flow through various trade–liberalisation agreements like the GATT and the North American Free Trade Agreement (NAFTA). On the one hand, this undermined the power of sovereign nation-states to plan their own national policies by a polycentric governance, while on the other, this enhanced the influence of various supranational institutions such as the NATO (North Atlantic Treaty Organization), WTO and OECD (Organization for Economic Cooperation and Development), along with transnational corporations such as the Coca-Cola Company, and global political associations and institutions such as the European Union, the United Nations, the Organization of African Unity, the Association of South East Asian Nations, the Common Market of the South, Amnesty International, Doctors Without Borders, the World Economic Forum, and the Union of Concerned Scientists.

Globalisation expanded intra-regional associations for promoting local culturalism and regional democracies through the formation of groups such as the Union of South American Nations (USAN), the African Union (AU), the Caribbean Community (CARICOM), the Arab League(AL), and the Union for the Mediterranean (UfM), comprising either neighbouring countries or countries in the same continent. There are also multilateral organisations such as the Renewable Energy and Energy Efficiency Partnership (REEEP), the World Association of Nuclear Operators (WANO), the Alliance for Financial Inclusion (AFI), the Alliance of Small

Island States (AOSIS), the Intergovernmental Organisation for International Carriage by Rail (OTIF), and the Community of Portuguese Language Countries (CPLP). This rising global civil society started advocating for a cosmopolitan democracy in order to acknowledge the plurality of identities through mutual acceptance and accountability. This cosmopolitan democracy of the future, according to David Held, would operate through the formation of a global parliament that would formulate a new charter of rights and duties, formally split political and economic interests, and give rise to a global legal system. The movement towards globalism did not leave even the Communist Bloc untouched. Deng Xiaoping in China was successful in forging a state-controlled embracing of market globalism under the pretext of 'learning advanced management and new technologies from foreign countries' (Wang 101). Mikhail Gorbachev in the Soviet Union installed a justice globalism based on his conviction 'that our country and the world need new thinking, a new global understanding, a new interpretation of the ideas of progress, humanism, and justice . . .' (693).

From a cultural perspective, some critics regard globalisation as an 'Americanisation of the world' where the cultural heterogeneity of the world is replaced by what George Ritzer calls 'McDonaldization'. Benjamin Barber coined the term 'McWorld' to refer to a colonising consumer capitalism propagated by American popular culture that threatens unique and diverse cultural traditions with a homogenised market actualised through globalisation. However, Francis Fukuyama welcomed the adoption of American lifestyles and techno-culture by people of different cultural lineages as a positive expansion of free market and democratic values. He also declared the 'end of history' marking the triumph of Western economic and political liberalism – which, according to Fukuyama, aimed at reducing poverty and inequality by strengthening global integration and thereby also strengthening democracy – over all other alternatives. On the other hand, while some critics have warned that there would be repercussions against the 'cultural synchronization' (Hamelink 3) promoted by globalisation, others feel that a clash of civilisations among the Eastern Orthodox, Confucian, Hindu, Judeo-Christian and Islamic populations (Huntington) has given rise to sub-state identities like the indigenous peoples' movements and ethno-nationalisms (Brysk). Ronald Robertson, however, has used 'glocalization' to illustrate a hybridity based on both difference and sameness, which is a visible outcome of globalisation in the cultural domain as manifested in fashion, dance, music, language, food and living patterns.

The idea of 'globality' has been analysed by a number of thinkers from a variety of perspectives. Some have pointed out that globality has brought about an 'advanced', 'high', 'radical' or 'super' modernity (Giddens, *The Consequences of Modernity*), or a 'modernization of modernization' that has given birth to a 'new' and 'reflexive' modernity (Beck). The cultural changes occurring due to global capitalism – seen as 'hypercapitalism' – have been often labelled as 'postmodernity' (Harvey), since 'the Global Age' (Albrow) no longer revolves around rationality or the fixation with the nation-state but is dominated by social experiences that are 'mediatized', 'informationalized', 'virtual', 'hyperreal' and 'simulated' (Peterson), leading to a 'risk society' marked by insecurities (Beck).

Globality, in contemporary times, has manifested itself through global finance and global communication – such as 'global outsourcing' for commodity production, promotion and sales; use of global credit cards; digital money; and entering into global agreements like the Paris Convention for the Protection of Industrial Property (1883), the Berne Convention for the Protection of Literary and Artistic Works (1886), the Madrid Agreement for the International Registration of Marks (1891), and the Agreement on Trade-Related Aspects of Intellectual Property Rights (1994). It also manifests in the creation of an 'e-world' of e-friendships, e-commerce, e-government and e-mails. Globality is also evident in transworld solidarities such as the observation of 'international days' like the World AIDS Day; preservation of World Heritage; learning of global languages; accomplishment of cooperative ventures such as connecting 'global cities' like Tokyo, London, New York and Singapore; the various trans-governmental endeavours of G7, G10, and G20 groups of countries; and transworld solidarities like that of socialist and communist internationals, pan-Africanism, the White Commonwealth, or women's solidarities during first-wave feminism. The benefits of globalisation is best evident in the robot-assisted trans-oceanic telesurgery that was performed on September 2001 on a patient in Strasbourg, France, by doctors in New York, USA. Transworld solidarities among cybercommunities following incidents like the 2012 Delhi Nirbhaya case or the 9/11 attacks, or the shared aims of the recent #MeToo movement, prove the fact that with the emergence of computer-supported social networks (CSSNs) resulting in the internet-mediated globalism, 'humankind in some respects becomes a "we", facing problems and opportunities where there are no "others"' (Giddens, *Modernity and Self-Identity* 27), further eroding the boundaries of nationalism.

International sports and arts organisations have also been involved in strengthening international peace and harmony, and solidarities beyond national boundaries. For instance, the International Olympic Committee (IOC), set up in 1894, is actively engaged in the 'Fighting For Peace in the Favelas of Rio de Janeiro' project in Brazil, 'Preventing Youth Violence in Colombia: A Joint IOC–War Child Project' in Colombia, and a project called 'Building Resilience through Sport in Violence-Affected Communities of Jamaica' in Jamaica. In collaboration with the UNHCR, IOC has implemented 'Sport for Protection' programmes in Colombia, Ethiopia, the Democratic Republic of Congo, Jordan, Mexico and Rwanda, and in September 2017, during its 131st Session in Lima, Peru, IOC launched the Olympic Refuge Foundation to support the displaced around the world. There are a number of organisations of artists, musicians and dancers, which have been striving towards globality: the International Music Council (IMC), founded in 1949, has its network in 150 countries; Freemuse – The World Forum on Music and Censorship (1998) advocates and defends artistic freedom; Musicians Without Borders was founded in 1999 to draw on music, dance and theatre for world peace and social change; World Dance Alliance (WDA) was set up in 1990 to provide a platform to dancers worldwide; International Theatre Institute (ITI) was established for training performing artists across the globe for peace and mutual understanding through global exchanges, daCi (Dance and the Child International, 1978) is committed to involving children and youth in dancing on an international scale.

The effect of globalisation on higher education institutions can be understood from the efforts put in by most universities around the world to set up 'global campuses' with special focus on interdisciplinary and comparative scholarship, and to establish new centres that specialise in foreign languages, development studies, comparative literatures, translation studies, area studies, human rights, conflict management and peace studies, and comparative cultural studies. For instance, new scholarship in translation studies aims at a panlingual globalisation through interlingual projects such as the ones undertaken by the University of Washington's Turing Center in collaboration with the Utilika Foundation in 2006. Theorists have variously questioned the idea of nationalism in the context of such panlingual experiments. For instance, in her attempt to address, '[w]hen and how does the love of mother tongue, the love of my little corner of ground become the nation thing?' (*Nationalism and the Imagination* 13), Spivak concludes that the 'nation thing' that is the outcome of a 'rock-bottom comfort in one's language and one's home' (15), can be resisted by reading diverse works of imagination in translation, since while experiencing one's mother tongue being translated simultaneously with the translation of others' mother tongues, the nationalism – that works by 'recoding . . . underived private as the antonym of the public sphere' (18) – can be flouted by not giving importance to the 'underived private'.

Globalism has had an impact on traditional academic disciplines too. For example, departments of English studies have moved beyond canonical representatives of a mono-national literary space towards incorporation of New World literatures of writers writing across cultures. Examples include writers such as Pico Iyer (Indian, British and American), Inez Baranay (Australian and Hungarian), Amin Maalouf (Lebanese, Arabic and French), Alberto Manguel (Argentinian, Canadian and French), Michael Ondaatje (Sri Lankan and Canadian), Brian Castro (Chinese, Portuguese and Australian), Ilija Trojanow (Bulgarian, German and Kenyan), and Tim Parks (English and Italian), who have been producing transnational literatures based on a 'cosmopolitics', 'thinking and feeling beyond the nation' (Cheah and Robbins). Their work reflects a global modernity that can 'no longer be approached as a dialogue internal to Europe or EuroAmerica' but has been evolving as 'a global discourse in which many participate, producing different formulations of the modern as lived and envisaged within their local social environments' (Dirlik 17). The literatures of these transcultural writers is characterised by 'dispatriation', 'a kind of detachment in viewpoint of, not severance of interest in, the birthland' (Dagnino 6). As an example of how 'the pressing reality of new global dynamics challenges postcolonial intellectuals to think beyond the premises of their original quest' (Ponzanesi xiii), one can recall Ngũgĩ wa Thiong'o's effort to liberate 'works of imagination . . . out of nationalist prisons and find welcoming fans outside the geographic walls' (wa Thiong'o 58), using a 'globalectic' reading as the 'way of approaching any text from whatever times and places to allow its content and themes form a free conversation with other texts of one's time and place' (60). Such readings are based on the conviction that all creative works 'are amazingly antinational even where the author may think he or she is espousing national themes. People identify with a good tale and the characters irrespective of the tale's region of origins' (58).

In the context of globalisation, claims have been made about the increasing universality of civil society groups functioning mainly through international non-government organisations (NGOs) who have emerged as significant actors at grassroots. The internationalisation of NGO activism has resulted in a firm focus on transnational collective actions and campaigns concerned with issues such as disarmament, drug addiction, illiteracy, social justice, poverty, animal rights, sustainable development, HIV/AIDS, women's rights, child abuse, environment protection, violation of human rights, etc. Despite the criticisms levelled against NGOs for their failure to effectively play their role as agents for mobilising transformation and social change, and as critics of government policies, they have, at least in a Gramscian sense, provided a space where people, the state and the market interact, and where people can organise movements against the hegemony of both the state and the market.

Globalisation has also inspired a collective state-sponsored rise of supraterritorial alliances – for example, the Council of Europe, the League of Arab States, the African Union and the European Union. Along with international organisations such as the BIS (Bank for International Settlements) and the Commonwealth, several intercontinental transregional projects like the Association of South East Asian Nations (1980), the Andean Pact (1983), and the Gulf Cooperation Council (1989) were initiated by such alliances. Interconnectivity among various local bodies was also made possible when the International Union of Local Authorities (IULA), the World Associations of Cities and Local Authorities Coordination (WACLAC) and the World Federation of United Towns (UTO) together decided to form the World Organization of United Cities and Local Governments, in 2004. Globalisation has also accelerated the growth of non-national, non-territorial, issue-based collective actions in times of wars, epidemics, famines and natural disasters – for example, the efforts to provide relief during the Indian Ocean tsunami of 26 December 2004 and the Kerala floods of August 2018, and the donations raised from the satellite transmission of Live Aid pop concerts for twenty drought-stricken countries of Africa in July 1985. Globally mobile civil societies, businesses, and media and governance personalities have been increasingly identifying with one another as 'a transnational managerial class' (Strange 138). According to Nicholas Negroponte, the emerging global generation is 'released from the limitation of geographic proximity as the sole basis of friendship, collaboration, play, and neighborhood' (230).

The connectivity promoted by globalisation has also helped the underprivileged, marginal and working classes to form transworld solidarities. For instance, LaVía Campesina, with members from eighty-one countries as of 2018, has provided a global platform to peasant struggles since 1993. The historical concurrence of the gender and sexuality revolution with the emergence of supraterritorial domains is also noteworthy. Since 1978, with the formation of the International Lesbian and Gay Association (ILGA), various transworld organisations, like Amnesty International, have provided support to sexual minorities. According to one Black activist based in São Paulo (qtd. in Carnciro), 'Globalization provides us with an opportunity to recognize that people of African descent throughout the world form a community of destiny and face similar problems. My identity as a person of African descent can be greater than my national identity'.

The spread of terrorist networks and anti-terror operations provide another facet of transworld networks. By 2002, the British Army had its presence in over eighty countries; and around 250,000 US troops were stationed in 120 countries in 2005; just as some paramilitary groups like the Irish Republican Army (IRA) and the Al-Qaeda have dispersed themselves across the planet.

Globalisation, however, cannot announce the end of the 'national project' when it comes to its role in defining one's identity. Globalisation has witnessed a proliferation of micro-nationalisms within nation-states. For example, the aboriginal Hawaiian identity was spurred by apprehensions about global tourism; indigenous activism in Amazonia was strengthened through people's resistance to global deforestation; and the North American Free Trade Agreement (NAFTA) of 1994 triggered the Zapatista rebellion in Mexico. Also, monolingualism has often challenged the multicultural/multilingual character of globality through cumulative majoritarian sentiments, as shown by the English-only movement in the United States and the French-only movement in Quebec, Canada. Unlike micro-nations who struggle to secure their rights within statist hegemonies, some regionalist macro-nationalist movements – like the pan-Arab, pan-Asian and pan-Turkish movements – have developed ideas of nationhood that are 'above' the state.

Diasporas are another interesting factor in discussions around nationalism and globalisation. For instance, the Armenian and Chinese diasporas have given impetus to globalisation by their efforts to link the countries of their origin with their new settlements. The following section addresses such diasporas.

'SOFT BORDER' AND DIASPORIC COMMUNITIES

The term 'diaspora' has become an inclusive reference for guest-workers, immigrants, refugees, expatriates and travellers. Diaspora consciousness, characterised by a dual or multiple identification with more than one nation-state, is shaped among the globally dispersed yet collectively self-identified ethnic groups by their transnational associations with territorial states where such groups currently reside as well as with their homeland-states of origin. In the words of James Clifford, 'The empowering paradox of diaspora is that dwelling here assumes a solidarity and connection there. But there is not necessarily a single place or an exclusivist nation. . . . [It is] the connection [elsewhere] that makes a difference [here]' (322). According to Robin Cohen, 'Transnational bonds no longer have to be cemented by migration or by exclusive territorial claims. In the age of cyberspace, a diaspora can, to some degree, be held together or re-created through the mind, through cultural artefacts and through a shared imagination' (516). In this context, the idea of 'transnationalism' has also seen the transformation from the nationalist notion of a 'melting pot', where diasporic communities were expected to be gradually appropriated by the dominant culture of the host state, towards the liberal democratic ideology of 'multiculturalism', where a state tries to cater to the needs of multiple nations within its borders. An apt example for this is the gradual change in the outlook among the Zionists of Israel where using any language other than Hebrew used to be considered anti-national, who now permit the use of English, Russian, Arabic or Yiddish as medium of instruction along with Hebrew.

In the transnational move from 'home' towards a 'home-away-from-home', and while representing 'cultural specificity and difference, packaged for transnational consumption' through 'microelectronic transnationalism' (Spivak, 'Who Claims Alterity?' 276), diaspora embodies a hyphenated identity 'in the electronic media in particular, (where) the politics of desire and imagination are always in contest with the politics of heritage and nostalgia' (Appadurai and Breckenridge iii). While Mary Kaldor has hinted at the presence of both reactionary ethno-nationalists and cosmopolitan anti-nationalists within diasporas, Arjun Appadurai observes that the 'new patriotisms' of diasporic transnational communities 'also involve various rather puzzling new forms of linkage between diasporic nationalisms, delocalized political communications and revitalized political commitments at both ends of the diasporic process' (220).

Christian Joppke and Ewa Morawska have pointed out that '[a]lthough not a new phenomenon in the history of international migration, contemporary immigrant transnationalism, of course, is not an exact replica of the old, but a different configuration of circumstances' (20). The differences can be understood in terms of the rise of multiculturalism, advances in communications, government outreach programmes for emigrants like the granting of dual citizenship or providing favourable conditions as the Government of India does for non-resident Indians (NRIs) to use their foreign-honed capital and skills to invest in Indian industries. However, despite the changes that transnationality enforces on the diaspora, 'there seems to be a basic inability to move on from the core ideas and concepts of the national imagination. In the discussion of transnational futures, the fundamental reference point continues to be the stubborn and insistent idea of "imagined community"' (Robins and Aksoy 183).

Theorists have formulated various classifications of diaspora depending on the extent, impact and modes of transnationalism on a wide variety of diasporic groups such as forced migrants (Castles), return migrants (Thomas-Hope), undocumented migrants (Hagan), retirement migrants (King et al.), refugees and asylum seekers (Koser), highly skilled workers (Vertovec), religious representatives servicing migrants (Riccio), IT professionals employed through global 'body shopping' (Xiang), and specialists drawn back from diasporas to add to the development of their homelands (Meyer and Brown). Roger Rouse has described the 'habitus' of dual orientation reproduced by migrants as 'bifocality' or 'a dual frame of reference', on the basis of which they continuously compare their situations in the host society abroad to their situations in their home society. Katy Gardner's study on the Sylhetis in Britain and Bangladesh show that in everyday discourse, *desh* (home) is used to refer to the locus of personal, religious and social identity, while *bidesh* (foreignness) is associated with material and economic benefits. Gardner shows how the *desh–bidesh* paradox ultimately becomes a part of the 'local mental maps (that) involve a geography of power, in which locations are points along a continuum, with different types of empowerment to be found at each' (5).

In the context of diaspora, transnational lives acquire cosmopolitan cultural competences, which sociologists have linked to various concepts such as 'creolisation', 'translation', 'cut 'n' mix', 'crossover', 'hyphenated identity', 'multidirectional shifts in identity', 'hybridity', 'bricolage', 'syncretism', 'multiculture', 'third space', 'multiple cultural competence', 'ghettoising', 'transculturation', 'diasporic consciousness' and 'pragmatic manipulation of multiplicity' (Amit-Talai). Although transnational diasporic communities are studied within the framework of a 'transnational social field' (Glick Schiller et al.), 'translocality' (Appadurai, 'The Production of Locality'), 'transnational social space' (Pries) or 'transnational village' (Levitt, *The Transnational Villagers*), research among Indian Americans by Sunaina Marr Maira has revealed how constant struggles to negotiate the everydayness of migrant life remains central to the lives of second-generation immigrants: 'second-generation youth culture becomes a site of struggles to define notions of authenticity that, while drawing on transnational imaginings of "India", also work to position these youth in relation to hierarchies of race, class, gender, and nationalism that mark them as "local"' (23). Peggy Levitt uses the example of one of her informants in her study, Pratik, a Gujarati engineer living in Boston, to show how he 'has assimilated into mainstream economic life in the US but rejects membership in its cultural and religious institutions. And at the same time, he is active in the economic and religious life of his sending community. He purposefully picks and chooses where and what he will be involved in, so far achieving mobility in both contexts', and thereby, combines efficiently and selectively his transnational involvements ('Keeping Feet in Both Worlds' 194).

On the other hand, home countries often deploy diasporic communities in nation-building processes, mainly through launching various outreach governmental policies such as extending voting rights, special consular services and providing parliamentary representation. Governments also attempt to involve the diaspora during moments of national crisis. For example, diaspora communities contributed generously to victims of the

Gujarat earthquake in 2001 and during the earthquake in Turkey in 1999. In such cases, concern for the homeland, along with the insecurities of being a minority in the host country, often gives birth to an awareness of one's own identity which had been otherwise overlooked. During Penny Logan's research on the religious and cultural practices of Gujaratis in Britain, 'many adults reported that they had become more aware of their religion in Britain, as a result of belonging to a minority group in a predominantly irreligious society. They could no longer take their religion and their children's assumption of it for granted' (124). According to Chetan Bhatt, religious nationalism based on a revivalist agenda popularised in India by the Vishwa Hindu Parishad (VHP), the Rashtriya Swayamsevak Sangh (RSS) and the Bharatiya Janata Party (BJP), 'has relied extensively on its followers in the US, Britain, Canada and Europe to generate global support and funds for its political ventures in India' (155). Many fundamentalist Islamicist groups have adopted various modes of electronic and Internet-mediated communication to channelise resources, funds and support from diasporic communities. However, Susan Paul Pattie highlights another facet of diasporic responses to home in her study of the ambivalence that characterises the response of Armenians in diaspora to the Armenian Apostolic Church: 'Looking at their diaspora situation, Armenians in Cyprus and London place great value on this continuing, seemingly unchanging aspect of the Church. Yet at the same time the old presentation is not always understood and, worse, not even experienced, as attendance and participation dwindle with each new generation' (231).

Such contrasts in diasporic responses to nationalism leads to an important question – can the notion of nationhood be ever eliminated or at least renovated with various reformative initiatives? Critics like Hannah Arendt (1906–75) have shown no confidence in the probability of a future humanitarian transformation of the nation-state. However, others like Jean-Luc Nancy have tried to show how communities have always been 'singular plural' and that it is possible to have a country like India comprising widely varying communities. Genomics has provided data to prove that every nation is in fact a blend of people with multiple genetic origins. Thus, Kwame Anthony Appiah advocates the possibility of a cosmopolitan patriot who 'can entertain the possibility of a world in which everyone is a rooted cosmopolitan, attached to a home of one's own, with its own cultural particularities, but taking pleasure from the presence of other, different places that are home to other, different people' (16). This notion of the cosmopolitan patriot would also resolve the debate on whether nationhood is voluntary or involuntary. For Ernst Renan, a nation is the outcome of an 'everyday plebiscite' (qtd. in Pecora 175), while for Margalit and Raz, 'Qualification for membership (of a nation) is usually determined by non-voluntary criteria. One cannot choose to belong. One belongs because of who one is' (447).

TRANSNATIONAL FOCUS ON ENVIRONMENT AND TERRORISM

Globalisation is often given credit for creating a trans-planetary awareness, through international environmental NGOs like the World Wide Fund for Nature (WWF) and Greenpeace, about ecological catastrophes such as global warming, the depletion of natural resources, climate change, loss of biological diversity, excessive world population growth, nuclear holocaust, species extinction, acid rain, ecologically unsustainable development, and GM (genetically modified) food crops. The United Nations has sponsored global summits related to environmentalism at various venues across the globe – Stockholm (1972), Rio de Janeiro (1992), Johannesburg (2002), etc. The grave threat of the depletion of the ozone layer was addressed at the 1985 Vienna Convention and the 1987 Montreal Protocol. Since 1994, the Global Environment Facility (GEF), along with United Nations Environment Programme (UNEP), United Nations Development Programme (UNDP) and the World Bank, has been trying to assist poor countries in making investments that would benefit ecological integrity. The WWF and the World Conservation Union (IUCN) collaborated with UNEP in 1980 to launch a World Conservation Strategy that formulated guidelines for various states. Similarly, the World Resources Institute (WRI) framed the Tropical Forestry

Action Plan jointly with UNDP and the UN Food and Agriculture Organization (FAO) in 1985. Since 1997, Global Forest Watch has been trying to stop illegal logging in countries across the world. The Intergovernmental Panel on Climate Change was set up in 1988 by the International Council of Scientific Unions, UNEP and the World Meteorological Organization. The Secretariat for the Convention on International Trade in Endangered Species of Wild Fauna and Flora (CITES) has undertaken collaborative measures with the WWF and the IUCN. The IUCN, UNEP and WRI have jointly organised the Biodiversity Conservation Strategy Programme. The Jakarta Mandate (1995), Kyoto Protocol (1997) and Rotterdam Convention (1998) are some of the international treaties that are significant in this context. Thus, concerns about environmental issues is a key foundation for a significant amount of transnational cooperation.

The future of the solidarity among nations is mainly centred around transnational concerns regarding the environment and the threat posed by global terrorism. Ecoglobalism and the war against terror have often toned down unilateral management capacities of nation-states and created new imperatives for states to cooperate internationally in terms of policy convergence through effective supranational governance or common-interest coalitions. However, such cooperation has always been heavily lopsided affairs as is evident from the Euro-American dominance of the numerous international pacts and protocols that have been put into place till date. The social inequalities and ecological devastations resulting from 'the systematic exclusion of people of color from environmental decisions affecting their communities' (Bryant 5) can be described as 'environmental racism'. Another aspect of environmental racism is the 'garbage imperialism' practised by countries of the Global North who try to dump hazardous and toxic industrial wastes in countries of the Global South. The latter group has risen up to challenge this. Even though solidarities among the G77 (formed in 1964) group of countries – comprising developing nations including representatives from the African states, the Least Developed Countries and the Alliance of Small-Island States (AOSIS) – have weakened, after the 2009 Conference of Parties

(COP) meeting of the United Nations Framework Convention on Climate Change (UNFCCC), nations of the Global South asserted 'the ability to present a collective voice from the South' (Beer 86). They are united by a common perception of the 'inadequacy of Northern action on climate change, . . . [a] collective sense of an "unjust world order," . . . [and a] trust deficit towards developing countries' (86). Although the G8 countries account for 47 per cent of World Carbon emission, studies supported by the United States often project poverty and underdevelopment of developing countries as the major cause of pollution. This attitude ultimately led to President Donald Trump withdrawing the United States from the Paris climate agreement in 2017, calling the accord signed by 195 nations in 2015 'draconian', while reaffirming that he 'was elected to represent the citizens of Pittsburgh, not Paris'. From the Trump administration's point of view, the accord was dangerous for American economy and sovereignty. However, America reentered the Paris Agreement under the leadership of President Joe Bidden, with effect from 19 February 2021.

The globalisation of a 'weapon culture', according to Mary Kaldor, can be outlined through 'the rigidification of the alliances in Europe and the establishment of integrated command systems, together with a global network of military connections through military assistance, arms sales and training' along with 'a whole set of new arrangements . . . which constitute an intensification of transnationalization in the military sphere' (Kaldor, *New and Old Wars* 139). Contractors like the MPR and DynCorp, and private security organisations 'have expanded to a degree that they outnumber most national armies' (Mandel 8). This naturalisation of militarism is often done by linking ammunition with issues related to human rights and global peace – Zoltan Grossman has illustrated how the US military in most of their post–Second-World-War interventions in other countries has proclaimed that the 'interventions were carried out in the name of "freedom" and "democracy," [although] nearly all of them in fact defended dictatorships controlled by pro-U.S. elites' (Web, n. p.). The Gulf War of 1990, initiated by President George H. W. Bush, violated the Westphalian model and proclaimed the birth of a 'new world order' where the global leaders would no longer disengage themselves from cross-border acts which they recognise as unjust and as internal matters of those affected states. According to Thomas P. M. Barnett, former professor of military strategy at the US Naval War College and former Assistant for Strategic Futures in the Pentagon's Office of Force Transformations, 'Globalization is this country's [US'] gift to history. . . . In short, we the people needs to become we the planet' (*The Pentagon's New Map* 50). In the context of this global militarism, Ferguson and Turnbull observed the evolution of 'political language' through which '"winning wars" has been replaced by "defending national security". "Merchants of death" have become respectable defense contractors. These euphemisms do more than conceal violence, they enable it, by both what they do not say and their open-ended promise. . . . "War" is not just more frank than "national security"; "war" suggests the possibility of peace' (87).

Militarism also thrives in populist speeches delivered by so-called upholders of justice globalism. The invoking of 'the people' by justice globalists while asserting their dissent against corporate-led globalisation often ends up denoting only a national population, where militarism is frequently validated for the sake of the safety of the national 'people'. One may argue that such national-populist narratives are evident in the positions taken by India's Prime Minister Narendra Modi. Such narratives are in tune with a global trend popularised by Austria's Jörg Haider, Australia's Pauline Hanson, France's Jean-Marie Le Pen, Italy's Umberto Bossi, Holland's Pim Fortuyn, New Zealand's Winston Peters, Switzerland's Christoph Blocher, or America's Patrick Buchanan, to name a few. On the other hand, jihadist globalists like Osama bin Laden, or the Taliban and ISIS, intersect their militant version of political Islam with a parallel populist rhetoric that treats 'the people' as the *umma* (a single global community of believers) of *tawhid* (who believes in the absolute oneness of God and His creation), and represent their jihad as struggle against what they label as 'Satanic acts of aggression' – the 'presence of American troops on the Arabian peninsula' for transnational corporate interests, 'the ongoing Israeli oppression of the Palestinian people, the 1993 American operations against Muslim warlords in Somalia, the Western indifference to the slaughter of thousands of Bosnian Muslims during the 1991–95 Yugoslav Civil War, and the economic sanctions imposed by the West on Iraq after the first Gulf War' (Steger 223).

The recent environment of global insecurity, for some critics, is engineered by compromises made by certain nation-states, like Colombia or Pakistan, who have a vested interest in promoting terrorism. For some others like Boot, the rise of a global militancy has to be understood in connection with the rise of the 'American Empire' founded on a 'superpower syndrome' (Boot 27–30). Based on Manfred B. Steger's definition of 'imperial globalism' as the 'neoconservative inclination to shape the globe in its own image by military means' (231), Martin Shaw has argued, 'It is clearly plausible to define the Bush administration's kind of globalism as "imperial" in character' (28).

The extent of global terrorism can be understood from the fact that in the year 2017 alone, a total of 2926 people were killed in the first twenty terrorist attacks of that year which included the attack by Al-Shabaab in Mogadishu, Somalia, on 14 October; the 24 November attack on Beir al-Abd, Egypt, by the Sinai Province of the Islamic State; the 16 February attack in Sehwan, Pakistan; and the 31 May attack on Kabul, Afghanistan, by the Khorasan Chapter of the Islamic State (Institute for Economics and Peace 81). The spread and intensity of the threat has also inspired efforts to bridge the divides of nationalism to address the problem. There are several transnational initiatives that have tried to build global partnerships to counter terrorism – such as the Tokyo Convention on Offences and Certain Other Acts Committed on Board Aircraft (1963), the Hague Convention for the Suppression of Unlawful Seizure of Aircraft (1970), the New York Convention on the Prevention and Punishment of Crimes against Internationally Protected Persons, Including Diplomatic Agents (1973), the New York International Convention Against the Taking of Hostages (1979), the Vienna Convention on the Physical Protection of Nuclear Material (1979), the New York International Convention for the Suppression of Terrorist Bombings (1997), the New York International Convention for the Suppression of Financing of Terrorism (1999), the New York International Convention for the Suppression of Acts of Nuclear Terrorism (2005), the Convention of the Organization of the Islamic Conference on Combating International Terrorism at Ouagadougou (1999), the Minsk Treaty on Cooperation among the States Members of the Commonwealth of Independent States in Combating Terrorism (1999), the SAARC Regional Convention on the Suppression of Terrorism at Kathmandu (1987), the ASEAN Convention on Counter Terrorism at Cebu (2007), the Convention on the Suppression of Unlawful Acts Relating to International Civil Aviation (2010), and the Protocol to the Convention on Offences and Certain other Acts Committed on Board Aircraft adopted by the OSCE (Organization for Security and Co-operation in Europe) countries (2014).

Although we are yet to see nuanced scholarship analysing post-Hiroshima and post-Nagasaki accounts (similar to the intensive academic attention on the Holocaust, Partition narratives or trauma studies), the post–9/11 era has witnessed academicians, social thinkers, political leaders, creative personalities, activists and worldwide media coming together to understand the 'Global War on Terror'. This transnational collective against terrorism, however, as delineated by Barnett, is closely interlinked with the 'military–market nexus':

> I express this interrelationship (of the military and the market) in the form of a "ten commandments of globalization": (1) Look for resources and ye shall find, but . . . (2) No stability, no markets; (3) No growth, no stability; (4) No resources, no growth; (5) No infrastructure, no resources; (6) No money, no infrastructure; (7) No rules, no money; (8) No security, no rules; (9) No Leviathan (American military force), no security; and (10) No (American) will, no Leviathan. Understanding the military-market link is not just good business, it is good national security strategy. (*Blueprint for Action* xvii)

Moreover, the resurgence of patriotic sentiments after every terrorist attack on nation-states – as revealed by the popularity of the Hindi film *Uri* (based on the Indian Army's surgical strike in retaliation to the 2016 terror strike in Uri), and the upsurge of hypernationalism after the 2019 Pulwama terror attack in Kashmir – is regarded by some commentators as the 'collapse of globalism' on account of a worldwide revival of nationalism (Saul).

THE NATIONALIST BACKLASH: CLOSING BORDERS AND THE RHETORIC OF ISOLATIONISM

Globalisation, rather than bridging economic inequalities among nations, has increased the asymmetrical power relations among nation-states through 'corporate globalisation' or 'globalisation-from-above' where corporate giants often record profits that surpass the GDP of an entire nation-state. In 2017, Trinidad and Tobago's GDP was less than the profits declared by Starbucks Corporation; New Guinea's GDP was less than McDonald's revenue; Mercadona's (Spanish supermarket chain) income was more than Nepal's GDP; Inditex's (Spanish clothing company) profits exceeded Paraguay's GDP; and Johnson and Johnson generated more profits than Ethiopia's GDP (Belinchón and Moynihan). Bypassing the Global South, the headquarters of most of the topmost TNCs (transnational corporations) of the year 2018, such as the Sinopec Group, Toyota Motor, Royal Dutch Shell, Microsoft, Apple, Amazon.com, Alibaba and Tencent, are geographically concentrated in the 'US (126), China (120), Japan (52), Germany (32), France (28), UK (21), South Korea (16), Netherlands (15), Switzerland (14) and Canada (12)' (Ventura, Web, n. p.). All these facts add to the resentment against globalisation that had already been felt during the 1997 financial crisis in South East Asia when – on account of crony capitalism promoted by the US-dominated IMF, along with the measures adopted by the US to recover from the 1990 recession – Thailand, Indonesia, South Korea, Malaysia, Philippines, Hong Kong and Laos faced an economic disaster, while China, Vietnam, Taiwan, Singapore and Brunei suffered from significant economic setbacks. Greece and Spain were among the worst sufferers of the global recession emerging out of the 2008 US financial crisis that resulted in more than 10,000 'economic suicides' due to monetary indebtedness and loss of property and jobs (Haiken). The 'Welcome to Hell' protest against globalisation, First-World imperialism and capitalism, outside the Hamburg venue of the G20 meet in July 2017, exposed the unrelieved rage against the 'dogmatic slumber of the leaders of the free world, represented at this G20 summit' which, according to the protesters, 'is the origin of our current dystopian nightmare (wars, terrorism, the refugee crisis and climate change)'

(Horvat, Web, n. p.). In the context of this neo-imperialism of the First World, it is important to reiterate Fanon's insistence on the formation of independent nations in the Third World as alternatives to Anglo-American liberalism and Soviet communism, on the basis of the argument that '[i]t is at the heart of national consciousness that international consciousness lives and grows' (248).

The Western world has witnessed a rise in Islamophobia and Arabophobia since the Six Days War of 1967. This was exacerbated by a series of events – the 1973 OPEC (Organisation of Petroleum Exporting Countries) oil embargo, the Gulf Wars, the attack on the World Trade Centre in 1993 and the 9/11 terrorist attack. This Islamophobia manifested itself in the USA PATRIOT Act and in the military operations in Iraq and Afghanistan, and thereafter, 'representations of "terrorism" and "Islamic fundamentalism" have increasingly replaced other representations . . . and have become more fervently deployed in anti-Arab state policies and everyday patterns of engagement than ever before' (Naber 4). In a context of heightened terrorist threats, aggressive postures adopted by nuclear states like North Korea, campaigns of 'global assassination' (like the drone campaign) and intolerance (for instance, the Boycott, Divestment, Sanctions [BDS] movement), giving rise to social hostilities (in countries such as India, Israel and Russia, as per Pew Research Center's Social Hostilities Index), the optimistic internationalist dream of a global village remains far from being realised. British Prime Minister Theresa May's move to document EU citizens residing in Britain, the ISIS-instigated Syrian and Middle Eastern refugee crisis in Europe, followed by the proposed ban on immigration in Trump's America (a country which once inspired John F. Kennedy's memorably titled book, *A Nation of Immigrants*), all point to a closing of borders again.

Even though countries like Iraq, Turkey, Lebanon, Jordan, Egypt and Libya – and later on, Germany and Sweden – provided asylum to a significant number of Syrian refugees, despite refusals from Israel and the US, the 'Long Summer of Migration' ended with repressive reforms of the EU refugee policy after the 2015 terrorist attacks in Paris. Refugees were regularly linked to 'Islamic terrorism' and, ultimately, the Aegean and Balkan routes were blocked in March 2016 by an agreement between Turkey and the EU. In Germany, the PEGIDA movement (Patriotic Europeans Against the Islamisation of the Occident), along with the right-wing Alternative for Germany (AfD) party, incited widespread violence, engineering more than a thousand attacks on refugee homes in 2015 (Friedrich and Kuhn). This attitude was also reflected by the nationalist political leadership in Europe. Mark Rutte, the Dutch Prime Minister, after his re-election in 2017, felt that there was 'something wrong with our country', and asserted that 'the silent majority' would no longer endure immigrants who come to 'abuse our freedom' (Ramesh). Addressing the refugee issue as a 'migration crisis' or 'refugee crisis', the unwilling global leaders further contributed to incidents like the tragic drowning of around 800 refugees on 19 April 2015 near the island of Lampedusa in Italy. Seventy-one dead bodies of refugees were found on 28 August 2015 in Austria. The body of three-year-old Aylan Kurdi washed up on a beach near Bodrum in Turkey on 3 September 2015 and became an enduring image of the magnitude of the tragedy. The Rohingya Muslims from the Rakhine state of Myanmar, victims of a massive human rights violation and genocide, were refused citizenship rights and treated as 'illegal immigrants' from Bangladesh by the state of Myanmar. They fled to camps near Cox's Bazar in Bangladesh in 2017. The Bangladesh government, of late, has been planning to move around 100,000 Rohingyas to Bhashan Char, an island infamous for cyclones and floods, while Malaysia, Indonesia and Thailand have all turned away boats overcrowded with Rohingyas attempting to seek shelter. The central government of India, on the one hand, initiated 'Operation *Insaniyat*' to provide relief and assistance for refugee camps in Bangladesh, but on the other, announced that it would deport Rohingyas living in India, although the West Bengal government has maintained a humanitarian stance and provided assistance to the refugees.

Policies aimed at wider national interests are often in conflict with the vision propounded by globalisation. China's domestic and international policies are an interesting example. While it has banned Muslims of the Xinjiang Uyghur Autonomous Region in western China from giving their children names which reveal their religious identity, it has nurtured ties with many Muslim-dominated countries in the Indian Ocean Region (IOR) for strategic reasons. China also tried to strengthen its geopolitical power through models like the 'String of Pearls' (propound by Booz Allen Hamilton in 2005) and the Maritime Silk Road (put forward by President Xi Jinping in October 2013).

The rise of 'academic nationalism' too has affected the spirit of universalism intrinsic to globalism. As hooks observed, the practise of higher education has always been seeped in sectarian and narrow focuses: 'If we examine critically the traditional role of the university . . . it is painfully clear that biases that uphold and maintain White supremacy, imperialism, sexism, and racism have distorted education so that it is no longer about the practice of freedom' (29). The slowdown of the enthusiasm around globalisation can also be traced in popular culture, best exemplified by films and documentaries such as *Toni Erdmann* (2016), *Cyberbully* (2015), *The True Cost* (2015), *The Big Short* (2015), *Men, Women & Children* (2014), *Trash* (2014), *Cloud Atlas* (2012), *Fast Food Nation* (2006) and *Lost in Translation* (2003). Scholars have also suggested that, contrary to the popular notion of a transnational media system 'domesticating the foreign' in a 'global newsroom', most of the current media content – including that of outlets such as Al Jazeera and CNN – remain 'firmly in the grip of nation-states' (Hafez 173). In a constant race to capture geo-cultural and geo-linguistic markets, they assist in the 'regionalization of globalization' by regularly focusing on regionalist and nationalist agendas.

The violation of a harmonious spirit of internationalism is evident in the protectionist populism prevalent in nation-states across the world. This has contributed to the rise of schismatic behaviours in recent times. There are several such tragic instances – the shooting inside the gay club Pulse in Orlando, Florida, on 12 June 2016; the attack during the Friday prayers at Al Noor and Linwood mosques in Christchurch, New Zealand, on 15 March 2019, by a white supremacist; the 2019 Kaduna State massacre of Christians in Nigeria. Contemporary political and cultural events show a systematic rejection of liberal nationalism that underlies globalisation – the increasing popularity of anti-refugee rhetoric in

European countries like France, Italy, Slovenia, Hungary, Poland, Germany, Czech Republic, Finland and the Netherlands; the attacks on women's rights by the ruling Law and Justice Party in Poland; the attacks on Muslim homes and business by the Sinhalese Buddhist nationalists in Sri Lanka in March 2018; the ban announced by the All India Cine Workers Association on Pakistani artistes and actors working in India, after the Pulwama terrorist attack; and the Pakistan's foreign minister's decision to skip the 2019 summit of the Organisation of Islamic Cooperation (OIC) at Abu Dhabi, protesting against OIC's decision to invite India. All these point to an insistence on implementing an 'isolationist nationalism' publicised through a rhetoric of supremacy and estrangement from other nations (Atkins).

REFERENCES

Albrow, Martin. *The Global Age: State and Society Beyond Modernity*. Cambridge: Polity Press, 1996. Print.

Amit-Talai, V. 'Conclusion: The "Multi" Cultural of Youth'. *Youth Cultures.* Ed. V. Amit-Talai, and H. Wulff. London: Routledge, 1995. 223–33. Print.

Appadurai, Arjun. *Modernity at Large: Cultural Dimensions of Globalization*. Minneapolis: U of Minnesota P, 1996. Print.

---. 'The Production of Locality'. *Counterworks*. Ed. R. Fardon. London: Routledge, 1995. 204–25. Print.

Appadurai, Arjun, and Carol Breckenridge. 'On Moving Targets'. *Public Culture* 2 (1989): i–iv. Print.

Appiah, Kwame Anthony. *Cosmopolitanism*. London: Penguin, 2007. Print.

Ashcroft, Bill. 'Globalization, the Transnation and Utopia'. *Narrating the (Trans)Nation: The Dialectics of Culture and Identity*. Ed. Krishna Sen, and Sudeshna Chakravarty. Kolkata: Dasgupta and Co., 2008. 1–24. Print.

Atkins, David. 'Trump's Isolationist Nationalism Is a Mask for White Supremacy'. *Washington Monthly*. 7 April 2019. <https://washingtonmonthly.com/2019/03/30/trumps-isolationist-nationalism-is-a-mask-for-white-supremacy/>.

Barber, Benjamin. *Jihad vs. McWorld.* New York: Ballantine, 1996. Print.

Barnett, Thomas P. M. *Blueprint for Action: A Future Worth Creating.* New York: G. P. Putnam's Sons, 2005. Print.

---. *The Pentagon's New Map: War and Peace in the Twenty First Century.* New York: G. P. Putnam's Sons, 2004. Print.

Beck, Ulrich. *Risk Society: Towards a New Modernity*. London: Sage, 1992. Print.

Beer, C. T. 'Climate Justice, the Global South, and Policy Preferences of Kenyan Environmental NGOs'. *The Global South* 8.2 (2014): 84–100. Print.

Belinchón, Fernando, and Ruqayyah Moynihan. '25 Giant Companies that are Bigger than Entire Countries'. *Business Insider*. Web. 2 April 2019. <https://www.businessinsider.com/25-giant-companies-that-earn-more-than-entire-countries-2018-7?IR=T>.

Bhatt, Chetan. *Liberation and Purity: Race, New Religious Movements and the Ethics of Postmodernity*. London: UCL Press, 1997. Print.

Boot, Max. 'The Case for American Empire'. *Weekly Standard,* 29 October 2001. Print.

Bryant, Bunyan, ed. *Environmental Justice: Issues, Problems, and Solutions.* Washington DC: Island Press, 1995. Print.

Brysk, Alison. *From Tribal Village to Global Village: Indian Rights and International Relations in Latin America*. Stanford: Stanford UP, 2000. Print.

Carneiro, S. Executive Coordinator of Geledes – Black Woman's Institute. Interviewed by Jan Aart Scholte. 2002. in Porto Alegre, Brazil, 1 February. Cited in *Globalization: A Critical Introduction* by Jan Aart Scholte. London: Red Globe Press, 2019. 249. Print.

Castles, Stephen. 'Towards a Sociology of Forced Migration and Social Transformation'. *Sociology* 37.1 (2003): 13–34. Print.

Cheah, Pheng, and Bruce Robbins, ed. *Cosmopolitics: Thinking and Feeling Beyond the Nation*. U of Minneapolis: Minnesota Press, 1998. Print.

Clifford, James. 'Traveling Cultures'. *Cultural Studies*. Ed. L. Grossberg, C. Nelson and P. Treichler. New York: Routledge, 1992. 96–116. Print.

Cohen, Robin. 'Diasporas and the Nation-state: From Victims to Challengers'. *International Affairs* 72 (1996): 507–20. Print.

Dagnino, Arianna. 'Transcultural Writers and Transcultural Literature in the Age of Global Modernity'. *Transnational Literature* 4.2 (2012): 1–14. Web. 20 February 2020. <http://fhrc.flinders.edu.au/transnational/home.html>.

Dirlik, Arif. 'Modernity as History: Post-Revolutionary China, Globalization and the Question of Modernity'. *Social History* 27.1 (2002): 16–39. Print.

Durkheim, E. *Professional Ethics and Civic Morals*. London: Routledge and Kegan Paul, 1992. Print.

Fanon, Frantz. *The Wretched of the Earth*. Harmondsworth: Penguin, 1967. Print.

Ferguson, Kathy E., and Phyllis Turnbull. 'Globalizing Militaries'. *Rethinking Globalism*. Ed. Manfred B. Steger. Maryland: Rowman and Littlefield, 2004. Print.

Friedan, Thomas L. *The World is Flat: A Brief History of the Twenty-First Century*. New York: Farrar, Straus and Giroux, 2005. Print.

Friedrich, S., and G. Kuhn. 'Between Capital and Volk'. *Jacobin*. Web. 4 April 2019. <https://jacobinmag.com/2017/06/germany-afd-cdu-immigrants-merkel-xenophobia-neoliberalism>.

Fukuyama, Francis. *The End of History and the Last Man*. London: Hamish Hamilton, 1992. Print.

Gardner, Katy. 'Death of a Migrant: Transnational Death Rituals and Gender among British Sylhetis'. *Global Networks* 2.3 (2002): 191–204. Print.

Giddens, Anthony. 'Desh-Bidesh: Sylheti Images of Home and Away'. *Man* 28.1 (1993): 1–15. Print.

---. *Modernity and Self-Identity: Self and Society in the Late Modern Age*. Cambridge: Polity Press, 1991. Print.

---. *The Consequences of Modernity*. Cambridge: Polity, 1990. Print.

Glick Schiller, Nina, Linda Basch, and Cristina Blanc-Szanton. 'Transnationalism: A New Analytic Framework for Understanding Migration'. *Toward a Transnational Perspective on Migration.* Ed. N. Glick Schiller, L. Basch, and C. Blanc-Szanton. New York: New York Academy of Sciences, 1992. 1–24. Print.

Gorbachev, Mikhail. *Memoirs*. New York: Doubleday, 1996. Print.

Grossman, Zoltan. 'A Briefing on the History of US Military Interventions'. Web. 2 April 2019. <https://sites.evergreen.edu/zoltan/interventions/>.

Hafez, Kai. *The Myth of Media Globalization*. Trans. Alex Skinner. Cambridge: Polity Press, 2007. Print.

Hagan, Jacqueline M. *Deciding to be Legal: A Maya Community in Houston*. Philadelphia: Temple UP, 1994. Print.

Haiken, Melanie. 'More than 10,000 Suicides Tied to Economic Crisis, Study Says'. *Forbes. Com*. Web. 2 April 2019. <https://www.forbes.com/sites/melaniehaiken/2014/06/12/more-than-10000-suicides-tied-to-economic-crisis-study-says/#64da9ec57ae2>.

Hamelink, Cees J. *Cultural Autonomy in Global Communications*. New York: Longmans, 1983. Print.

Hardt, Michael, and Antonio Negri. *Empire*. Cambridge: Harvard UP, 2000. Print.

Harvey, David. *The Condition of Postmodernity: An Inquiry into the Conditions of Cultural Change*. Oxford: Blackwell, 1989. Print.

Held, David. *Democracy and the Global Order: From the Modern State to Cosmopolitan Governance*. Cambridge: Polity Press, 1995. Print.

hooks, bell. *Teaching to Transgress: Education as the Practice of Freedom*. New York: Routledge, 1994. Print.

Horvat, Srećko. 'We Came to Hamburg to Protest about G20 – and Found a Dystopian Nightmare. *The Guardian*. Web. 3 April 2019. <https://www.theguardian.com/commentisfree/2017/jul/06/hamburg-protest-g20-dystopian-nightmare-security-disunity-politics>.

Huntington, Samuel P. *The Clash of Civilizations and the Remaking of World Order*. New York: Simon & Schuster, 1996. Print.

Institute for Economics and Peace. *Global Terrorism Index 2018: Measuring the Impact of Terrorism*. Web. 2 April 2019. <http://visionofhumanity.org/reports>.

Itzigsohn, J., and S. Giorguli-Saucedo. 'Immigrant Incorporation and Sociocultural Transnationalism'. *International Migration Review* 36.3 (2002): 766–98. Print.

Itzigsohn, J., C. Dore Cabral, E. Hernández Medina, and O. Vázquez. 'Mapping Dominican Transnationalism: Narrow and Broad

Transnational Practices'. *Ethnic and Racial Studies* 22.2 (1999): 316–39. Print.

Joppke, Christian, and Ewa Morawska. 'Integrating Immigrants in Liberal Nationstates: Policies and Practices'. *Toward Assimilation and Citizenship*. Ed. C. Joppke and E. Morawska. Basingstoke: Palgrave, 2003. 1–36. Print.

Kaldor, Mary. 'Cosmopolitanism versus Nationalism: The New Divide?'. *Europe's New Nationalism*. Ed. R. Caplan, and J. Feffer. Oxford: Oxford UP. 42–58. Print.

---. *New and Old Wars: Organized Violence in a Global Era*. Stanford: Stanford UP, 1991. Print.

King, Russell, Anthony M. Warnes, and Allan M. Williams. 'International Retirement Migration in Europe'. *International Journal of Population Geography* 4.2 (1998): 91–111. Print.

Koser, Khalid. 'From Refugees to Transnational Communities?'. *New Approaches to Migration*. Ed. N. Al-Ali, and K. Koser. London: Routledge, 2002. 138–52. Print.

Laitin, David D. *Nations, States and Violence*. Oxford: Oxford UP, 2007. Print.

Levitt, Peggy. 'Keeping Feet in Both Worlds: Transnational Practices and Immigrant Incorporation in the United States'. *Toward Assimilation and Citizenship*. Ed. C. Joppke, and E. Morawska. Basingstoke: Palgrave, 2003. 177–94. Print.

---. *The Transnational Villagers*. Berkeley: U of California P, 2001. Print.

Logan, Penny. *Practicing Hinduism: The Experience of Gujarati Adults and Children in Britain.* Unpublished report, Thomas Coram Research Unit, University of London Institute of Education, 1988. Print.

Maira, S. Marr. *Desis in the House: Indian American Youth Culture in New York City*. Philadelphia: Temple UP, 2002. Print.

Mandel, Robert. *Armies without States: The Privatization of Security*. Boulder: Lynne Rienner, 2002. Print.

Marder, Michael. 'The Coronavirus Is Us'. *The New York Times*. Web. 3 March 2020. <https://www.nytimes.com/2020/03/03/opinion/the-coronavirus-is-us.html>.

Margalit, Avishai, and Joseph Raz. 'National Self-Determination'. *Journal of Philosophy* 87.9 (1990): 439–61. Print.

Meyer, Jean Baptiste, and Mercy Brown. 'Scientific Diasporas: A New Approach to the Brain Drain'. Paris: UNESCO-MOST Discussion Paper No. 41, 1999. Print.

Naber, Nadine. 'Introduction: Arab Americans and US Racial Formations'. *Race and Arab Americans Before and After 9/11: From Invisible Citizens to Visible Subjects*. Ed. Amaney A. Jamal, and Nadine Naber. Syracuse: Syracuse UP, 2008. 1–45. Print.

Negroponte, Nicholas. *Being Digital*. London: Hodder and Stoughton, 1995. Print.

Nixon, Richard. *Public Papers of the Presidents of the United States*. Washington: United States Government Printing Office, 1975. Print.

Pattie, Susan Paul. *Faith in History: Armenians Rebuilding Community*. Washington: Smithsonian Institution Press, 1997. Print.

Pecora, Vincent P., ed. *Nations and Identities, Classical Readings*. Malden: Blackwell Publishers, 2001. Print.

Peterson, V. Spike. *A Critical Rewriting of Global Political Economy: Integrating Reproductive, Productive, and Virtual Economies*. London: Routledge, 2003. Print.

Pew Research Center. 'Appendix B: Social Hostilities Index'. *Global Uptick in Government Restrictions on Religion in 2016*. Web. 3 April 2019. <https://www.pewresearch.org/wp-content/uploads/sites/7/2018/06/APPENDIX-B-1.pdf>.

Ponzanesi, Sandra. *Paradoxes of Postcolonial Culture: Contemporary Women Writers of the Indian and Afro-Italian Diaspora*. Albany: State U of New York P, 2004. Print.

Portes, Alejandro. 'Conclusion: Theoretical Convergences and Empirical Evidence in the Study of Immigrant Transnationalism'. *International Migration Review* 37.3 (2003): 874–92. Print.

Pries, Ludger, ed. *Migration and Transnational Social Spaces*. Aldershot: Ashgate, 1999. Print.

Ramesh, Randeep. 'Geert Wilders was Beaten, but at the Cost of Fuelling Racism in the Netherlands'. *The Guardian*. Web. 5 April 2019 <https://www.theguardian.com/commentisfree/2017/mar/17/geert-wilders-racism-netherlands-far-right>.

Riccio, Bruno. 'Senegalese Transmigrants and the Construction of Immigration in Emilia-Romagna (Italy)'. DPhil Diss. U of Sussex, 1999. Print.

Ritzer, George. *The McDonaldization of Society*. Newbury Park: Pine Forge Press, 1993. Print.

Robertson, Roland. *Globalization: Social Theory and Global Culture*. London: Sage, 1992. Print.

Robins, Kevin, and Asu Aksoy. 'Parting from Phantoms: What is at Issue in the Development of Transnational Television from Turkey'. *Worlds on the Move*. Ed. J. Friedman, and S. Randeria. London: I. B. Taurus, 2004. 179–206. Print.

Rouse, Roger. 'Questions of Identity: Personhood and Collectivity in Transnational Migration to the United States'. *Critique of Anthropology* 15.4 (1995): 351–80. Print.

Saul, John Ralston. 'The Collapse of Globalism and the Rebirth of Nationalism'. *Harper's Magazine* (March 2005): 33–43. Print.

Shaw, Martin. 'The Political Structure of a Global World: The Role of the United States'. *The Paradox of a Global USA*. Ed. Bruce Mazlish, Nayan Chanda, and Kenneth Weisbrode. Stanford: Stanford UP, 2007. Print.

Smith, M. P., and L. E. Guarnizo, ed. *Transnationalism from Below*. New Brunswick: Transaction Publishers, 1998. Print.

Spivak, Gayatri Chakravorty. *Nationalism and the Imagination*. London: Seagull Books, 2010. Print.

---. 'Who Claims Alterity?'. *Remaking History*. Ed. B. Kruger, and P. Mariani. Seattle: Bay, 1989. 269–92. Print.

Steger, Manfred B. *The Rise of the Global Imaginary: Political Ideologies from the French Revolution to the Global War on Terror*. New York: Oxford UP, 2008. Print.

Strange, Susan. *States and Markets*. London: Pinter, 1994. Print.

Thomas-Hope, Elizabeth. 'Transnational Strategies in the Readjustment of Return Migrants to the Caribbean'. Paper at the Annual Meeting of the American Association of Geographers, New Orleans, 2003. Print.

Ventura, Luca. 'World's Largest Companies 2018'. *Global Finance*. Web. 2 April 2019. <https://www.gfmag.com/global-data/economic-data/largest-companies>.

Vertovec, Steven. 'Transnational Networks and Skilled Labour Migration'. Oxford: ESRC Transnational Communities Programme Working Paper WPTC-02-02, 2002. Print.

wa Thiong'o, Ngũgĩ. *Globalectics: Theory and the Politics of Knowing*. New York: Columbia UP, 2012. Print.

Wang, Yanlai. *China's Economic Development and Democratization.* Aldershot: Ashgate, 2003. Print.

Welsch, Wolfgang. 'Transculturality – the Puzzling Form of Cultures Today'. *Spaces of Culture: City, Nation, World*. Ed. Mike Featherstone, and Scott Lash. London: Sage, 1999. 194–213. Print.

Xiang, Biao. 'Structuration of Indian Information Technology Professionals' Migration to Australia: An Ethnographic Study'. *International Migration* 39 (2001): 73–88. Print.

Chapter Four

The Nation and Its Discontents

ETHNIC SUBNATIONALISMS, NEO-NATIONHOOD, NEW NATIONALISM, STATELESS NATIONS, AND THE CYBERSTATE

'ONE SHOULD BE A NATIONALIST': THE RESURGENCE OF NATIONALISM IN THE TWENTY-FIRST CENTURY

A multiculturalism based on acknowledging 'forms of differentiated citizenship that allow groups to express their distinct identities and practices' within a multinational state (Ivison 2) has been the guiding principle for most countries in their functioning as welfare states from the 1970s till the mid-90s. It allowed 'for the relevance of culture without making culture a determinant of action' (Phillips 131). Philosophers like Will Kymlicka expected that solidarity and stability among a heterogeneous population can be secured on the basis of a 'multicultural liberal nationalism' (Kymlicka). The exuberant transcultural bond in multination states such as Canada, Australia or the United States was exemplified as manifestations of an inclusive 'multicultural nationalism' that combined the 'unifying intentions of nationalism with the pluralizing ambitions of multiculturalism' (Gordon-Walker 7). But, eventually, as a reaction against the fact that 'the inclusion and participation of everyone in social and political institutions . . . requires the articulation of special rights that attend to group differences in order to undermine oppression and disadvantage' (Young 251), multiculturalism was criticised as a movement 'that radicalizes and Nietzscheanizes the liberal idea of tolerance – thus turning that ideal against liberalism – by tending to deny the possibility of universal truth', and contributing to 'a comprehensive redistribution . . . of wealth as of self-esteem . . . not so much to individuals as to various marginalized groups' (Melzer et al. 4). However, such criticisms based on liberal egalitarianism fail to realise that a supposedly fair and difference-blind state under the camouflage of neutrality actually operates as a highly discriminatory tool of the national elite who produce a common identity of social cohesion, disseminated through an assimilative majoritarian nationalism, only to fortify their cultural hegemony. Multiculturalism, on the contrary, seeks to protect minorities from such excesses of nationalism (Raz).

Towards the end of the twentieth century, with a range of debates aimed at distinguishing between national minorities and immigrant minorities within multinational states, Joppke identified a 'retreat of multiculturalism', while Tilly saw the return of 'state led nationalism on one side, (and) state seeking nationalism on the other' (133). Yael Tamir, in her 2019 book, pondered on the active role that every state must take for a nationalism that has to 'constantly be created, nurtured, supported, and reinvented' towards constructing a 'political we' – without which 'states disintegrate' (21). For instance, countries such as Germany, Sweden and Switzerland, which demonstrate robust bonds of nationalism, are considered to be peacefully prosperous and liberal, while countries like Somalia, Afghanistan and Congo have been treated as 'failed states' due to the lack of such strong sense of nationalism (Harari). Taking this argument further is Yoram Hazony, the Israeli philosopher, who declares that the nation-state is the best form of political order. Using this to argue for Israel's legitimacy as a sovereign national state, against Iran's consistent challenge to the very existence of Israel, and while acknowledging the Israeli raid on the Gaza Freedom Flotilla and the Israeli control of the Gaza Strip, Hazony persuasively claims that 'one should be a nationalist'. With nations turning more inward – echoing the twentieth-century totalitarian regimes of Idi Amin (1971–79) of Uganda, the military junta (1976–83) of Argentina, and the Uruguayan dictatorship (1973–84) – there seems to be a rise in the number of authoritarian regimes in the twenty-first century. Many instances from the last two decades attest to this alarming trend: the reimposition of military rule in Myanmar in February 2021, based on the allegation that the government led by Aung San Suu Kyi had held elections flouting democratic principles; Gurbanguly Berdimuhamedov's self-declaration as 'head of all Turkmen' in Turkmenistan; the 2013 declaration of Ilham Aliyev as the President of Azerbaijan, a day before voting had actually started; Nursultan Nazarbayev's prolonged rule in Kazakhstan, from 1990 till he handed over power to his daughter in 2019; and the Russian referendum, in 2020, that cleared the way for Vladimir Putin to continue his rule until 2036.

Recent events including the Brexit move in the United Kingdom seem to validate Samuel Huntington's notion of the 'clash of civilisations'. This rise of national chauvinism is evident in Deng Xiaoping's comment: 'Actually, national sovereignty is far more important than human rights' (334). One may list a number of recent events that point to the realpolitik that puts national pride before all other considerations: the suspension of Julian Assange's Ecuadorean citizenship based on an exposé that linked Ecuadorian President Lenin Moreno to a corruption scandal; the death of Daphne Caruana Galizia, whose Panama Papers investigations focused on corruption in Malta, in an explosion in 2017; the savage killing of Jamal Khashoggi, a prominent Saudi Arabian journalist and critic of the Saudi government, in the Saudi consulate in Istanbul in October 2018. As John Bew suggests, such events illustrate 'the new era of realpolitik into which 21st century international relations is sinking like quicksand. The nation state is back with a vengeance, baring its claws and teeth, just as the soothing post-Cold War notion of an "international community" fades further from view' (Web, n. p.).

Another aspect of this re-emergence of the nation-state is the anti-globalisation discourse that has gained popularity through events like the formation of Ejército Zapatista de Liberación Nacional (Zapatista Army of National Liberation, EZLN). The spokesman for EZLN, Subcomandante Marcos, has described the Zapatista movement as a revolutionary action against 'a world war' of neoliberal globalisation, towards 'recovering the concept of nation and homeland' (qtd. in Báez 169). Other such examples include alter-globalisation initiatives like the formation of a community-based media network against the global 'media dictatorship', initiated by the Venezuelan leader Hugo Chávez who advocated a 'twenty-first century socialism' through the 'Bolivarian Revolution'; and the recommendation by members of the European New Right (ENR) to 'return to a direct democracy, organic and communitarian' (De Herte). They recommend programmes like the International Eurasianist movement in Europe and other places (Umland), to resist the homogenising sea-based American mercantile 'Atlanticism' through providing regional autonomy to distinctive land-based 'civilisations'.

The reason for this worldwide shift towards nationalism – despite assurances of multicultural accommodation in most nation-states through constitutionalism or through 'desentimentalising the national identity' (for instance, in post-Tudjman Croatia or post-junta Argentina) – can be understood on the basis of an ambivalence that marks the actions of advocates of globalisation and multiculturalism. We may understand this ambivalence by taking a few famous examples. The Trump administration in the United States tried to maintain a cordial diplomatic relationship with North Korea's Kim Jong Un, despite the latter pursuing its nuclear weapons programme and supplying chemical weapons in the civil war in Yemen. The United States simultaneously withdrew unilaterally from the 2015 Joint Comprehensive Plan of Action (JCPOA), popularly known as the Iran Nuclear Deal, and formally recognised Jerusalem as the capital of Israel, ignoring demands made by the Hamas. Another example is that of the Facebook founder Mark Zuckerberg. A few months after the publication of his manifesto on Facebook's role in building a global community that is supportive, safe, informed, civically engaged and inclusive, the Cambridge Analytica scandal exposed that data provided to Facebook by users were used by third party actors for manipulating elections around the world. Another apt case to illustrate the underlying suspicion for globalism is World Bank's promotion of privatisation of basic utilities such as water supplies on the pretext of ensuring distributive equality. In Bolivia, for instance, this led to Aguas de Elimani, a French company, monopolising the supply system, and slum dwellers of El Alto residing above the water pipe were compelled to pay a heavy 'connection fee' (Schultz). Many radical alternatives such as the BRICS countries' lobbying for 'a new institutional foundation beside that of the Global North—the New Development Bank against the World Bank; the Contingency Reserve Arrangement against the IMF', failed because they could provide 'no ideological alternative to imperialism' (Prashad 43).

Moreover, as pointed out by Kymlicka and Banting, far from 'eroding national solidarity', multiculturalism can be deployed as a neo-nationalist 'tool of nation-building' for 'relegitimating nationhood' (302). Multiculturalism takes into account the concerns of minority identities while trying to reconfigure them towards the inception of a cross-cultural shared identity by using 'permissible' forms of nation-building and identity modifications (302). Suppression of intracultural mobilisers of differences, as revealed through the maneuvers like the Danish People's Party's campaign for 'Denmark for the Danish', India's National Register of Citizens (NRC), President Trump's 'America First' drive, or Angela Merkel's declaration that multiculturalism has 'failed utterly' (Noack), together with the emphasis on so-called community cohesion and integration, and the disappearance of the term multiculturalism from contemporary political rhetoric, indicate that the twenty-first-century nation-state would function meticulously by 'demarcating by specific categories who is included and who is excluded' (Marx 103). Multicultural democracies are witnessing increasing tensions related to claims of authenticity – the 'real citizen' vs. the 'outsider'. Traditions of the majority often get political patronage through institutional safeguards, although '[t]here are no cultural reasons that can tell us, which language deserves protection at which costs to its members and to outsiders . . . which religious restrictions of liberties for members should be tolerated and which shouldn't' (Baubock 15–16). Conservative nationalist policies based on partisan consensus on bracketing some sections of the population as possible non-natives have given birth to a new wave of nationalism that 'thrives on the perception that the culturally defined nation is in danger of becoming a minority on its "own" territory (the homeland) due to birth rate differentials, immigration flows, or assimilation' (Arel 77). The minorities, in the process, have become double victims of an internal minorisation by the 'mainstream'/majority, while being labelled as outcasts by governments for their 'failure' to get assimilated into the proclaimed 'state culture'.

MAJORITARIAN NATIONALISM AND AFFLICTED MINORITIES

Based on Harris Mylonas's observation that '[l]egitimate authority in modern national states is connected to popular rule, to majorities' and that '[n]ation-building is the process through which these majorities are constructed' (17), 'majoritarianism' can be associated with the authoritarian emergence of a majority elite governing the national state as a 'core group'. This group, in an alliance with the military and the administrative capacity to enforce its decisions as a 'national type' within the boundaries of the nation-state, can designate anyone, representing the 'non-core group' and refusing to abide by the 'national type', as the minoritised Other of the 'nationalizing state' (23–24). As Basharat Peer demonstrates, the twenty-first century is witness to militant nationalisms based on a revisionist summoning up of majoritarian values that persecute peripheral populaces. The Subaltern Studies Collective has shown that nationalisms based on majoritarian views promote discrimination against those who are minoritised on the basis of race, religion, caste, gender and sexuality, class, disabilities, and taboos attached with several categorised identities. These categorised identities include sex workers, persons who are HIV-positive, obese people, slum dwellers (for example, people of Dharavi in Mumbai; Khayelitsha in Cape Town, South Africa; Ciudad Neza in Mexico City, Mexico; and Orangi Town in Karachi, Pakistan), people engaged in manual scavenging (for instance, the *safai karamcharis* of India), etc. Our contemporary history is replete with incidents that illustrate majoritarian politics of nationalism trying to stifle voices of dissent: the crackdown on more than two hundred lawyers and activists during the '709 Crackdown' of 2015 in China; Nguyen Van Tuc's arrest in September 2017 in Vietnam, for his affiliation with the 'Brotherhood for Democracy'; detention of women human rights champions like Nasrin Sotoudeh (Iran), Loujain al-Hathloul (Saudi Arabia); murders of women activists like Su'ad Al-Ali (Iraq), Juana Ramírez Santiago (Guatemala), and Mariam UyAcob, Elisa Badayos and Annaliza Dinopol Gallardo Capinpin (Philippines), Guadalupe Campanur Tapia (Mexico), and Marielle Franco (Brazil); the murders of M. M. Kalburgi, Narendra Dabholkar, Govind Pansare and Gauri Lankesh in India; the harassment faced by Tamil writer Perumal Murugan in India. Human rights activists have also decried the arrests of lawyers and activists like Sudha Bharadwaj, Arun Ferreira, Vernon Gonsalves, Varavara Rao and Gautam Navlakha, and the raids on Father Stan Swamy, K. Satyanarayana, Anand Teltumbde, Kranti Tekula and others. The growing discontent against majoritarianism is also exemplified by many recent events. The Dalit march to 'Save Constitution, Save Dalit Rights' held on 20 December 2018 in New Delhi, organised by Dalit Shoshan Mukti Manch (DSMM), is a case in point. The march was in response to the atrocities faced by the oppressed castes revealed by the suicide of the Dalit leader and student Rohith Vemula of the University of Hyderabad, or the honour killing of P. Pranay Kumar, a Dalit Christian, by his upper-caste in-laws in Nalgonda district of Telangana. Such acts of resistance highlight the blatant domination, exploitation and stigmatisation of the Dalit subaltern in India – about 65 per cent of the alleged hate crimes documented by Amnesty India's 'Halt the Hate' website in 2018 were against Dalits. Other instances include the Kisan Long March by farmers of Maharashtra, organised by the All India Kisan Sabha, in March 2018; the Hirak movement in the Rif region in northern Morocco, demanding development and job creation for the region; and anti-government protests known as the New Arab Spring protests (2018–19). In India, the resistance by the Other Backward Classes (OBC) and the Dalit Bahujan is useful in debunking the overstated claims of homogeneity made by the 'mainstream' majority.

In the United States and Europe, majoritarian nationalisms are often taken over by white supremacists. Killings of Black Americans across the United States in the 'Red Summer' of 1919, or the anxiety over the 'pan-Orientalism' of Mongolian races spreading 'yellow peril' 'towards a war of rule or ruin against the white race' (*Chicago*

Tribune 1915), are instances of racial tensions fuelled by white supremacists. These racial tensions are responsible for the dejected lives, marked by constraints, stigma and spatial confinement, of the people of colour in the ghettos – particularly in America and Europe – that are often referred to as 'inner-city areas', 'low-opportunity areas', 'high-poverty neighborhoods' or 'underclass communities'. Such racial tensions have resurfaced in the wake of the resurgence of nationalism. As *The Guardian* reported in 2016, racist confrontations spiked in the United Kingdom in the immediate aftermath of the Brexit referendum: such as posting messages like 'Leave the EU: No more Polish vermin' in the letterboxes of Huntingdon's Polish families, or a racist asking a tram passenger in Manchester to 'Get off the . . . tram now. Get back to Africa'. In another report in 2015, *The Guardian* reported that '(o)verall in 2015, black people were killed at twice the rate of white, Hispanic and native Americans. About 25% of the African Americans killed were unarmed, compared with 17% of white people'. Such trends and recent incidents of xenophobia, such as the Johannesburg violence of May 2009, justify the coinage of the term 'new racism' (Bonilla-Silva). In times of polarised campaigns where *being white* is given priority over all other forms of identity, resistant movements like the Black Lives Matter (BLM) are more pertinent than ever.

Majoritarian cultural nationalism is firmly embedded in a patriarchal revivalism, and women and sexual minorities are always its victims. We have recently been witness to a shocking array of cyber harassment – sexist posts, slut shaming and victim blaming – and regressive traditions such as breast ironing, female genital mutilation and the perpetuation of female sexual slavery. Women are not safe even among close family and friends. As illustrated in a BBC report on femicide, 'More than half of the 87,000 women killed in 2017 were reported as dying at the hands of those closest to them. Of that figure, approximately 30,000 women were killed by an intimate partner and another 20,000 by a relative' ('The Women Killed on One Day around the World'). Global resistance movements like 'Slut Walk', the #MeToo campaign, and #womensmarch (2017); regional movements like the #TotalShutdown march in South Africa (2018), the 'Rage against Rape' protest in Nepal, the movement against institutionalised sexism in Santiago in 2018, and Pakistan's #GirlsAtDhabas movement of 2016; together with the movements in India such as the Pink Chaddi Campaign of 2009 against Sri Ram Sena's attack on women inside a pub in Mangalore, the 'Why Loiter' movement of 2015, the 'Women's Wall' in support of women's right to enter the Sabarimala temple in Kerala, the nude protest in Manipur in 2004 against the rape and killing of Thangjam Manorama Devi allegedly by a member of the Assam Rifles, alongside the fight against the 'everyday sexism' practised by misogynist hypermasculine men in power, validate the rise of a fourth wave of feminism. India, especially, has been witness to incidents that illustrate a gendered nationalism and nation-state: to point to a few – the initial ban on Alankrita Shrivastava's film *Lipstick Under My Burkha*; the sexual assault on Soni Sori, a tribal schoolteacher suspected of having Maoist links, in police custody in Bastar in 2011; the Kherlanji massacre of 2006; the arrest of twenty-two-year-old climate activist Disha Ravi, for her alleged links with the 'toolkit' supporting the Indian farmers' protests in 2021; the 2007 honour killing of Manoj and Babli ordered by a *khap panchayat* in Haryana; and the maltreatment of Muslim women during the Muzaffarnagar riots of 2013. This gendered nationalism also excludes the queer and the homosexual from the national fold. In 2017, mass arrests and detentions were carried out in Azerbaijan to suppress transgender women and gay/bisexual men. In another instance, in Uganda, the police closed down the Queer Kampala International Film Festival in 2017. As a survey in the United States showed, 'Suicide attempts, intimate partner violence (IPV), and other forms of inter-personal violence occur at comparable or higher rates among LGBT people relative to the general population. Lifetime suicide attempts are two to four times more common among LGB youth and adults than among heterosexuals, and are over five to eight times more common among transgender adults than the general population' (Conron et al. 2).

Another facet of the resurgent nationalism is religious majoritarianism which has been widening the gulf between religious sects. For instance, a sunni bloc made up of Saudi Arabia, the Gulf states, parts of Egypt and Turkey, has been locked in a brutal confrontation with a shia bloc comprising Iran, Nuri al-Maliki's central and southern Iraq, parts of Syria under the control of Bashar al-Assad, and the militias of Hamas in Gaza and Hezbollah in Lebanon. On the other hand, it has, in many cases, undermined secular nationalism in countries such as India: the mob lynching of Mohammed Akhlaq in Uttar Pradesh on 28 September 2015 is a case in point. The devastating escalation of intolerance was also evident in the series of bombings targeting the Christian community in Sri Lanka on 21 April 2019. Majoritarianism also promotes an aggressive abhorrence for those who are seen as the 'Other' of the majority idealism: the Centre for Study of Society and Secularism (CSSS) estimated that from January 2014 to 31 July 2018, there have been 109 incidents of mob lynching in India. In response to these majoritarian tendencies, the resistance offered by the minorities has resulted in three types of substate nationalisms: independentist (secessionist), autonomist and pro-federation nationalisms (Lluch), the manifestations of which are evident in various countries around the world.

AUTONOMY AND SECESSIONIST MOVEMENTS WITH THE MOBILISATION OF NEO-NATIONHOOD

A defensive nationalism – to protect the threatened linguistic, cultural and historical identity of a particular minority community in a multinational state – can give rise to a state-seeking neo-nationhood based on minority nationalism, aimed at self-determination through either secession or autonomy. This results in the federalisation of the unitary state or in carving out a new federation out of the existing federal state. Such forms of defensive nationalism are a reaction to dominant state-led nationalisms that do not grant desired freedom to minority communities – 'when the symbolism of flags, currencies, names, public holidays, national anthems, public funds for cultural activities and the content of school curricula bear on a minority's fragile presence in the public political culture' (Seglow 158). This demand for autonomy as the 'Other' of governmentality can be regarded as a 'politics of the governed' (Chatterjee), whose 'existence is in contradistinction to the existence of the governmental realities of this world' (Samaddar 10). The liberal perspective on the minority right to self-determination holds secession as a legitimate response only when the minority group becomes the victim of persistent and serious violation of human rights at the hand of the nation-state. However, this provision seems inadequate when there are countries like Turkey, Japan or Greece where governments deny even the existence of national minorities within their borders. Also, theorists have been divided on the question whether a decentralised accommodative federalism curbs secessionist drives by granting more autonomy through the recognition of minority nationhood, or it paves the way to more pronounced moves towards secession by emboldening neo-nationhoods and by inspiring minorities to transform symbolic nationalisms to instrumental nationalisms.

There are many examples of successful mobilisation of neo-nationhoods where hitherto minoritised 'nation-groups' have been able to shape sovereign national states for themselves: the breakup of Yugoslavia into seven independent states – Bosnia and Herzegovina, Croatia, Kosovo, Macedonia, Montenegro, Serbia and Slovenia; East Timor's secession from Indonesia to emerge as an independent nation on 20 May 2002; and the birth of South Sudan, after it gained independence from Sudan on 9 July 2011. Instances where a movement for self-determination has been limited to attaining greater autonomy within a host state is well elucidated by Quebec nationalism. Quebec nationalism renounced its ambition to create a nation-state, as revealed by the outcomes of the referendums of 1980 and 1995 on the issue of Quebec sovereignty. There are more such instances: Scotland's decision to remain within the United Kingdom in the 2014 referendum on independence; the 2013 referendum in the Falkland Islands which decided in favour of retaining their status as a British overseas territory; the downscaling of the vernacular nationalism which had formed the basis of a separatist movement in the Basque Country of Spain, towards a demand for greater autonomy in the form of campaigns such as 'right to decide' in 2018; and the Dalai Lama's advocacy, since the late 1980s, for greater autonomy for Tibet within China, as an act of acknowledging the minority micro-nationalism. Many nation-states have taken steps to assuage neo-nationhoods by granting greater autonomy to minority groups or by forming autonomous territorial units – such as Gagauzia in Moldova, Vojvodina in Serbia, the Dutch region of Flanders which was given autonomy by Belgium, the northern regions of Veneto and Lombardy in Italy, and Greenland which was given autonomy by Denmark in 2009. There are many examples of states democratically accommodating diverse cultural minorities within their boundaries, such as Ethiopia granting territorial autonomy to various national minorities resulting in the formation of nine ethno-linguistic Regional States and two city administrations. On the other hand, there are states that take a counter-secession attitude to sub-nationalist tendencies. An important example is the Spanish central government's reluctance to recognise the result of the 2017 referendum in Catalonia where the people of the region voted for complete independence from Spain. Similarly, countries like Turkey, Iraq and the United States have refused to acknowledge the result of the 2017 referendum which clearly showed that Iraqi Kurds wanted to secede from Iraq and shape an independent state. While some movements for self-determination have received international support – like in the case of the formation of Bangladesh – others have failed to get international recognition. Unrecognised states like Crimea, South Ossetia, North Cyprus, Abkhazia, Somaliland and Bougainville fall in the latter category. The Tamils in Sri Lanka have also fought a long unsuccessful struggle for a separate Tamil *Eelam*. Other ongoing struggles for secession include protests against deferred referendums in several parts of the world (for instance, in Northern Ireland and Kashmir); the violent struggle in Cameroon's Anglophone regions for the creation of a republic called Ambazonia; Thailand's PULO (the Pattani United Liberation Organization) demanding the formation of an independent Muslim state; Philippines's Moro National Liberation Front (MNLF) struggling for a Moro homeland; and Pakistan's Baloch National Movement (BNM) for an independent Baluchistan. India has also witnessed several groups that have sought to secede from the state – the Khalistan Liberation Front (KLF) for 'independent Khalistan', Naga National Council (NNG), National Socialist Council of Nagaland (NSCN), Mizo National Front (MNF), People's Liberation Army of Manipur (PLA), People's Revolutionary Party of Kangleipak (PREPAK), All Tripura Tribal Force (ATTF), United Liberation Front of Assam (ULFA), etc. Secessionist drives in the United States, like the Calexit campaign seeking independence for California, gained momentum after the election of President Donald Trump. Minority nationalism is often accompanied by assertions of cultural subnationalism – for instance, the idea of *Kashmiriyat*. Such aspirations of sovereignty based on minority nationalism is often labelled as 'antinational' (May, 'The Crypto Anarchist Manifesto') by the national polity. However, according to some thinkers like Michael Hechter, '[I]t is not that these groups actually uncover evidence of their ancient cultural past as an independent people; most often such culture is created contemporaneously to legitimate demands for the present day goal of independence, or the achievement of economic equality' (38–39).

INTERNAL COLONISATION AND THE RISE OF INDIGENOUS NATIONALISM

'Internal colonisation' is one of the continuing modes of colonialism operating in postcolonial states. To understand internal colonisation, colonialism needs to be conceived as operating simultaneously 'then and there', 'here and now' and 'here and there' (Alexander 251), on account of the diffusion of past colonial tackles back into domestic spaces. This has considerable significance in the biopolitics of the new state in providing a 'break into the domain of life . . . the break between what must live and what must die' (Foucault 254). Internal colonisation is a discriminatory provenance of governmentality displayed by the state's 'geographically-based pattern of subordination of a differentiated population, located within the dominant power or country' (Pinderhughes 236). Persistent marginalisation of Native Americans in the United States or the Inuit community in Canada, despite many proactive laws instituted in the twentieth century, is a classic example of internal colonialism. The peoples of the 'Fourth World' (to use the evocative phrase coined by Manuel and Posluns) are the worst victims of postcolonial state power, as are the native communities who are designated as 'tribes' in South and Central

America, 'aborigines' in Australia, and 'tribals'/'adivasis'/'janajatis'/'vanavasis' in India.

In India, these highly contentious nomenclatures, such as 'tribes of India', were made accessible by British colonisers who thought 'knowledge of subject races or orientals is what makes their management easy and profitable; knowledge gives power, more power requires more knowledge' (Said 36). While expounding the 'link between classification and colonialism' (156), Gyan Prakash has exposed how the colonisers 'classified' groups of people with definite dissimilarities 'according to races and tribes, [who] should sit each in his own stall, should receive and converse with the Public, and submit to being photographed, printed, and taken off in casts, and otherwise reasonably dealt with, in the interests of science' (158). Colonial anthropology characterised 'tribes' in terms of racial inferiority, barbarism and primitivism, to justify the hegemonic 'civilising missions'. Indian anthropologists, on the other hand, tried, in the first half of the twentieth century, to appropriate the 'tribal people' into the nationalist discourse on the basis of a 'Hindu' nationalism. This is outlined in M. N. Srinivas's theory of 'Sanskritisation' through which a 'tribal or other group, changes its customs, ritual ideology and way of life in the direction of a high, and frequently, "twice born caste"' (6). Arjun Appadurai's critique of all 'officially enforced labeling activities' (326) shows that colonial anthropological practices were imbibed by the builders of the postcolonial Indian nation-state. This is revealed in the conferring of administrative categories such as 'scheduled tribes' on indigenous communities, based on a revisionist re-inscription of primitivism, aloofness and overall 'backwardness'. Thus, the inability of the postcolonial Indian ethnography to bring the history of the people classified as 'tribals'/'aboriginals' out of the 'waiting-room of history' has resulted in a 'provincializing' of the Western modernity, in negotiation with a Hindu cultural nationalism. This has, on one hand, re-labelled these subaltern 'tribes' as backward, isolated 'Other' of the civilised citizens, and on the other, strengthened the Hindu nationalist's 'mission civilisation' aimed at erasing alternatives offered by the 'native modernity' of traditions, in order to facilitate the 'mainstreaming' of the 'tribal'/'indigenous' communities whose ties to the state have mostly remained tenuous (Beteille). The common experience of indigenous knowledge being obliterated by the coloniser's antipathy – which has continued into the post-independence era – inspired diverse native communities of postcolonial states to formulate an indigenous nationalism, or a pan-aboriginal nationalism, aimed at self-determination and sustaining cultural and customary traditions. Such indigenous nationalisms are circulated through a lingua franca (usually the consequence of an enforced learning of the coloniser's language) towards building up a solidarity based on their shared sense of an organic belongingness with the land, ecology and 'alternative modernities' of a 'tribal' ontology as opposed to the 'mainstream' modernity. Indigenous nationalists strive for self-governance by dismissing the statist 'mainstream' paternalism which, they accuse, have subsumed indigenous knowledges and cultures by enforcing a strictly codified national culture. They also point to economic deprivation as the major cause of disaffection, especially among the 'tribals' of northeast India, Jharkhand and Chhattisgarh.

As Ngũgĩ waThiang'o points out, to resist internal colonialism in a neocolonial state where indigenous people are given education in 'other peoples' languages rather than their own', they 'have to speak the united language of struggle contained in each of their languages. They must discover their various tongues to sing the song: "A people united can never be defeated"' (3). There are many instances of linguistic reforms undertaken by indigenous nationalists: such as the Meitei people of Manipur reclaiming the Meitei script that was substituted with Bengali under the influence of the Hindu missionary Shantidas Gosai; and replacing the convention of writing Santali in the Latin script by using the newly framed OlChiki script by Pandit Raghunath Murmu in 1925. Based on 'the ethno-poetics and performance of the shaman' where there was no splitting of 'the artistic from the functional, the sacred from the secular, arts from everyday life' (Anzaldua 88), tribal nationalism has motivated indigenous communities to save their religion, culture and world views from getting coopted by corporate, capital and market forces. This is manifested in aboriginal global movements like the 'indigenista' movement popular in Mexico, Bolivia,

Peru, Brazil and other Latin American countries. Other regional uprisings of this kind include, the Native Hawaiian struggles for self-government; the Taíno revolt for land rights; the Chamorro resistance for jurisdictional integrity in Guam; the struggle of the Igorot for land rights in the Philippines; the struggle of the Ainu people for official recognition which lasted until 2008 when they were accepted as indigenous people in Japan; the Makah insurgency for whaling rights in the United States; the 'Sit at Home' protest by the Indigenous People of Biafra (IPOB) for a separate homeland for the Igbo people in Nigeria; the movement for self-governance by the indigenous communities of Bougainville in Papua New Guinea; the Maori struggles for intellectual property rights; the fight for independence by New Caledonia's indigenous Kanaks; the political tension between the natives of Orang Asli and the Malay state; the ongoing insurgencies by 'hill tribes' in Bangladesh, Thailand, Vietnam and Cambodia for their indigenous status; and efforts by nomadic communities like the Hui of China to attain 'indigenous' status. In Canada, experiences of injustice gave rise to the 2012 'Idle No More' movement whose 'goals are to build indigenous sovereignty, to repair the relationship between indigenous peoples of Canada (First Nations, Métis, and Inuit), the crown [sic], and the government [sic] of Canada from a grassroots framework, and to protect the environment for all Canadians to enjoy for generations to come' (Charleyboy, Web, n. p.).

Several important measures have been taken to promote the indigenous cause by the United Nations (UN), various international solidarity organisations (such as the Amazon Coalition, Cultural Survival, Rainforest Action, and The Legal Defense Fund) and indigenous organisations and forums (that include Ford, Oxfam, Coordinating Body for Indigenous Organizations of the Amazonian Basin [COICA], The South and Meso American Indian Rights Center [SAIIC], and others). However, in many countries, indigenous people are losing their control over native resources and are being deprived of forest rights due to the nexus between the state and the global bourgeoisie who, under the pretext of development, destroy the tribal habitus, degrade the ecology and displace indigenous people from their native homelands.

In India, various eco-indigenist movements have emerged in recent times like 'Save the Teesta'; 'Narmada Bachao Andolan'; and people's protests in Kashipur block of Rayagada district in Odisha against the establishment of a mining industry, and to protect *jal*, *jamin* and *jangal* (water, land and forests). An indigenous eco-nationalism, or green nationalism, is the basis of such ecological activisms. It emerges from the nature-mediated attachment of the indigenous people with their ancient territories. It is an instinct towards protecting the indigenous natural environment from being attenuated, and managing and harnessing natural resources to enrich local economies through endogenous endeavours. The indigenous populations of India continue to fight injustice on several fronts. To recall a few recent examples: the plight of dispossessed tribals whose homes are going to be submerged in the so-called developmental scheme of the Indira Sagar Polavaram National Multi-purpose Project in the Godavari region of Andhra Pradesh and Telangana; the adivasi people of Dantewada, Bijapur and Sukma, who were forced to evacuate their villages and live in relief camps from where adivasi girls were allegedly sold into states with poor sex ratio like Haryana; the rise of radical-left elements labelled as 'Naxalite' or 'Maoist' in *janajati*-dominated areas like Sarguja, Bastar, Dhantar, Kankar, Koriya and Korbahave, to name a few in Chhattisgarh alone (Moini), against the exploitation of the adivasis by industrialists and state machineries (for example, the Salwa Judum which was terminated in 2011 after the Supreme Court found it unconstitutional).

ETHNIC SUBNATIONALISMS AND REGIONAL MOVEMENTS IN INDIA

Ethnonationalism – as a disposition of the peripherals founded on 'a mixture of the idea of a pure state from an ethnic point of view with a populist rhetoric, and with the aspiration to safety as in the times of the dictatorship' (Michnik, Web, n. p.) – has given rise to ethnic conflicts in countries around the world. To cite a few examples: the conflict between ethnic minorities such as the Druese, Buluchs, Cophs and the Berbers, and the dominant

Saharouis, Kurds and Palestinians in the Arab world and Western Asia; the catastrophic conflicts in the Horn of Africa; or the ethno-political struggles in Chad, Burundi, Angola and other places. India represents a linguistic federalism where the country is divided into multiple linguistic states. Scholars like Wilkinson have observed that, in India, language-related violence has declined over time, in comparison to violence related to religious conflicts. However, the interminable ethnoterritorial conflicts, with increasing demands for ethnoregional autonomy among the ethnic communities in India, justifies the observations made by Gurharpal Singh: 'The process of nation- and state-building has created a sharp divide between the core and peripheral regions. This division is better understood if India is seen as an ethnic democracy where hegemonic and violent control is exercised over minorities, especially in peripheral regions, thereby creating the conditions for the resilience of ethno-nationalist separatist movements in the latter region' (35). As Hale noted in another context, 'explaining separatism . . . largely boils down to explaining the rise of national consciousness' (58). Both these comments can be read alongside Anderson's observation that people who politically epitomise visible 'sub-nationalisms' within the borders of 'old nations' would challenge the dominant nationalistic impulse in future by the 'dream of shedding [their] sub-ness one day' (*Imagined Communities* 3), and Moltchanova's definition of nation 'as collective agents with a particular type of political culture *that does not require the possession of the state* but that is based upon the shared end of acquiring or maintaining effective agency in relation to the capacity of the group to control its own political future' (14; emphasis added). Based on these observations, it can be argued that the regional movements in India towards ethnolinguistic autonomy – which either pose the threat of a possible division within, or successfully divide, an existing federal state, to add new states within the Indian federation – are consequences of expanding ethnic subnationalisms of marginalised ethnic minorities who are obliged to protect, through self-governance, their 'ethno-nationalist resources—distinctiveness, historical collectivity, and a sense of destiny' (Singh 43).

The political struggles that led to the formation of regional states like Meghalaya, Mizoram or Telangana – which were directed against a national polity that 'is constituted and functions as a "defensive democracy"' (Smooha 447) – can be perceived as movements for enhancing the ethnic democracy of unacknowledged ethnolinguistic communities who, as noncore ethnic groups, had been enjoying some of the rights, albeit not all the rights, bestowed on other ethnolinguistic groups who possessed their own federal states. One can easily comprehend the reasons behind the escalation of vernacular nationalism in India when one acknowledges its linguistic diversity. Apart from its dominant languages, India has around forty-two endangered languages, like Jarawa, Lamongse, Luro, Muot, Onge, Pu, Sanenyo, Sentilese, Shompen and Takahanyilang (in Andaman and Nicobar Islands), Mra and Na (in Arunachal Pradesh), Tai Nora and Tai Rong (in Assam), Nihali (in Maharashtra), Toto (in West Bengal), etc., along with numerous large linguistic groups – like the speakers of the Bhili and Santali languages – with no federal states. Vernacular nationalism struggles against the linguistic imperialism enhanced through 'linguicism', that is 'ideologies, structures and practices which are used to legitimate, effectuate, regulate and reproduce an unequal division of power and resources (both material and immaterial) between groups which are defined on the basis of language' (Skutnabb-Kangas 13). In this context, one is reminded of the Gorkha poet Manprasad Subba's avowal:

> Now
> I don't want to sing what the
> Mainstream wants me to
> Until my own melody is not given
> A chord in its composition. (Subba and Pradhan)

Economic exploitation was the major factor behind movements for state formation in case of states like Jharkhand and Chhattisgarh, while Uttarakhand was formed to address concerns of dissident communities of Kumaon and Garhwal who had struggled to assert their *pahari* identity. Most of the ethno-nationalist regional movements in India – with exceptions like that of Naga secessionist movements for a proposed 'Nagalim' – have been based on a 'nested nationalism' characterised by a double allegiance to the federal state and the national state. The movement demanding a separate Kamtapur in the northern part of West Bengal by the Rajbongshi people is mainly based on ethnolinguistic claims. Demands for forming a Saurashtra state in southern Gujarat, and Kongu Nadu in southern Tamil Nadu, are made to address economic negligence; whereas the agitations demanding the formation of a Bodoland state in northern Assam, or a separate state of Ladakh in eastern Jammu and Kashmir, are founded on ethnic subnationalisms of culturally minoritised ethnic communities. The movement for a separate Gorkhaland in the areas surrounding the Darjeeling hills of West Bengal, through the formation of a neo-ethnic Gorkha identity fashioned out of cross-ethnic solidarities among different ethnic communities like the Lepcha, Limbu, Rai, Newar, Thami, Kami, Damai, etc., for a common goal, underscores a multi-ethnic interculturalism. It also highlights the fact that the Nepali-speaking communities of India are negotiating to gain 'the sacred stuff of recognition to affirm their being-in-and-of-India' (Middleton 22).

POPULIST ISOLATIONISM OF THE NEW NATIONALISM

Our recent history has seen the transformation of diasporic nationalism to a 'radical diasporism'. Diasporic nationalism privileges the 'Diaspora, a dissociation of ethnicities and political hegemonies as the only social structure that even begins to make possible a maintenance of cultural identity in a world grown thoroughly and inextricably interdependent' and gives birth to the consciousness 'that peoples and lands are not naturally and organically connected' (Boyarin and Boyarin 723). The transformation to a radical diasporism is characterised by an emerging émigré nationalism that, contradicting the notion of 'long-distance nationalism' as 'a serious politics that is at the same time radically unaccountable' (Anderson, 'Long Distance Nationalism' 74), plays an important role in 'defining the national identity and political ethos' (Shain 8). This has led to the emergence, from the late twentieth century onwards, of an aggressively partisan 'new nationalism' emanating mainly from Western countries and subverting earlier ideals of liberal nationalism. The central idea of this new nationalism can be traced back to a speech delivered by the American President Theodore Roosevelt in September 1910, where he argued that the first duty of the state is to benefit its own people and preserve its own culture. New nationalism thus aligns itself with a populist conservatism that is nativist and protectionist, and therefore promotes anti-globalisation, anti-immigration, anti-multiculturalism and anti-cosmopolitanism. Prime contemporary instances of new nationalism include Brexit; Donald Trump's rise to American presidency based on slogans such as 'Hire American', 'Buy American' and 'America First'; the growing clout of right-wing political parties like Alternative for Germany (AfD), Spain's Vox party, Austria's The Freedom Party (FPÖ), the neo-Nazi Sweden Democrats, and People's Party of Estonia (EKRE); along with the mounting influence of right-wing populist leaders in the European Union countries (Viktor Orbán in Hungary, Matteo Salvini in Italy, Marine Le Pen in France, to name a few). Examples from the Global South will include the many instances of Islamic and Hindutva nationalisms. New nationalism, which is isolationist in its essence and is completely centred on the state, eventually degenerates into chauvinism and jingoism, and protracts through interstate rivalries. President Trump's declaration of national emergency on 15 February 2019, in a bid to get the billions needed for building the US–Mexico border wall, or the Indian government's September 2018 circular to higher educational institutes to celebrate 29 September as 'Surgical Strikes Day' to commemorate Indian Army's successful strikes across the Line of Control in Pakistan-occupied Kashmir, are some cases in point.

According to Jacques Rancière, 'Populism is the convenient name under which is dissimulated the exacerbated contradiction between popular legitimacy and expert legitimacy, . . . This name at once masks and reveals the intense wish of the oligarch: to govern without people' (80). There are many contemporary leaders who have been termed populist for their political positions: Nigel Farage and Jeremy Corbyn in the United Kingdom, Pablo Iglesias in Spain, Evo Morales in Bolivia, Donald Trump and Bernie Sanders in the United States, Rafael Correa in Ecuador, Hugo Chávez in Venezuela, Narendra Modi in India, and Néstor Kirchner in Argentina. Citing that '[i]n 2018, the governments of eight countries of the European Union (Austria, Belgium, Denmark, Finland, Italy, Poland, Hungary, and Slovakia) are led by far-right, nationalist, and xenophobic parties', Enzo Traverso branded the 'present moment a period of *postfascism*' (12), to refer to the continuity of fascism which has undergone transformations and is operating through 'populism'. Populism, according to Pierre Rosanvallon, is a 'pathological' form of politics, and the 'pure politics of the unpolitical' (22). He further claims that the rise of the 'unpolitical' (or 'anti-politics') by means of totalitarian 'populism' signals that representative democracy is 'paralysed', and in due course, 'vampirized' by a 'counterdemocracy' (24). The 'anti-politics' of new nationalism was revealed when under the pretext of Donald Trump's 'zero-tolerance' policy against illegal migration, around two thousand children were separated from their parents who had illegally crossed the US–Mexico border, and the traumatised kids were kept in cages in Texas (BBC, 'Trump Migrant Separation Policy'). Analysing the reasons behind the emergence of the 'dysfunctional age' of an isolationist new nationalism, Pankaj Mishra observes that the commonality between radical Islamists and Hindutva nationalists, angry Trumpites and splitting Brexiters, is 'an experience of meaninglessness converted quickly into anarchist ideology' (297). He argues that the aftermath of 'the history of modernization [that] is largely one of carnage and bedlam' (17), gives birth to 'the culture that stokes unappeasable vanity and shallow narcissism' (330).

Critics have observed that the Hindutva nationalism in India argues, on the basis of 'nativism', that 'states should be inhabited exclusively by members of the native group ("the [Hindu] nation") and that non-native elements (persons and ideas) are fundamentally threatening to the nation-state' (Mudde 22). Dibyesh Anand has described it as 'schizophrenic nationalism' which tries to retain an image of a tolerant Hindu while generating violence and terror through social mobilisation, politics of imagination, ontological insecurity and cultural transformation (1). Sikata Banerjee has called it 'muscular nationalism' where nationalism is equated with engineering a macho identity out of the fear for a hypermasculine enemy. This echoes Anand's 'porno-nationalism' of 'obsessive preoccupation with the predatory sexuality of the putative Muslim figure and the dangers to the integrity of the Hindu bodies' (Anand 1). Kinnvall has used the term 'anxious nationalism' while referring to the politics of imagining a pure self and a polluted Other through the reconstruction of religious, racial and gendered stratifications (294).

STATELESS NATIONS AMID NATION-STATES

The term 'stateless nation' stands for a community recognised as a unique nation but has no nation-state of its own, such as the Tibetans, Kurds, Yazidis, Bhupalese and Chakmas. Palestine can also be termed a stateless nation since it is yet to be recognised by the United States. A stateless nation may sometimes have a government in exile. On the basis of the data that only a mere three per cent of the world's six thousand national groups have their separate sovereign states (Minahan xx), and given the fact that 'stateless nations are the overwhelming majority of nations and only a small number of states represented in the UN are technically nation-states' (Nimni, 'Stateless Nations in a World of Nation-States' 55), critics have argued that the term 'nation-state' – which is expected to convey the presence of one (cultural) nation within one state – is essentially a 'misnomer' (Govier 269). The policies involving 'consociationalism' (Lijphart) – that is, to form a governance of coalition, encompassing mutual representation across cultural divides – of the multinational host state, aimed at preserving individual rights, in effect, mostly end up in alienating, demoralising and destroying the cultural identity of minoritised stateless nations (Nimni, 'Constitutional or Agonistic Patriotism?' 98–99). This is because consociationalism casts the counter-unifying nationalism of the proto-nation as reprehensible separatist nationalism. The possible 'normalisation' of stateless nations into nation-states through secession is a complicated remedy. On the one hand, the route is generally obstructed by the veto power exercised by the host nation (with a few exceptions like Slovakia and Singapore), and on the other hand, as pointed out by Stephane Dion, all secessionist attempts might not be permitted to materialise on the ground since the world lacks enough 'portions of real estate' to accommodate a sovereign territorial state for each and every community that perceive themselves as a nation. The alternative model of national cultural autonomy (NCA) given to stateless nations is often rendered ineffective by the encroachment of governmental mechanisms of the dominant state. This problem was observed in Kashmir where the Indian government continued to dominate even when the state had autonomy as per its special status.

There are numerous examples of stateless nations, or contested claims to nationhood, in South Asia: Dimasa, Gond, Kashmiri, Koch-Rajbongshi, Karbi, Kuki, Sindhi, Tibetan, Zomi (in India); Pashtun, Baloch, Kho, Mujahir, and Saraiki (in Pakistan); Aimaq, Brahui, Balawari, Hazara, Waziri, South Turkestani, and Yusufzai (in Afghanistan); Bhupalese (of Bhutan); Bhutia (in Nepal); Jumma, Chakma, and Tripuri (of Bangladesh); and Tamil (in Sri Lanka), among many others. Their stateless nationalisms have gained visibility through the formation of organisations such as Balawaristan National Front (BNF), Balochistan Government in Exile, Free Hazaristan (Azad Hazaristan), Karbi National Liberation Army (KNLA), and Muhajir Nation, along with the establishment of global platforms such as the Unrepresented Nations and Peoples Organization (UNPO).

CYBERSTATE AND DISENCHANTMENT

Cyberspace has been perceived as a sovereign 'cyberstate', which can overcome the restrictions imposed by nation-states and create domains of digital democracy by providing open access to knowledge, online platforms and opinions. As Barlow declared, defending the cyberstate, 'the global social space' created by the cyberstate is 'naturally independent of the tyrannies you [government] seek to impose on us': 'You have no moral right to rule us, nor do you possess any methods of enforcement we have true reason to fear' (Barlow 28). Extensive use of encryption technologies and transactions taking place behind the mask of encryption, allowing online businesses to escape the attention of traditional nation-states, has led to a thriving 'crypto anarchy' (May). Moreover, 'being at home' through cyber 'homepages' – as opposed to being an 'outsider within' one's situatedness bounded by a nation-state – and by changing the location of internet profiles or by opening multiple profiles in different locations, the 'multi-locale diasporas [that] are not necessarily defined by a specific geopolitical boundary' violate the stereotyped notion of a 'physical return and attachment to land' (Clifford 305).

Cyberspace allows ways to overcome obligations imposed by citizenship rules. Cyberspace's 'particular mix of special metaphors and the dynamics of instantaneous communication' help build 'a sense of belonging' and 'a new kind of conversational space opens up' (Turkle 34). This new space can overcome 'the hierarchies and "unfreedoms" of gendered and racially marked identities' (Seidler 20) associated with the 'national identity'. Michel de Certeau argues that within the cyberstate, 'without leaving the place where he [the digital citizen] has no choice but to live and which lays down its law for him, he establishes . . . a degree of plurality and creativity' (30). Digital citizens who rely on technology to function and participate in all sphere of society, thereby, are supposed to attain an 'informed citizenship' (Garnham). Through various 'e-concepts' (like e-democracy, e-campaigning, e-government, etc.), digital democracy affirms 'the right of everyday people to actively contribute to their culture' (Jenkins 136) by taking part in various debates related to citizens' involvement with institutionalised politics. Haraway uses a transhuman notion of 'cyber nation' where '[w]e are all chimeras, theorized and fabricated hybrids of machine and organism; in short, we are cyborgs. The cyborg is our ontology; it gives us our politics' (150).

However, while it provided freedom from old hierarchies, the cyberstate has created new kinds of social divides – for example, between 'digital natives' of urban India and 'digital immigrants' of rural India. The 'Net Generation' has also been criticised for the threat of evolving a 'GM nation', or creating a further divide between the 'gene rich' and the 'gene poor' (Silver) on the basis of their ability to afford expensive technologies related to genetic engineering and the 'morphological freedom' to modify one's body. Digital technologies have also evolved to become tools for state repression and surveillance strategies. Digitised record-keeping, and use of advanced information and communications technology and biometry for mass surveillance and border control, have become widespread since the early years of the twenty-first century. Under the pretext of 'national security', they are often deployed to harass and victimise activists who raise their voice against state-sponsored injustices and wars for instance, against environmental activists where 'the "terrorist" label functions as the important alarm that justifies a range of heavy repressive measures' (Miraneau 88). Using the excuse of 'exceptional circumstances', these measures are used to harass nonconformist individuals, ignoring the worth of dissenting voices in a democratic culture, through command and not through consultation or consent (Agamben). Contemporary state surveillance deploys second-generation biometrics and a range of projects like INDECT (an intelligent information system supporting observation, search and detection for security of citizens in urban environments), SAMURAI (a system for monitoring suspicious and abnormal behaviour using network cameras for situation awareness enhancement), ADABTS (Automatic Detection of Abnormal Behavior and Threats in Crowded Spaces), etc. However, while they have been protecting citizens from attacks from adversaries of the state, they have also increased chances of discrimination and stigmatisation of innocent citizens through erroneous or false interpretation of biometric characteristics. There have also been cases where the individual's right to privacy was violated through leaks where personal data was transmitted to unauthorised agencies. In this backdrop, one needs to affirm that right to privacy 'in liberal societies is valued and needed for the sake of individual liberty and autonomy, that is, for the sake of both freedom for each individual to fulfill himself, and thus ultimately for the sake of a life that is rewarding' (Rössler 44).

REFERENCES

Agamben, Giorgio. *State of Exception*. Chicago: U of Chicago P, 2005. Print.

Ahmed, Hilal. 'Two Readings of Ayodhya Verdict: legalizing Hindutva or Separating Site from Structure'. *The Print*. Web. 9 November 2019. <https://theprint.in/opinion/two-readings-of-ayodhya-verdict-legalising-hindutva-or-separating-site-from-structure/318704/>.

Alexander, M. Jacqui. *Pedagogies of Crossing: Meditations on Feminism, Sexual Politics, Memory, and the Sacred*. Durham: Duke UP, 2006. Print.

Anand, Dibyesh. *Hindu Nationalism in India and the Politics of Fear*. London: Palgrave, 2011. Print.

Anderson, Benedict. *Imagined Communities: Reflections on the Origins and Spread of Nationalism*. London: Verso, 1991. Print.

---. 'Long Distance Nationalism'. *The Spectre of Comparisons: Nationalism, Southeast Asia and the World*. London: Verso, 1998. 58–76. Print.

Anzaldua, Gloria E. *Borderlands/*La Frontera*: The New Mestiza*. San Francisco: Cardinal, 1999. Print.

Appadurai, Arjun. 'Number in the Colonial Imagination'. *Orientalism and the Post-Colonial Predicament*. Ed. Carol A. Breckenridge, and Peter van der Veer. Philadelphia: U of Pennsylvania P, 1993. 314–39. Print.

Arel, Dominique. 'Political Stability in Multinational Democracies: Comparing Language Dynamics in Brussels, Montreal and Barcelona'. *Multinational Democracies*. Ed. Alain Galgon, and James Tully. Cambridge: Cambridge UP, 2001. 65–89. Print.

Báez, René. *Conversaciones con Marcos*. Quito: Eskeletra Editorial, 1996. Print.

Banerjee, Sikata. *Muscular Nationalism: Gender, Violence and Empire in India and Ireland, 1914–2004*. New York: New York UP, 2012. Print.

Barlow, John Perry. 'A Declaration of the Independence of Cyberspace'. *Crypto Anarchy, Cyberstates, and Pirate Utopias*. Ed. Peter Ludlow. Cambridge: The MIT Press, 2001. 27–30. Print.

Baubock, Rainer. 'Beyond Culturalism and Statism'. *Eurosphere Working Paper No. 6* (2008). Print.

BBC. 'The Women Killed on One Day around the World'. 25 November 2018. Web. 03 March 2020. <https://www.bbc.com/news/world46292919?ocid=socialflow_facebook&ns_mchannel=social&ns_source=facebook>.

---. 'Trump Migrant Separation Policy: Children "In Cages" in Texas'. 18 June 2018. Web. 20 April 2020. <https://www.bbc.com/news/world-us-canada-44518942>.

Beteille, Andre. 'The Concept of Tribe with Special Reference to India'. *Journal of European Sociology* 27 (1986): 297–318. Print.

Bew, John. 'Revenge of the Nation State'. *New Statesman*, 09 November 2018. Web. 9 April 2019. <https://www.newstatesman.com/2018/11/revenge-nation-state>.

Bonilla-Silva, Eduardo. Foreword. *Critical Pedagogy and Race*. Ed. Z. Leonardo. Oxford: Blackwell, 2005. Print.

Boyarin, Daniel, and Jonathan Boyarin. 'Diaspora: Generation and Ground of Jewish Identity'. *Critical Inquiry* 19.4 (1993): 693–725. Print.

Charleyboy, Lisa. 'Idle No More: Canada's Indigenous People are Demanding a Better Deal'.11 January 2013. *The Guardian*. Web. 19 April 2020. <https://www.theguardian.com/commentisfree/2013/jan/11/canada-indigenous-people-demand-better-deal>.

Chatterjee, Partha. *The Politics of the Governed: Reflections on Popular Politics in Most of the World*. New York: Columbia UP, 2004. Print.

Chicago Tribune. 'Thinks Americans Ignorant of Japan Question', 6 March 1915. Print.

Clifford, James. 'Diasporas'. *Cultural Anthropology* 9.3 (1994): 302–38. Print.

Conron, K. J., S. K. Goldberg, A. R. Flores, W. Luhur, W. Tashman, and A. P. Romero. *Gun Violence and LGBT Adults: Findings from the General Social Survey and the Cooperative Congressional Election Survey*. Los Angeles: The Williams Institute, 2018. Print.

CSSS Team. 'India, the New Lynchdom'. *Newsclick*. Web. 10 April 2020. <https://www.newsclick.in/india-new-lynchdom>.

de Carteau, Michel. *The Practice of Everyday Life*. Tr. Steven Rendell. California: U of California P, 1998. Print.

De Herte, Robert. 'L'heure de la micropolitique' [The Hour of Micropolitics]. *Éléments pour la civilization européenne* [Elements for European Civilisation], March 2001. Print.

Dion, Stephane. 'Why is Secession Difficult in Well-established Democracies?: Lessons from Quebec'. *British Journal of Political Science* 26.2 (1996): 269–83. Print.

Foucault, Michel. *Society Must be Defended: Lectures at the Collège de France 1975–1976*. London: Penguin, 2004. Print.

Garnham, Nicholas. 'Amartya Sen's "Capabilities" Approach to the Evaluation of Welfare: Its Application to Communication'. *Communication, Citizenship and Social Policy. Rethinking the Limits of Welfare State*. Ed. A. Calabrese, and J. Burgelman. New York: Rowan and Littlefield, 1999. 113–24. Print.

Gordon-Walker, Caitlin. *Exhibiting Nation: Multicultural Nationalism (and Its Limits) in Canada's Museums*. Vancouver: U of British Columbia P, 2016. Print.

Govier, Trudy. *Social Trust and Human Communities*. Montreal: McGill-Queen's UP, 1997. Print.

Hale, Henry E. *The Foundations of Ethnic Politics: Separatism of States and Nations in Eurasia and the World*. New York: Cambridge UP, 2008. Print.

Harari, Yuval Noah. *21 Lessons for the 21st Century*. London: Jonathan Cape, 2018. Print.

Haraway, Donna. *Simians, Cyborgs and Women: The Reinvention of Nature*. New York: Routledge, 1991. Print.

Hazony, Yoram. *The Virtue of Nationalism*. New York: Basic Books, 2018. Print.

Hechter, Michael. *Internal Colonialism: The Celtic Fringe in British National Development, 1536–1966*. London: Routledge and Kegan Paul, 1975. Print.

Ivison, Duncan. 'Introduction: Multiculturalism as a Public Ideal'. *The Ashgate Research Companion to Multiculturalism*. Ed. D Ivison. Burlington: Ashgate, 2010. 1–16. Print.

Jenkins, Henry. *Convergence Culture: Where Old and New Media Collide*. New York: New York UP, 2008. Print.

Joppke, Christian. 'The Retreat of Multiculturalism in the Liberal State: Theory and Policy'. *British Journal of Sociology* 55.2 (2004): 237–57. Print.

Kinnvall, Catarina. 'Populism, Ontological Insecurity and Hindutva: Modi and the Masculinization of Indian Politics'. *Cambridge Review of International Affairs* 32.3 (2019): 283–302. Print.

Kymlicka, Will. 'Solidarity in Diverse Societies: Beyond Neoliberal Multiculturalism and Welfare Chauvinism'. *Comparative Migration Studies* 3.4 (2015): 1–19. Print.

Kymlicka, Will, and Keith Banting. 'Immigration, Multiculturalism, and the Welfare State'. *Ethics and International Affairs* 20.3 (2006): 281–304. Print.

Lijphart, Arend. *Democracy in Plural Societies: A Comparative Exploration*. New Haven: Yale UP, 1997. Print.

Lluch, Jaime. *Visions of Sovereignty: Nationalism and Accommodation in Multinational Democracies*. Philadelphia: U of Pennsylvania P, 2014. Print.

Marx, Anthony. 'The Nation-State and Its Exclusions'. *Political Science Quarterly* 117.1 (2002): 103–26. Print.

May, Stephen. *Language and Minority Rights: Ethnicity, Nationalism and the Politics of Language*. London: Longman, 2001. Print.

May, Timothy C. 'The Crypto Anarchist Manifesto'. *Crypto Anarchy, Cyberstates, and Pirate Utopias*. Ed. Peter Ludlow. Cambridge: The MIT Press, 2001. 61–64. Print.

Melzer, Arthur M., Jerry Weinberger, and M. Richard Zinman. 'Introduction'. *Multiculturalism and American Democracy*. Lawrence: UP of Kansas, 1998. 1–14. Print.

Michnik, Adam. 'Schirinowski, *mon amour*'. *Der Spiegel*. Web. 19 April 2020. <https://www.spiegel.de/spiegel/print/d-13683174.html>.

Middleton, Townsend. 'States of Difference: Refiguring Ethnicity and Its "Crisis" at India's Borders'. *Political Geography* 35.1 (2013): 14–24. Print.

Minahan, James. *Encyclopaedia of the Stateless Nations: S–Z*. Westport: Greenwood Press, 2002. Print.

Miraneau, M. 'The Criminalisation of Environmental Activism'. *Studia Universitatis Babes-Bolyai* 2 (2014): 87–103. Print.

Mishra, Pankaj. *Age of Anger: A History of the Present*. New York: Farrar, Straus and Giroux, 2017. Print.

Moini, Midhat. 'Naxal-Hit Areas of Chhattisgarh See Sharp Decline in Population'. *DownToEarth*. 17 August 2015. Web. 19 April 2020. <https://www.downtoearth.org.in/news/naxalhit-areas-of-chhattisgarh-see-sharp-decline-in-population--44683>.

Moltchanova, Anna. *National Self-Determination and Justice in Multinational States*. London: Springer, 2009. Print.

Mudde, Cas. *The Populist Radical Right in Europe*. Cambridge: Cambridge UP, 2007. Print.

Mylonas, Harris. *The Politics of Nation-Building: Making Co-nationals, Refugees, and Minorities*. Cambridge: Cambridge UP, 2012. Print.

Nimni, Ephraim. 'Constitutional or Agonistic Patriotism?: The Dilemmas of Liberal Nation-states'. *Constituting Communities: Political Solutions to Cultural Conflict*. Ed. Per Mouritsen, and Knud

Erik Jørgensen. Basingstoke: Palgrave Macmillan, 2008. 94–116. Print.

--. 'Stateless Nations in a World of Nation-States'. *Routledge Handbook of Ethnic Conflict*. Ed. Karl Cordell, and Stefan Wolff. London: Routledge, 2011. Print.

Noack, Rick. 'Angela Merkel: German Chancellor Says Multiculturalism is a Sham'. *The Independent*, 14 December 2015. Web. 9 April 2019. <https://www.independent.co.uk/news/world/europe/angela-merkel-german-chancellor-says-multiculturalism-is-a-sham-a6773111.html>.

Peer, Basharat. *A Question of Order: India, Turkey and the Return of Strongmen.* Columbia Global Reports, 2017. Print.

Phillips, Anne. *Multiculturalism Without Culture*. Princeton: Princeton UP, 2007. Print.

Pinderhughes, Charles. 'Toward a New Theory of Internal Colonialism'. *Socialism and Democracy* 25.1 (2011): 235–56. Print.

Prakash, Gyan. 'Science "Gone Native" in Colonial India'. *Representations* 40 (1992): 153–78. Print.

Prashad, Vijay. 'In the Ruins of the Present'. Tricontinental Working Document, No. 1. March 2018. Print.

Rancière, Jacques. *Hatred of Democracy.* London: Verso, 2006. Print.

Raz, Joseph. 'Multiculturalism'. *Ratio Juris* 11.3 (1998): 193–205. Print.

Rosanvallon, Pierre. *Counter-Democracy: Politics in an Age of Distrust.* Cambridge: Cambridge UP, 2008. Print.

Rössler, Beate. *The Value of Privacy*. Cambridge: Polity Press, 2005. Print.

Said, Edward W. *Orientalism: Western Conceptions of the Orient*. London: Penguin, 1995. Print.

Samaddar, Ranabir, ed. *The Politics of Autonomy: Indian Experiences*. New Delhi: Sage, 2005. Print.

Schultz, J. 'The Politics of Water in Bolivia'. *The Nation*. Web. 9 April 2019. <http://www.thenation.com/doc/20050214/shultz>.

Seglow, J. 'Multiculturalism'. *Political Concepts*. Ed. R. Bellamy, and A. Mason. Manchester: Manchester UP, 2002. 156–68. Print.

Seidler, V. 'Embodied Knowledge and Virtual Space'. *The Virtual Embodied: Presence/Practice/Technology*. Ed. J. Wood. New York: Routledge, 1998. 15–29. Print.

Shain, Yossi. *Marketing the American Creed Abroad: Diasporas in the U.S. and their Homelands*. Cambridge: Cambridge UP, 1999. Print.

Silver, Lee. *Remaking Eden: Designing Human Life in the New Millennium*. London: Weidenfeld and Nicholson, 1998. Print.

Singh, Gurharpal. *Ethnic Conflict in India*. New York: St. Martin's, 2000. Print.

Skutnabb-Kangas, Tove. 'Multilingualism and the Education of Minority Children'. *Minority Education: From Shame to Struggle*. Ed. T. Skutnabb-Kangas, and J. Cummins. Clevedon: Multilingual Matters, 1988. 9–44. Print.

Smooha, Sammy. 'The Model of Ethnic Democracy: Israel as a Jewish and Democratic State'. *Nations and Nationalism* 8.4 (2002): 447–48. Print.

Srinivas, M. N. *Social Change in Modern India*. Berkeley: U of California P, 1966. Print.

Subba, Manprasad, and Kumar Pradhan, trans. *Voices from the Margin*. Siliguri: Sunchari Publications, 2009. Print.

Tamir, Yael. *Why Nationalism*. Princeton: Princeton UP, 2019. Print.

The Guardian. 'A Frenzy of Hatred: How to Understand Brexit Racism'. 29 June 2016. Web. 2 April 2020. <http://www.theguardian.com/politics/2016/jun/29/frenzy-hatred-brexit-racism-abusereferendum-celebratory-lasting-damage>.

---. 'Young Black Men Killed by US Police at Highest Rate in Year at 1,134 Deaths'. 31 December 2015. Web. 2 April 2020. <https://www.theguardian.com/us-news/2015/dec/31/the-countedpolice-killings-2015-young-black-men>.

Tilly, Charles. 'States and Nationalism in Europe 1492–1992'. *Theory and Society* 23 (1994): 131–46. Print.

Traverso, Enzo. *The New Faces of Fascism: Populism and the Far Right*. Tr. David Broder. London: Verso, 2019. Print.

Turkle, Sherry. *Life on the Screen: Identity in the Age of the Internet*. New York: Simon and Schuster, 1995. Print.

Umland, Andreas. 'Fascist Tendencies in Russia's Political Establishment'. *History News Network,* 29 May 2009. Print.

wa Thiong'o, Ngũgĩ. *Decolonising the Mind: The Politics of Language in African Literature*. Oxford: James Curry and Heinemann, 1986. Print.

Wilkinson, Steven I. 'Which Group Identities Lead to the Most Violence?: Evidence from India'. *Order, Conflict, and Violence*. Ed. S. N. Kalyvas, I. Shapiro, and T. Masoud. Cambridge: Cambridge UP, 2008. 271–300. Print.

Xiaoping, Deng. *Selected Works of Deng Xiaoping: Vol. 3 (1982–1992)*. Beijing: Foreign Languages Press, 1994. Print.

Young, Iris. 'Polity and Group Difference: A Critique of the Ideal of Universal Citizenship'. *Ethics* 99.2 (1989): 250–74. Print.

Zuckerberg, Mark. 'Building Global Community'. *Facebook*. 16 February 2017. Web. 9 April 2019. <https://www.facebook.com/notes/mark-zuckerberg/building-global-community/10154544292806634/>.

Chapter Five

Narrating/Imagining the Nation

A BRIEF SURVEY OF THE INDIAN ENGLISH WRITER'S NEGOTIATIONS WITH THE NATION AND NATIONALISMS

Partha Chatterjee has problematised the normalisation of the nation-state as the sole reference for framing a 'political community' where 'the state became the nation's singular representative embodiment, the only legitimate form of community' (*The Nation and Its Fragments* 236). This is done at the cost of suppressing alternative forms of collective affiliations based on 'love, kinship, austerity, sacrifice' (237), etc. Chatterjee, however, acknowledges the purpose of the Indian state as the definitive 'site of strategic manoeuvres, resistance and appropriation by different groups and classes' ('Introduction' 15) for working out 'new forms of democratic institutions and practices in the mediating field of political society that lies between civil society and the nation-state' ('Beyond the Nation? Or Within?' 34). A national identity based on the state is often tenuous. The intra-nation conflicts within the Indian state attest to this. The 'Assamese nationalism [that] has always ranged itself against the outsider' (Hazarika 26–27) as '*bidekhi*' or foreigner is one of many such instances. However, this state-determined national identity, in due course, can produce a composite subjectivity of 'the collective man': a '"cultural-social" unity through which a multiplicity of dispersed wills, with heterogeneous aims, are welded together with a single aim' (Gramsci 349).

Nation as a metaphor for unison, according to Brennan, emerged out of the synthesis between the political thought and the literary language of an age: 'Nations, then, are imaginary constructs that depend for their existence on an apparatus of cultural fictions in which imaginative literature plays a decisive role' (qtd. in Bhabha 49). The narrative form of the novel, which was instrumental in spreading colonial and imperialist ideologies, has paradoxically become a derivative nationalist discourse for resisting the empire and reflecting the heterogeneous character of the nation: 'It was the *novel* that historically accompanied the rise of nations by objectifying the "one, yet many" of national life, and by mimicking the structure of the nation, a clearly bordered jumble of languages and styles' (49). In the case of postcolonial India, where modernity has been evolving through the 'paradigm of the national/modern' – 'the double discourse of the national and the modern' (Kapur 288) – the discussion of the novel as a narrative of the nation has a particular significance. On the one hand, the heterogeneous and dialogic language that the novel provides helps in signifying the alternative narratives of Indian modernity. For Ashis Nandy, for instance, India's modernity is not a mere replica of the West, and 'is neither pre-modern nor anti-modern but only non-modern' (76). On the other hand, the novel is also a site for narrating the 'national allegories' of 'heterogeneous time' (Chatterjee, 'The Nation in Heterogeneous Time' 402), while the social realist traditions of the novel (specifically, in the 'progressive literature' encouraged by the All-India Progressive Writers' Association, or AIPWA) brings out the many modern evocations of the nation-state. The reason behind such multiplicity and variety in these narratives is the fact that, as Aijaz Ahmad points out, India as a nation-state exists not as a concrete and closed entity but as a 'process . . . a terrain of struggle which condenses all social struggles, so that every organized force in society attempts to endow it with specific meanings and attributes' (*Lineages of the Present* 145). Homi K. Bhabha poses an interesting question in this context, 'If the ambivalent figure of the nation is a problem of its transitional history, its conceptual indeterminacy, its wavering between vocabularies, then what effect does this have on narratives and discourses that signify a sense of "nationness"' (2).

Fictional narratives of the Indian 'nation' have tried to address the diversity of India either by inventing a language based on an imagined tolerance and accommodation, or by critiquing the imagined idea of 'unity in diversity' by revealing the hardships of those who are not the nation's normative citizens, for instance, Dalits, tribal communities, the proletariat, women, queer persons, the differently abled, and the minorities. Addressing the debate whether Indian English fictions are capable of narrating Indian sensibilities, Aijaz Ahmad has rightly pointed out that, 'the only *national* literary intelligentsia that exists in India today—an intelligentsia constituted as a distinct social stratum and dispersed in all parts of the country, which brings to bear on its vocation and its work a *shared* body of knowledge, *shared* presumptions and a *shared* language of mutual exchange is the one that is fairly well grounded in English' (*In Theory* 278; original emphasis). Focusing on this *national* dimension of the Indian novels written in English, Priyamvada Gopal observes that

> the anglophone Indian novel is part of a heterogeneous corpus in which certain dominant trends, shared concerns, and recurrent themes are, nevertheless, discernible. It is a genre that has been distinguished from its inception by a preoccupation with both history and nation as these come together to shape what political scientist, Sunil Khilnani (1997) terms, after Nehru, "the idea of India". (5)

Meenakshi Mukherjee has pointed at 'the anxiety of Indianness', considering how 'when it comes to English fiction originating in our country, not only does the issue of Indianness become a favourite essentialising obsession in academic writings and the book review circuit, the writers themselves do not seem unaffected by it' (2607). Raja Rao's anxious elaboration on the nativisation of English is a case in point: 'One has to convey in a language that is not one's own the spirit that is one's own . . . yet English is not really an alien language to us. It is the language of our intellectual make-up, like Sanskrit or Persian was before' (*Kanthapura* v).

The following section will briefly look at some of the well-known novels in Indian Writing in English that have thematically engaged with the idea of an Indian nation.

INDIAN ENGLISH NOVELS AND THE IDEA OF THE NATION: A BRIEF SURVEY

Freedom and Fracture

The history of pre-colonial India and the nation's struggle for independence have been themes of abiding interest for Indian writers in English. Mughal India in general and the legend of Shah Jahan and Begum Mumtaz in particular, are the central focus of Indu Sundaresan's trilogy – *The Twentieth Wife* (2002), *The Feast of Roses* (2003) and *The Shadow Princess* (2010). *The Queen of Kittur* (2012) by Basavaraj Naikarre constructs Rani Chennamma's resistance against the East India Company, while *Rani* (2007) by Jaishree Misra focuses on the patriotic zeal of the Queen of Jhansi. Based on revisiting India's first war of independence of 1857, works like Soshee Chunder Dutt's *Shunkur: A Tale of the Indian Mutiny of 1857* (1885), Qurratulain Hyder's *Rain of Fire* (1959), Manohar Malgonkar's *The Devil's Wind* (1972), Ruskin Bond's *A Flight of Pigeons* (1978), Khushwant Singh's *Delhi* (1990), and Vikram Chandra's *Red Earth and Pouring Rain* (1995) belong to the category known as 'Mutiny fiction'. An impassioned anticolonialism underlines novels such as Lal Behari Day's *Bengal Peasant Life* (*Govinda Samanta*) (1874) where the colonisers are criticised as exploiters whose 'only object is to make money and then run away to merry England as fast as steam can carry them' (208). This refusal to give in to colonial oppression also marks the works of Easterine Kire Iralu who gives an account of the Nagas' battle with the British army as well as with the Japanese who attempted to invade India during the Second World War in *A Naga Village Remembered* (2003) and *Mari* (2010), respectively. K. S. Venkataramani's *The Patriot: A Novel of New India in the Making* (1932) has the Oxford-educated Kandan resigning from the ICS to enter the civil disobedience movement of the 1930s. Bhabani Bhattacharya's *So Many Hungers* (1947) describes the Bengal famine and the Quit India Movement of 1942. K. A. Abbas's *Tomorrow is Ours: A Novel of the India of Today* (1943) combines issues of nationalism and the need for sociocultural reforms through its female protagonist, Parvati. His *Inquilab: A Novel of Indian Revolution* (1955) provides a panorama of the Indian political scenario during the 1920s and 30s.

'Gandhian fictions', eulogising the Mahatma while narrating the Indian struggle for freedom and post-independence nation-building, are exemplified by Raja Rao's *Kanthapura* (1938), Mulk Raj Anand's *Untouchable* (1935) and R. K. Narayan's *The Guide* (1958). Iyengar described *Kanthapura* as 'a veritable grammar of the Gandhian myth – the myth that is but a poetic translation of the reality' (396). *Untouchable* describes Bakha, the Dalit protagonist, finding hope and upliftment through Gandhi, 'by far the greatest liberating force of our age' (142). Raju in *The Guide* is transformed into a sage like Gandhi: 'He is like Mahatma. When Mahatma Gandhi went without food, how many things happened in India! This is a man like that' (102). There were voices of disapproval as well. Khushwant Singh's *I Shall Not Hear the Nightingale* (1959) portrays its unheroic hero, Sher Singh, who 'loves the dog more than his own relations' (219), as a possible 'future prime minister of India' (142), implicitly critiquing nationalist leaders. *A Bend in the Ganges* (1964) by Manohar Malgonkar portrays Debi who, in the context of the post-Partition turmoil, questions, 'Had Gandhi envisaged a freedom that would be accompanied by so much suffering . . . ? . . .Who had won, Gandhi or the British? . . . Or had they both lost . . . ?' (355).

Ahmed Ali's *Twilight in Delhi* (1940), located within 'a larger Indian world in which English officials are being bombed while troops kill those who participate in Gandhi's non-cooperation movement' (King 246), addressed Muslim lives in the context of colonialism. According to Sugata Bose and Ayesha Jalal, 'the colossal human tragedy of the partition and its continuing aftermath has been better conveyed by the more sensitive creative writers and artists – for example in Saadat Hasan Manto's short stories and Ritwik Ghatak's films – than by historians' (164). Khushwant Singh's *Train to Pakistan* (1956), the first Partition novel in Indian Writing in English, provides a realistic account of the genocide during the traumatic period of Partition: 'Trainloads of dead people came to Mano Majra. . . . The river was flooded with corpses. Muslims were evacuated, and in their place, refugees have come from Pakistan' (191–92). Mumtaz Shah Nawaz's *The Heart Divided* (1947) underscored that 'the division of India had already taken place . . . In the heart, i.e., in the universe of emotions and relations' (Kumar vi). Zohra, in the novel, interrogates: 'Is there not a greater law than the law of communities? The law of humanity that denies any barrier between man and man . . . [A]re you going to build your nationalism upon the flimsy foundation of communal barriers?' (Shah Nawaz 186–87). Novels like *Sunlight on a Broken Column* (1951) by Attia Hossain, Anita Desai's *Clear Light of Day* (1980), *Some Inner Fury* (1956) by Kamala Markandaya, Chaman Nahal's *Azadi* (1975), H. S. Gill's *Ashes and Petals* (1978), *A Time to be Happy* (1957) by Nayantara Sahgal, *Looking Through Glass* (1995) by Mukul Kesavan, Jaina Sanga's *Silk Fish Opium* (2012), and Siddhartha Deb's *The Point of Return* (2002), focus on the fracture that Partition caused in India's social and cultural fabric. Amitav Ghosh's narrative of Partition in *The Shadow Lines* (1988) is 'marked by a growing sense that the logic of the modern nation-state is necessarily at odds with various forms of subcontinental commonality', which, in turn, suggests 'that to be "Indian" is to perversely, and perhaps unsuccessfully, define oneself against one's mirror-image from across the borders' (Kaul 270). Another moment of national crisis, the Chinese invasion of 1962, is dealt with in Bhabani Bhattacharya's *Shadow from Ladakh* (1966) and Arun Joshi's *The Apprentice* (1974).

Unity and Disjunction

India's nationalism, as Chatterjee has remarked, is bestowed with a 'spiritual domain [in which] the East was superior to the West' (*The Nation and Its Fragments* 120). Writers of Indian English fictions have been fairly conscious of this distinctiveness. For instance, Rama's 'Indianness' in *The Serpent and the Rope* (1960) – despite his assertions that 'India is wheresoever you see, hear, touch, taste, smell' (389) and 'Wheresoever I am is my country' (402) – is not complete without his spiritual quest: 'I lie on my bed and sob. Sometimes singing some chant of Sankara, I burst into sobs' (402). The central character in Arun Joshi's *The Strange Case of Billy Biswas* (1971) renounces his American and Delhi lives to become almost a saint in the woods of the Maikala Hills. Ruth Prawer Jhabvala's *The House Holder* (1960) and *A Backward Place* (1965) also contrast Indian ethos with the Western ones. Humanyun Kabir's *Men and*

Rivers (1945), Khawaja Ahmad Abbas's *Defeat for Death* (1944), K. Nagarajan's *The Chronicles of Kedaram* (1961), Gurcharan Das's *A Fine Family* (1990), Chaman Nahal's *The Salt of Life* (1990) and *The Triumph of the Tricolour* (1993), and M. J. Akbar's *Blood Brothers* (2006) have contributed to imagining a harmonious national unity amid diversity. Later on, Amitav Ghosh in *The Hungry Tide* (2004), Kiran Desai in *The Inheritance of Loss* (2006), Siddharth Chowdhury in *Patna Roughcut* (2005), Sree Vatsan's *Countryside Album* (2007) and Sarita Mandanna's *Tiger Hills* (2010) tried to draw attention to the local/regional Indian concerns in times of globality, while novels such as Hari Kunzru's *Transmission* (2005) and Rana Dasgupta's *Tokyo Cancelled* (2005) globalised the local. In contrast, there are 'national allegories' in Pankaj Mishra's *The Romantics* (1999) and Kiran Nagarkar's *Cuckold* (1997) where events of the past are invoked to expose the impoverished contemporary citizens of India. Ruchir Joshi's *The Last Jet-Engine Laugh* (2000) – where Netaji Subhas Chandra Bose is shown as victorious over both Gandhi and Nehru – is probably the most provocative of this lot.

Rushdie's *Midnight's Children* (1981) and *The Satanic Verses* (1988), Shashi Tharoor's *The Great Indian Novel* (1989) and *The Riot* (2001), Vikram Seth's *A Suitable Boy* (1993), and Rohinton Mistry's *A Fine Balance* (1996) are major novels that have critically engaged with the raptures in Indian polity, beginning with 'the breakdown of the Nehruvian secular consensus', followed by 'the National Emergency (1975–77)' and 'the rise to prominence of an alternative national ideology, Hindutva, based on the supremacy of Hindu religion and culture' (Srivastava 2). These novels engaged with history either through fantasised rewritings of popular myths and epics, narrating history through a magic-realist mode, or by deploying a realistic documentary mode, bringing out the fact that 'no longer was the postcolonial writer limited to anticolonial resistance – he was now an adversary of his own government, no less' (Sunder Rajan 210).

India, through Rushdie's 'chutnification', was presented as an 'imagined community':

> . . . quite imaginary . . . a mythical land, a country which would never exist except by the efforts of a phenomenal collective will—except in a dream we all agreed to dream; it was a mass

> fantasy shared in varying degrees by Bengali and Punjabi, Madrasi and Jat, and would periodically need the sanctification and renewal which can only be provided by rituals of blood. (Rushdie 112)

On the other hand, through the 'khichrification' of Indian vernaculars in *A Suitable Boy*, Seth provides 'an awareness and even a celebration of the cultural Indianness of the Indian novel in English, which remains unparalleled' (Trivedi, 'Translation as Recovery' 31). Seth used music as a metaphor for negotiating the diversities of the Indian nation without surrendering to the capitalist homogenisation. This leaves hope for a harmonious future based on listening to the 'Other'. In Nayantara Sahgal's *Lesser Breeds* (2003), one comes across this witty sketch:

> What is an Indian. . . . A specimen to gawk at, not a normal chap who joins military pacts and lets his markets get flooded with advanced tomato ketchup. We don't have jolly golfing Generals heading our governments and Colonels overthrowing them with coups . . . we're not even a theocracy. Rank outsiders is what we are, unlovable as halitosis. But do the world's rulers pat our little bottoms and say Never mind if you're god-awful freaks, at least you've got democracy? Not at all. Every few years their think-tanks predict we're about to fall apart. It's so affronting when we don't. Hell hath no fury like a think tank scorned. (362)

But the narrator, Ved Vyas, of the 'historiographic' *The Great Indian Novel*, replaces all objective notions of a national identity with subjective impressions of 'Indianness': 'This is my story of the India I know, with its biases, selections, omissions, distortions, all mine. But you cannot derive your cosmogony from a single birth, Ganapathi. Every Indian must forever carry with him, in his head and heart, his own history of India' (Tharoor 373). These differences in attitudes and perceptions justify the observation that 'post-independence literature, especially fiction, was forced to account for a perplexing reality. On the one hand freedom had been won. . . . But on the other hand, writers and intellectuals generally felt that the only change effected by independence was the change in the colour of the exploiters' skin. Writers varied widely in their reactions' (Coppola 3).

'Emergency novels' – such as Balwant Gargi's *The Naked Triangle* (1979), O. V. Vijayan's *The Saga of Dharmapuri* (1988), Ranjit Lal's *The Crow Chronicles* (1996), and Anees Salim's *The Vicks Mango Tree* (2012) – are complemented by works like Pratap Sharma's *Days of the Turban* (1986) and Rafiq Zakaria's *The Price of Power* (1987) which present accounts of the post-Emergency era. Radhika Oberoi's *Stillborn Season* (2018), Vikram Kapur's *The Assassinations: A Novel of 1984* (2017), and Anita Rau Badami's *Can You Hear the Nightbird Call?* (2006) depict the anti-Sikh riots of 1984, while Githa Hariharan's *In Times of Siege* (2003), Meher Pestonji's *Pervez – A Novel* (2002), and *The Solitude of Emperors* (2007) by David Davidar, chronicle the violence that erupted in the wake of the demolition of Babri Masjid. These works ruminate on a democratic society's slide into fascism: 'Can we not find it in ourselves to belong to an ancient civilization instead of to just a recent nation? To love "a land" instead of just patrolling a territory?' (Roy 285). Such 'dystopias' can also be read in Shiv K. Kumar's unmasking of the religious imperialism of fake gurus in *Two Mirrors at the Ashram* (2006), Upamanyu Chatterjee's ridiculing of an absurdist political project to construct a 'glorious nation' in *Weight Loss* (2006), or in Manjula Padmanabhan's *Escape* (2008) that outlines a future India ruled by cloned Generals and characterised by the elimination of women and the annihilation of nature through nuclear technology.

Subnationalist movements have inspired novels like Amandeep Sandhu's *Roll of Honour* (2012) and *Remember to Forget* (2012) by Neel Kamal Puri, where the authors write poignantly about the Khalistan movement. Neel Mukherjee in *The Lives of Others* (2014), Upamanyu Chatterjee in *English, August* (1988), and Jhumpa Lahiri in *The Lowland* (2013), engage with the Naxalite movement in West Bengal during the 1960s. The Indian army's handling of insurgent movements in the Northeast is discussed in novels like *The House with a Thousand Stories* (2013) by Aruni Kashyap, Mitra Phukan's *The Collector's Wife* (2005) and Siddhartha Deb's *Surface* (2005). One may discern a Bakhtinian 'heteroglossia' and 'polyphony' in Indian novelists' engagement with the issue of 'terrorism' and the nationalist backlash. Vikram Chandra's *Sacred Games* (2007) outlined a terrorist plot to attack India. Colonel Chowdhry's version of terrorists in Jaspreet Singh's *Chef* (2008) – as 'bloody men from bloody Islam, who are in touch with militants in Afghanistan and Pakistan, they have occupied the bloody mosques, sir. They want bloody azadi, sir' (59–60) – finds a sharp retort in Khalid's objection in *Jimmy the Terrorist* (2010), a novel by Omair Ahmad: 'Why don't you just admit that you beat me because I'm a Muslim?' (143). Aniruddha Bahal's *Bunker 13* (2003) and Salman Rushdie's *Shalimar the Clown* (2005) are anxious about the erosion of the composite tradition of '*kashmiriyat*'. *The Collaborator* (2010) by Mirza Waheed, *The Half Widow* (2012) by Shafi Ahmad, and *The Garden of Solitude* (2010) by Siddhartha Gigoo are tales of 'nerve-wracking terror' for Kashmiris who grew up in the 1990s and suffered the violence (Bharat 48).

Counter-narratives of an inclusive and secular nationhood can be found in Pawan K. Varma's *When Loss is Gain* (2012) and Tabish Khair's *Filming: A Love Story* (2007). The Indian tradition of 'bhakti' is the foundation of the hagiographic narrative in Basavaraj Naikar's *Light in the House* (2009) which pays tribute to Shishunala Sharif, while Amita Kanekar's *A Spoke in the Wheel* (2005) reverts to Buddhist and Vedic traditions. Tamil culture and music are central to *The Silent Raga* (2008) by Ameen Merchant. An Indian 'culinary nation' is imagined in Chitra Banerjee Divakaruni's *The Mistress of Spices* (1997). Domestic/family narratives, as repositories of alternative Indian histories, are featured in novels such as Arundhati Roy's *The God of Small Things* (1997), *The Blue Bedspread* (1999) by Raj Kamal Jha, Rupa Bajwa's *The Sari Shop* (2004), Padma Viswanathan's *The Toss of a Lemon* (2008), and Amit Chaudhuri's *A Strange and Sublime Address* (1991) and *Afternoon Raag* (1993). In these narratives, portrayals of domestic/personal spaces provide a larger view of the nation-state.

The Periphery Writes Back

Arundhati Roy has the following to say about the role of writers: 'We will be forced to ask ourselves some very uncomfortable questions about our values and traditions, our vision for the future, our responsibilities as citizens, the legitimacy of our "democratic institutions", the role of the state, the police, the army, the judiciary and the intellectual community' (198). Many Indians writing in English have questioned the injustices of class and caste inequalities. They were largely following the earlier generation of writers who discussed the exploitation of rural commoners and the erosion of traditional ethos in the wake of industrialisation and the introduction of technology. Mulk Raj Anand's 'village trilogy' (comprising *The Village* [1939], *Across the Black Waters* [1941] and *The Sword and the Sickle* [1942]), Sudhin Ghose's 'Balaram tetralogy' (which included *And Gazelles Leaping* [1949], *Cradle of the Clouds* [1951], *The Vermilion Boat* [1953], and *The Flame of the Forest* [1955]), Kamala Markandaya's *The Coffer Dams* (1969), Manohar Malgonkar's *Combat of Shadows* (1962), and Anita Desai's *The Village by the Sea* (1982), have found successors in works by novelists of later generations. Ashish Gupta's *Dying Traditions* (1992) and David Davidar's *The House of Blue Mangoes* (2002) depict internal migration of villagers. Aravind Adiga's *The White Tiger* (2008), Vikas Swarup's *Q & A* (2005) and *Six Suspects* (2008), and Tarun Tejpal's *The Story of My Assassins* (2009), provide accounts of the oppression of the poor in both villages and city-slums. An urban 'slumdog narrative' of Chennai is featured in Kavery Nambisan's *The Story that Must Not Be Told* (2008). R. K. Narayan condemned the 'Devadasi' tradition in *The Man-Eater of Malgudi* (1962) and the dowry system in *The Vendor of Sweets* (1967). Namita Gokhale's *Priya in Incredible Indyaa* (2011) is a parody of metropolitan elites, while Upamanyu Chatterjee's *The Mammaries of the Welfare State* (2000) is a satire on bureaucratic corruption in India.

Sara Newman has talked about the ethical dilemma (19) regarding issues of authenticity and possible 'misconception' (261) of a writer speaking on behalf of people with disabilities (particularly those with intellectual disabilities). However, there are a handful of novels that have highlighted the issues of the differently abled vis-à-vis the nation-state. Novels like *Ancient Promises* (2000) by Jaishree Misra, Pramila Balasundaram's *Sunny's Story* (2005), Jerry Pinto's *Em and the Big Hoom* (2012), Firdaus Kanga's *Trying to Grow* (1991), Vikram Seth's *An Equal Music* (1999), Susmita Bagchi's *Children of a Better God* (2010), and *Gods without Men* (2011) by Hari Kunzru, show a commitment to advocacy with regards to the rights of the differently abled.

'Minority fictions' in Indian Writing in English have revealed the contradictions within the Indian secular–nationalist discourse.

For example, Rohinton Mistry's *Family Matters* (2002), Shama Futehally's *Reaching Bombay Central* (2002), and Samina Ali's *Madras on Rainy Days* (2004). The deepening insecurity among the Indian minorities – in the backdrop of communal violence and heightened communal rhetoric questioning and vilifying even personal and culinary choices – is recorded in novels such as Githa Hariharan's *Fugitive Histories* (2009), Peggy Mohan's *The Youngest Suspect* (2012), Rukun Advani's *Beethoven Among the Cows* (1994) and Raj Kamal Jha's *Fireproof* (2007). The exodus of Kashmiri Pandits from the Valley features prominently in *The Tree with a Thousand Apples* (2017) by Sanchit Gupta, and Manan Kapoor's *The Lamentations of a Sombre Sky* (2016).

Allan Sealy's *The Trotter-Nama: A Chronicle* (1988), while presenting the marginalised status of Anglo-Indian communities, offers a critique of how Indian nationalists 'selectively appropriate[ed] and refurbish[ed] certain traditions and historical events, while discarding others as inappropriate or "backward" and constraining' (Srivastava 27). The Dalit consciousness about the exploitation by savarna castes – a realisation which Kancha Ilaiah Shepherd calls 'buffalo nationalism', suggesting that it equips the Dalit–Bahujan with the positive qualities of the productive beast – has prompted Indian English writers to engage with a 'literature of protest' against caste discrimination, exemplified by novels such as Cyrus Mistry's *Chronicle of a Corpse Bearer* (2012), Amitav Ghosh's *Sea of Poppies* (2010), Kancha Ilaiah Shepherd's *Untouchable God* (2013), Meena Kandasamy's *The Gypsy Goddess* (2014), and Srividya Natarajan's graphic novel, *A Gardener in the Wasteland: Jotiba Phule's Fight for Liberty* (2012). These 'trauma narratives' dealing with testimonies of postcolonial atrocities can align with the global human rights literature. Gita Mehta's *A River Sutra* (1993) presents a tribal world by the side of the Narmada river. Novels like *The Black Hill* (Mamang Dai, 2015), *A Bowstring Winter* (Dhruba Hazarika, 2006), *A Terrible Matriarchy* (Easterine Kire Iralu, 2007) and *Shadow Men* (Bijoya Sawian, 2010), while highlighting a shared humanity among people from different cultures, reveal that the Indian ethnic novel's 'literary universals' can serve as 'an antidote' to an 'annihilating, nonassimilative, separatist universalism' (Hogan and Pandit 207).

Writings of resistance against anti-women prejudices within the nationalist discourse can be found in feminist fictional works – for example, Shashi Deshpande's *In the Country of Deceit* (2008) that portrays a marital discord; Manju Kapur's depiction of women's longing for education and independence in *Difficult Daughters* (1998); Manjul Bajaj's portrayal of honour killing in *Come, Before Evening Falls* (2009); *Witness the Night* (2010) where Kishwar Desai focuses on female feticide; Chitra Banerjee Divakaruni's retelling of *The Mahabharata* from a woman's point of view in *The Palace of Illusions* (2008); and *Neti, Neti* (2009) where Anjum Hasan reveals women's experiences of multiple displacements. The Indian 'queer nation', with no tangible place in the 'mainstream' society, finds concrete existence in the stories narrated by novelists such as Shobhaa De (*Strange Obsession*, 1992), R. Raj Rao (*The Boyfriend*, 2003), Arundhati Roy (*The Ministry of Utmost Happiness*, 2017), Hoshang Merchant (*The Man Who Would be Queen*, 2011), Vivek Shraya (*She of the Mountains*, 2014), and Hansda Sowvendra Shekhar (*My Father's Garden*, 2019).

Indian literatures in English have also produced critiques of nationalist narratives of progress and advancement. Indra Sinha's *Animal's People* (2007), set against the backdrop of the Bhopal gas tragedy of 1984, attests to Harvey's argument that 'Capitalism is under the impulsion to eliminate all spatial barriers . . . but it can do so only through the production of a fixed space. Capitalism thereby produces a geographical landscape . . . only to have to destroy and rebuild the geographical landscape to accommodate accumulation at a later date' (59). On the other hand, Subham Basu's *Glian, the Son of Nature* (2007) and Nilanjana Roy's *The Wildings* (2012) are marked by a posthuman intimacy.

Expatriates' India

Novels by diasporic writers of Indian origin represent an 'imaginary homeland' by providing an 'imagined history'. These imaginaries help the expatriate, characterised by her/his uneasy relationships with both 'home' and the host country which renders her/him a 'specular border intellectual', move towards being a 'syncretic border intellectual' who reaches out to both the donor and recipient cultures (Jan Mohammed 97). This syncretism is depicted in M. G. Vassanji's novels – such as *The Gunny Sack* (2009), *The Book of Secrets* (1994) and *The In-Between World of Vikram Lall* (2003) – through the portrayal of 'transnational beings' or 'liminal personae' living in a multicultural state. This idea was also referred to by Tagore as a 'greater nationalism' which allows one to resist nationalist jingoism through a harmonious and amiable internationalism (*Greater India* 86). However, the dominant theme in Indian English diasporic fictions has been how 'the aspiration for "destiNations" has resulted not in hope but in "alieNations"' (Joshi, 'Nations and Alienations' 92). Bharati Mukherjee's *Wife* (1975) shows the frustration of a young housewife in an unfamiliar world. The theme of the breakdown of marital relationships due to 'migration stress' and 'acculturation stress' (Lozano-Vonrich 198) is central to Adarshir Vakil's *One Day* (2003), Sunetra Gupta's *Memories of Rain* (1992) and Amit Chaudhury's *New World* (2000). *Fury* (2001) by Salman Rushdie depicts immigrants caught up in the culture of globalisation. The 'girmit' experience of indentured plantation migrants is recorded in Anand Mulloo's *Watch Them Go Down* (1957). The trauma of the forced migration of Indian labourers in East Africa, Mauritius, Fiji, Trinidad, Jamaica, Guyana and Malaysia finds expression in novels such as K. S. Maniam's *In a Far Country* (1993) and *The Return* (1981). The experience of exile and the exile's conflicted relationship with the nation-state is also narrated in Naipaul's *A House for Mr Biswas* (1961): 'They continually talked of going back to India, but when the opportunity came, many refused, afraid of the unknown, afraid to leave the familiar temporariness' (174). This theme is also central to Cyril Dabydeen's *Dark Swirl* (1988).

As discussed above, loss of identity is a recurrent theme in the early diaspora writers, which might have provoked Peter van der Veer to observe that 'those who do not think of themselves as Indians before migration become Indians in the diaspora' (7). The younger generation of diasporic Indian novelists, however, treat 'hybrid identity' as a positive mode of self-identification. For instance, Shalini Akhil, in *The Bollywood Beauty* (2005), depicts Rupa, who lives in Fiji. Despite her arranged marriage to a 'Delhiite', Rupa is not 'really Indian' for her Australian-born cousin: 'Her great-grandfather had been, and his dad and his dad, but not anyone from her grandfather's generation down. They had not been born and bred in India. They were too far removed to be real Indians. They looked different. They ate different food. Hell, they even made up their own language' (309). To take another instance, the post-racist stand evident in Farrukh Dhondy's *The Siege of Babylon* (1989) and *Bombay Duck* (1990), can be read as a postnationalist position. On the other hand, the global rise of isolationism and the ineffectiveness of a global fraternity are anticipated in the tragic end of the Indian Guyanese couples in David Debydeen's *The Counting House* (1996).

Located outside the boundaries of the nation-state, the expatriate Indian writer continues to celebrate the 'Indian culture overseas' with her/his fellow *desi*s. This is revealed in *Life Isn't All Ha Ha Hee Hee* (Meera Syal, 2001), as well as in Meera Alexander's diasporic novel *Manhattan Music* (1997) which captures '*the simultaneity of geography* . . . the possibility of living here in body and elsewhere in mind and imagination' (Katrak 201; italics in the original). The nostalgic remembrance of India amid the immigrants' looking forward to her/his prospects in the adopted country – as delineated in novels like *Listening Now* (1998) by Anjana Appachana, and Bharati Kirchner's *Shiva Dancing* (1998) and *Sharmila's Book* (1999) – justify Bhikhu Parekh's observation: 'The Indian Diaspora is like the banyan tree . . . spreads out his roots in several soils, drawing nourishment from one when the rest dry up. Far from being homeless, he has several homes, and that is the only way he has increasingly come to feel at home in the world' (106).

TRANSLATING THE NATION

Harish Trivedi has divided the process of Indian writings getting translated into English into four phases – the Indological phase of translating classical literature; the neo-orientalist or post-orientalist phase of translating literatures of the Bhakti period; the national allegory phase of translating realistic vernacular texts into English; and the phase of internationalism/universalism of translating modernist Bhasha writers (*Colonial Transactions* 52). While studying the history of translating regional Indian literatures into English, G. N. Devy also identifies four phases – the colonial phase

(1776–1910), the revivalist phase (1876–1950), the nationalist phase (1902–29), and the formalist phase (1912 onwards) (*In Another Tongue* 120). 'The emergence of bhasha literatures', according to Devy, 'coincided with, even if it was not entirely caused by, a succession of Islamic rules in India. . . . The intimate contact with Islamic cultures created for the bhasha literatures new possibilities of continuous development' (*After Amnesia* 9). As observed by Priya Joshi, the widespread use of English in India gave birth to 'not just the literal translation of reams of printed matter', but the translation of bhasha literatures into English created 'a symbolic and metaphoric translation in which the Indian world was carried forth from one state to another through the act of reading and interpretation', turning Indians 'from consumers [of English] to producers of their own national self-image' (321). These translations included a large number of modern classics – such as Rabindranath Tagore's *The Home and the World* (1915; tr. Surendranath Tagore), Amrita Pritam's *Pinjar* (1950; tr. Khushwant Singh), Thakazhi Sivasankara Pillai's *Chemmeen: A Novel* (1962, tr. Narayana Menon), U. R. Ananthamurthy's *Samskara* (1965; tr. A. K. Ramanujan), Bibhutibhushan Bandopadhyay's *Song of the Road* (1968; tr. T. W. Clark and Tarapada Mukherji), Shridhar Pendse's *Wild Bapu of Garambi* (1968; tr. Ian Raeside), Manik Bandopadhyay's *The Puppet's Tale* (1968; tr. S. L. Ghosh); Premchand's *Godan: The Gift of a Cow* (1968; tr. Gordon Roadermal), and Aziz Ahmad's *The Shore and the Wave* (1971; tr. Ralph Russell), among many others. These works provided a picture of 'many Indias' where 'individuals live with multiple associations and . . . maneuver among multiple associations' (Gottschalk 134). This stress on multiplicity continues to be underscored by newer and recent translations: a few prominent examples will include Perumal Murugan's *Poonachi: Or the Story of a Black Goat* (2017; tr. N. Kalyan Raman) where a sociopolitical commentary is provided from the perspective of a goat; Vivek Shanbhag's *Ghachar Ghochar* (2015; tr. Srinath Perur), dealing with a dysfunctional family; and Subash Chandran's *A Preface to Man* (2016; tr. Fathima E. V.) which, through stories of more than three generations of a nair family, deals with questions of caste, gender and politics. Issues related to caste divisions and atrocities have received widespread attention through English translations of Dalit writings – such as Laxman Gaikwad's *The Branded* (1998; tr. P. A. Kolharkar), Bama Faustina's *Karukku* (2000; tr. Lakshmi Holmström), P. Sivakami's *The Grip of Change* (2006; tr. author), and Narayan's *The Araya Woman* (2010; tr. Catherine Thankamma). Narratives of subalternity have received global attention through translations of autobiographies such as *Me Hijra, Me Laxmi* by Laxminarayan Tripathi (2015; tr. R. Raj Rao and P. G. Joshi) and Nalini Jameela's *The Autobiography of a Sex Worker* (2005; tr. J. Devika). The Sahitya Akademi, while encouraging translations of vernacular Indian fictions into English, has contributed to augmenting the writers' 'quest for India': as Umashankar Joshi observes, 'the regional novels, presenting widely divergent aspects of the Indian social landscape, highlight India's innate unity in diversity and, above all, give their authors a sense of rootedness' (81). The attack on Perumal Murugan from right-wing groups after his *Madhorubhagan* (2010) was translated into English as *One Part Woman* (by Aniruddhan Vasudevan) in 2013, and the allegations of blasphemy, obscenity and defamation levelled against him, showed how translations can question regressive traditions that still persist in the name of communitarian legacy. As Sartre has argued, such debates show that a writer should never merely position herself/himself as a national ambassador or 'embark on national highways, even if he [or she] is furnished with a racing car' but display 'the strength to scandalize' by focusing on 'the need for justice' (287).

Translating National Culture through Other Forms of Art

Apart from the narratives by novelists and writers of autobiographies, 'India' has also been 'translated' through other forms of creative imaginings of its body politic. Many noted Indian filmmakers including Dadasaheb Phalke, Ritwik Ghatak, Satyajit Ray, Adoor Gopalakrishnan, Mrinal Sen, Shyam Benegal, Mani Ratnam, Mira Nair, Mani Kaul, Jahnu Barua, Mehboob Khan, and Gulzar have used cinema as a medium for narrating the nation. Paintings by artists such as Raja Ravi Varma, Abanindranath Tagore, Nandalal Bose, Jamini Roy, Abdur Rahman Chughtai, Zainul Abedin, Tyeb Mehta, Syed Haider Raza, S. L. Haldankar, S. Elayaraja, and Maqbool Fida Husain are marked with a keen nationalist fervour. Legends like M. S. Subbulakshmi, Bismillah Khan, Begum Akhtar, Ali Akbar

Khan, Vilayat Khan, Ravi Shankar, Bhimsen Joshi, Girija Devi and Bhupen Hazarika, to name a few, have translated and disseminated 'Indianness' musically. Udaya Shankar's cultural centre at Almora for dancers, actors and musicians is an example of a transcreative platform that strives to overcome the 'bigotry' of nationalism – the bigotry that, as Tagore pointed out, is 'born of the habit of a past generation' and cultivated 'in the name of Indian art' (Tagore, 'Art and Tradition' 54). Such initiatives have brought together regional and global artists and traditions, to foster an intimate bond between diverse national and international art forms.

REFERENCES

Ahmad, Aijaz. *In Theory: Nations, Classes, Literatures.* Delhi: Oxford UP, 1991. Print.

---. *Lineages of the Present: Ideology and Politics in Contemporary South Asia.* London: Verso, 2000. Print.

Ahmad, Omair. *Jimmy the Terrorist.* New Delhi: Penguin Viking, 2010. Print.

Akhil, Shalini. *The Bollywood Beauty.* Camberwell: Penguin, 2005. Print.

Anand, Mulk Raj. *Untouchable.* New Delhi: Penguin, 2001. Print.

Askari, Muhammad Hasan. 'A Novel by Ahmed Ali'. Trans. Carlo Coppola. *Annual of Urdu Studies* 9 (1994): 27–38. Print.

Bakhtin, M. M. *The Dialogic Imagination: Four Essays.* Trans. Caryl Emerson, and Michael Holquist. Austin: U of Texas P, 1981. Print.

Bhabha, Homi K., ed. *Nation and Narration.* London: Routledge, 1990. Print.

Bharat, Meenakshi. *Troubled Testimonies: Terrorism and the English Novel in India.* New Delhi: Routledge, 2016. Print.

Bose, Sugata, and Ayesha Jalal. *Modern South Asia: History, Culture, Political Economy.* New Delhi: Oxford UP, 2004. Print.

Chatterjee, Partha. 'Beyond the Nation? Or Within?'. *Economic and Political Weekly* 32.1–2 (1997): 30–34. Print.

---. 'Introduction'. *The Wages of Freedom: Fifty Years of the Indian Nation State.* Ed. Partha Chatterjee. New Delhi: Oxford UP, 1998: 1–20. Print.

---. *The Nation and Its Fragments: Colonial and Postcolonial Histories*. New Delhi: Oxford UP, 1993. Print.

---. 'The Nation in Heterogeneous Time'. *The Indian Economic and Social History Review* 38.4 (2001): 399–418. Print.

Coppola, Carlo. 'Politics and the Novel in India: A Perspective'. *Politics and the Novel in India*. Ed. Yogendra K. Malik. New Delhi: Orient Longman, 1978. 1–5. Print.

Day, Lal Behari. *Bengal Peasant Life* [*Govinda Samanta*]. Calcutta [Kolkata]: Editions Indian, 1969. Print.

Devy, G. N. *After Amnesia: Tradition and Change in Indian Literary Criticism*. Hyderabad: Orient BlackSwan, 1995. Print.

---. *In Another Tongue: Essays in Indian Literature*. Madras [Chennai]: Macmillan India, 1993. Print.

Gopal, Priyamvada. *The Indian English Novel: Nation, History and Narration*. New Delhi: Oxford UP, 2009. Print.

Gottschalk, Peter. *Beyond Hindu and Muslim: Multiple Identity in Narratives from Village India*. New York: Oxford UP, 2000. Print.

Gramsci, Antonio. *Selections from the Prison Notebooks*. Ed. and tr. Quintin Hoare, and Geoffrey Nowell Smith. Hyderabad: Orient Longman, 1996. Print.

Harvey, David. *Spaces of Hope*. Berkeley: U of California P, 2000. Print.

Hazarika, Sanjoy. *Rites of Passage: Border Crossings, Imagined Homelands, India's East and Bangladesh*. New Delhi: Penguin, 2000. Print.

Hogan, Patrick Colm, and Lalita Pandit, ed. *Literary India: Comparative Studies in Aesthetics, Colonialism and Culture*. Albany: State U of New York P, 1995. Print.

Iyengar, Srinivasa. *Indian Writing in English*. New Delhi: Sterling Publishers, 1962. Print.

Jan Mohammed, Abdul R. 'Worldliness-without-World, Homelessness-as-Home: Towards a Definition of the Specular Border Intellectual'. *Edward Said: A Critical Reader*. Oxford: Blackwell, 1992. 218–41. Print.

Joshi, Priya. 'Reading in the Public Eye: The Circulation of Fiction in Indian Libraries, c. 1835–1901'. *India's Literary History: Essays on the Nineteenth Century*. Ed. Stuart Blackburn, and Vasudha Dalmia. New Delhi: Permanent Black, 2004. Print.

Joshi, Rita. 'Nations and Alienations: Diaspora in Recent Indian Fiction'. *India International Centre Quarterly* 31.1 (2004): 83–93. Print.

Joshi, Ruchir. *The Last Jet-Engine Laugh*. London: Flamingo, 2001. Print.

Joshi, Umashankar. 'The Novelist's Quest for India'. *Indian Literature* 8.1 (1965): 58–81. Print.

Kapur, Geeta. *When Was Modernism: Essays on Contemporary Cultural Practice in India*. New Delhi: Tulika, 2000. Print.

Katrak, Ketu H. 'South Asian American Literature'. *An Interethnic Companion to Asian American Literature*. Ed. King-kok Cheung. Cambridge: Cambridge UP, 1997. 192–218. Print.

Kaul, Suvir. 'Separation Anxiety: Growing Up Inter/National in *The Shadow Lines*'. *The Shadow Lines*. CULT Educational ed. Delhi: Oxford UP, 1998. 268–86. Print.

King, Bruce. 'From Twilight to Midnight: Muslim Novels of India and Pakistan'. *The Worlds of Muslim Imagination*. Ed. Alamgir Hashmi. Islamabad: Gulmohar, 1986. 243–59. Print.

Kumar, Krishna. 'Foreword'. *The Heart Divided*. New Delhi: Penguin, 2004. v–vi. Print.

Lozano-Vonrich, Belisa. *The Seven Beliefs*. New York: HarperCollins, 2003. Print.

Malgonkar, Manohar. *A Bend in the Ganges*. New Delhi: Orient Paperbacks, 1974. Print.

Mukherjee, Meenakshi. 'The Anxiety of Indianness: Our Novels in English'. *Economic and Political Weekly* 28.48 (1993): 2607–11. Print.

Naipaul, V. S. *A House for Mr Biswas*. London: André Deutsch, 1961. Print.

Nandy, Ashis. *The Intimate Enemy: Loss and Recovery of Self Under Colonialism*. New Delhi: Oxford UP, 1988. Print.

Narayan, R. K. *The Guide*. Chennai: Indian Thought Publications, 2004. Print.

Newman, Sara. 'Disability and Life Writing: Reports from the Nineteenth-century Asylum'. *Journal of Literary and Cultural Disability Studies* 5.3 (2011): 261–78. Print.

Parekh, Bhikhu. 'Some Reflections on the Indian Diaspora'. *Journal of Contemporary Thought* 3 (1993): 105–51. Print.

Rao, Raja. *Kanthapura*. New Delhi: Oxford UP, 1989. Print.

---. *The Serpent and the Rope*. Delhi: Orient Paperbacks, 1968. Print.

Roy, Arundhati. *The Algebra of Infinite Justice*. New Delhi: Penguin Books India, 2002. Print.

Rushdie, Salman. *Midnight's Children*. London: Vintage, 1985. Print.

Sahgal, Nayantara. *Lesser Breeds: A Novel*. New Delhi: Harper Collins, 2003. Print.

Sartre, Jean-Paul. *'What Is Literature?' and Other Essays*. Cambridge: Harvard UP, 1988. Print.

Shah Nawaz, Mumtaz. *The Heart Divided*. New Delhi: Penguin, 2004. Print.

Singh, Jaspreet. *Chef*. Montreal: Vehicule Press, 2008. Print.

Singh, Khushwant. *I Shall Not Hear the Nightingale*. Bombay: IBH Publishing Co., 1973. Print.

---. *Train to Pakistan*. New Delhi: Ravi Dayal, 1988. Print.

Srivastava, Neelam. *Secularism in the Postcolonial Indian Novel: National and Cosmopolitan Narratives in English*. London: Routledge, 2008. Print.

Sunder Rajan, Rajeswari. 'After *Midnight's Children*: Some Notes on the New Indian Novel in English'. *Social Research* 78.1 (2011): 203–30. Print.

Tagore, Rabindranath. 'Art and Tradition'. *Art and Aesthetics: A Selection of Lectures, Essays and Letters*. Ed. Prithwish Neogy. Kolkata: Subarnarekha, 2005. Print.

---. *Greater India*. Madras: S. Ganesan, 1921. Print.

Tharoor, Shashi. *The Great Indian Novel*. New York: Arcade, 1989. Print.

Trivedi, Harish, *Colonial Transactions: English Literature and India*. Kolkata: Papyrus, 1993. Print.

---. 'Translation as Recovery: *A Suitable Boy* as *Koi Achcha-sa Ladaka*'. *The Book Review* 12.9 (1998): 30–31. Print.

van der Veer, Peter. 'Introduction: The Diasporic Imagination'. *Nation and Migration: The Politics of Space in the South Asian Diaspora*. Ed. Peter van der Veer. Philadelphia: U of Pennsylvania P, 1995: 1–16. Print.

Chapter Six

The Postnation

THE FUTURE OF NATIONALISM AND NATIONAL IDENTITIES, AND MOVEMENTS TOWARDS A PATRIOTIC PLANETARISM

The havoc wrecked by the two World Wars had a profound impact on the idea and practice of nationalisms across the world. It restrained generations who had had the haunting memories of devastations from forming alliances with other nation-states or from engaging in rivalries with enemy-states. Rather, the lessons learned from the war paved way for a 'critical nationalism' (Buttle) that undermined the importance of 'national identity' (the criteria that legitimises one's membership in the nation), 'national attachment' (one's fidelity to one's nation), 'national pride' (how one feels as a part of all national achievements), and 'national integrity' (how one is made to consider all other nation-states as possible threats to the state sovereignty of one's own nation-state), and popularised cooperational ideas like internationalism, globalism, and transnationalism. This 'critical nationalism' recognises and transverses the national boundedness of cultural 'groupism' with an 'affective cosmopolitics' of 'becoming-world' (Braidotti et al., 3–4). However, in the twenty-first century, where the new generation has no first-hand experience of the traumatic wars, there seems to be a renewed enthusiasm for hyper-nationalism among the 'populist nationalists' (who are characterised by a strong adherence to a national identity without a firm belief in national pluralism). Due to this hyper-nationalism, state-centricity has increasingly played a crucial role in the election of national leaders, who, in turn, have mostly been trying to instigate citizens with 'ultranationalist' ideals of national exceptionality or superiority (Bonikowski 20–23).

Moreover, as Alain Touraine has rightly observed, the post-globalisation era has witnessed the emergence of an 'introverted community' (12) which, out of an acute disillusionment at the failure in establishing an imagined cosmopolitan/transnational belongingness in the realms of international networks of technology, financial flows and information, has gradually reverted to traditional compartmentalised identities, and eventually joined hands with ideologues of isolationist ultranationalist movements. The emergence of 'homonationalism' as the 'US national homosexuality' is a case in point. As Puar points out, the emergence of homonationalism has signalled 'a collusion between American homosexuality and American nationalism that is generated both by nationalist rhetorics of patriotic inclusion and by gay and queer subjects themselves' (39) towards 'a process of racialization' (xi). This process validates white supremacy and Islamophobia.

While the debates on nationalisms rage on, there are instances of shared victimhood which calls for 'a collaborative morality', as defined by Lloyd (74), of interrelational cross-national engagements. There are many escalating worldwide issues which cannot be addressed as isolated internal concerns of a particular nation-state: the rigid social controls by the state giving rise to 'scattered hegemonies' (Grewal and Kaplan); the constant governmental surveillance which Paul Gilroy has called 'securocracy'; bio-genetic capitalism (Parisi) turning human life and human body into sites of profit and investment as a part of a 'necro-politics' which endorses 'the material destruction of human bodies and population' (Mbembe 19); the 'global civil war' (Duffield 149) between 'insured' and 'uninsured' humans of advanced and dysfunctional states; the 'infrastructural warfare' (Mbembe) where services like electricity, hospitals, roads and other necessities are in crisis; the large-scale logistical operations (Virilio) where a 'population' is categorised into 'rebels, child soldiers, victims or refugees, or civilians incapacitated by mutilation or massacred on the model of ancient sacrifices, while the "survivors", after a horrific exodus, are confined to camps and zones of exception' (Mbembe 34); and the 'ethnocidal violence' – to borrow from Arjun Appadurai ('Dead Certainty') – as a new form of warfare where kinsmen, friends and neighbours participate in mutilation, rape, lynching, sexual abuse and other kinds of violence.

Hence, as Guattari speculated, the need for a trans-continental solidarity, aimed at combating such universal suffering, is expected to evolve a 'chaosmosis' – 'that is to say being-one-with the vital processes of transformation alongside and with a multiplicity of human and non-human others' (Braidotti et al. 8) – and, thereby, debilitate the obsessive nation-centrism.

THE CORRODED NATIONAL IDENTITY

The weakening of the monopolistic sovereignty of the state by demands for a shared and negotiated sovereignty – particularly in 'non-nation states' like India where a state is shared by multi-nations – displays the shrinking authority of absolutist nation-states. The special autonomous status (revoked in 2019) that was granted to Jammu and Kashmir through Article 370 of the Indian Constitution was an initiative towards such a shared sovereignty. A shared sovereignty is based on the vision that '[a]ll the fundamental axiomatics of responsibility or decision (ethical, juridical, political) are grounded in the sovereignty of the subject, that is, the intentional auto-determination of the conscious self (which is free, autonomous, active, etc.)' (Derrida xix). The recent instances of civil-society protests in India, in the wake of events such as the revocation of the Kashmir autonomy and the riots in Delhi (2020), can also be read as gestures against a monopolistic national identity. Another recent instance is the protests in the US and the nationwide 'Black Lives Matter' protests against racism after the death of George Floyd. The ongoing negotiations between the Indian government and the Naga Council for a separate flag and a pan-Naga '*Yehzabo*' (Constitution) advocating polycentric governance are further examples of the corrosion of monopolistic nationalisms.

Citizenship, which used to be perceived as solely embedded within the 'national grip' of a particular nation-state, has been progressively inclining towards postnationalisation by its correspondences with various extra-state and non-/supra-national arrangements. This 'postnational citizenship' has resulted from both the 'multinationalisation' and 'denationalisation' of citizenship. There are many instances of such 'plurinationalisation' of citizenship: subnational affiliations within some nation-states to municipalities or federal states; supranational identities such as the European Union; extra-state belongingness seen in global diasporas and refugees; membership rights conferred by many liberal democratic states on long-term resident non-nationals; and instances of states that confer dual citizenship. This evolution in the concept of citizenship has paved way for postnational extraterritorial shifts in the notion of citizenship (Soysal; Bosniak).

The 'denationalisation' of citizenship has been outlined by critics in different ways. For Saskia Sassen, denationalisation takes place when the nation-state itself undergoes changes and reduces its role as a welfare state. Processes such as corporatisation, privatisation, inflow of foreign investment, and deregulation, which are often attached to globalisation, actually take place within the confines of the nation-state. They affect the institutional citizenship by allowing it to be 'connected to the national, as constructed historically, and is indeed profoundly imbricated with it', along with generating 'historically new terms of engagement' towards postnationality (Sassen 578). Theorists studying 'biological citizens' have shown that denationalisation of citizens can be understood in terms of how the poor in underdeveloped states are exploited by medical sciences. They are often accommodated under a 'medical citizenship' that is used to incorporate them into a global geography of experimentations related to drugs, commodified organ transplantation, globally traded tissues, etc. (Petryna). The weakening of national polities, through denationalisation, can also be understood as a result of the pressure exerted on nation-states to extend certain human rights to even those who are not the 'national citizens'. On the other hand, 'national citizens' are progressively inclined towards postnational solidarities, towards becoming 'world citizens', out of humanitarian convictions (Pogge). This trend points out the 'pathological nature' of nationalism, calling for 'more specific remedies or palliatives' (Gellner 10). This also marks the emergence of a critical consciousness that 'we need to take heed of the widening gap between post-national idea(l)s and the nationalist reality' (Wang 144). A plausible postnationalisation of citizenship can inspire one to transgress 'borders and boundaries both of the state and of the conceptual terrain mapped by states' (Schiller and Fouron 156).

COUNTER-CARTOGRAPHIES OF BELONGING

Julia Kristeva imagined 'nations without nationalism' where the gap between 'citizens' and 'foreigners' is minimised on the basis of a realisation that what we call a nation is actually a belongingness among the 'foreigners that we all are (within ourselves and in relation to others)' (47). Kristeva believed that eventually 'the very idea of nation, saturated through mingling of economies and cultures, might open up on other unions where the bond between human beings would be located, thus forcing political discourse to move away from national constraints' (76). In the same vein, in C. L. R. James's description of 'Ellis Island', while reinterpreting Herman Melville, one comes across a postnationalist counter-cartographic account: 'The whole of the world is represented on Ellis Island. Many sailors, but not only sailors; Germans, Italians, Latvians, Swedes, Filipinos, Malays, Chinese, Hindus, Pakistanis, West Indians, Englishmen, Australians, Danes, Yugoslavs, Greeks, Canadians, representatives of every Latin American country' (151). To borrow examples from cricket, the West Indies cricket team and teams in the Indian Premier League (IPL) exemplify a counter-nationalist belonging among men from different countries. What comes through in these transgressive examples is a postnational counter-cartography of belonging.

There is a burgeoning corpus of literature on postnational counter-cartographies. To give a few examples – Kastoryano's study of 'embryonic nations' that form transnational solidarities as 'transnational nations' on the basis of nationalisms without territorial boundaries; Robinson's 'transnational state' of global investors and a transnational capitalist class that look for uniformity in macroeconomic policies across borders; the 'transnational nation-state', as formulated by Schiller, that focuses on a transmigrant agency which influences the administrative state structure of both the states of departure and the transnational migrant settlement; the 'transnation' of diasporas who align themselves beyond the constrictions of national borders (Tololyan); the 'nation-superstate' formulated out of the 'cultural citizenship' of members who have their origins related to the nation but staying in different parts of the world (Choate); the 'Cross-border nationalism' (Pavlasek) among the Czech Protestant community in Serbia; the 'transborder nation' invented by the bureaucratic and political proclaiming of ethno-nationals beyond the territorial border of a state (Kim); the 'network nation' of groupings based on Computer-mediated Communication (CMC) systems (Hiltz and Turoff); and the 'virtual nation' (Levine), exemplified by the 'Bitnation' founded as a virtual sovereignty on 14 July 2014. Another interesting example of the postnational is the e-residency policy in Estonia established in 2015. It allows anyone from any part of the world to obtain a government-issued digital identity in order to access digital public services on par with those available for people who were born in Estonia.

'Postnation' can be understood as the transformation of nation-states into 'continent states' as manifested in continental solidarities like the European Union that has almost all the distinctive characteristics of a state – a parliament, a president, its own embassies, flag, currency, etc. (Sarmela). It is a movement towards becoming planetary states by sharing the aftereffects of post-local economic structures – transnational organisations operating on meritocracy; a worldwide unity emerging out of easy connectivity and mobility; ubiquitous governmental surveillance systems; solidarities aimed at promoting human rights across the world; increased dependence on technology; disintegration of traditional social structures like marriage, and traditional notions of reproduction and family; a widespread digital culture; and the universal impact of a postnational vision of humanity that advocates sustaining ecology and human rights by opposing all sorts of violence. There is a possibility that environmental nationalism may be hijacked by right-wing sectarianism (Sharma). However, one can hope that in the post–Covid-19 era, bioregional endeavours of 'ecological nationalisms' (Cederlof and Sivaramakrishnan) will be more sincerely interlinked with concerns of global risks, thereby promoting an ecological internationalism.

Postnationalism has been criticised for its 'moral poverty', as remarked by Hansen, for it devalues 'the importance of hard won rights that attach only to national citizenship' (14). On the other hand, philosophers like Nussbaum have been advocating a postnational cosmopolitanism through which 'one should always view the good of humanity as a whole as one's goal' (Nussbaum,

'Climate Change' 473). Nussbaum envisions a 'globally sensitive patriotism' which emphasises that 'when a nation is conceived around ideas of inclusion and human dignity, it can easily lead to a struggle for these ideas everywhere' ('Toward a Globally Sensitive Patriotism' 88). However, Nussbaum also wants to revise the notion of an abstract and rootless cosmopolitanism, and argues for an 'uneven dialectical oscillation within ourselves, as we accept the constraints of some strong duties to humanity, and then ask ourselves how far we are entitled to devote ourselves to the particular people and places whom we love' (80), which ultimately 'makes plenty of room for patriotism' (80). It will also make space for a celebration of diverse local human ways of being/becoming instead of a homogenous global humanism and, thereby, push for a situated cosmopolitanism in the form of a 'cosmopolitan patriot'. The cosmopolitan patriot celebrates 'the variety of human cultures'; is rooted 'loyal to one local society (or a few) that you count as home'; is a 'liberal convinced of the value of the individual; and patriotic celebrating the institutions of the state (or states) within which you live' (Appiah 633).

The postnationalist ethos of expansion and inclusiveness, which rejects globalisation's 'undifferentiated notion of culture', can be traced among various traditions: traditions of African American spirituality as underscored by Cornell West, the ideal of collective empathy in the Buddhist *sarvabhutadaya*, African humanism or *Ubuntu* (Cornell), the Upanishadic ideal of *vasudhaivakutumbakam* ('the world is one family'), or the Jaina notion of *syadvada* (interrelation among all things). To give more examples – Benjamin Lee's 'critical internationalism' which proposes a 'decentered vision' (575) developed through a 'comparative perspective' that can look 'beyond multiculturalism and international studies' (579); and the concept of 'postnational constellation', developed by Habermas, where the 'incorporation of each individual state into the binding cooperative procedures of a cosmopolitan community of states would have to be perceived as a part of states' own domestic policies' (55).

Many theorists have studied postnational cosmopolitanism using a variety of paradigms. Benita Parry describes 'global flows' towards an 'emergent *postcolonial* cosmopolitanism' (41, original emphasis); Paul Gilroy's planetary cosmopolitanism; Bhabha's 'vernacular cosmopolitans' who are 'translating between cultures, renegotiating traditions from a position where "locality" insists on its own terms, while entering into larger national and societal conversations' ('The Vernacular Cosmopolitan' 139), and 'subaltern secularism' (*The Location of Culture*); Avtar Brah's diasporic ethics; and Vandana Shiva's anti-global neohumanism. Extending the postnational vision, Weinbaum and Edwards have put forward the concept of a 'critical globality' that can associate globality with critical considerations for diverse national exceptionalisms and various forms of marginalisations related to class, race and unequal development (270). Taking into consideration the multisite context of global migration (where the refugees are kept in temporary camps of the host state, deported to their source state, from where they again try to migrate to a foreign state), Laguerre has framed the idea of a 'cosmonation'. It is a transborder 'cultural demographic collectivity' that represents a 'transfrontier social formation' by 'those who do not have a collective homeland' (25). Surveying a range of such theories, a postnational solidarity seems to be best articulated as a discursively negotiated

> . . . networked practice composed of a vast web of actors who labour to create nodes of commonality and points of intersection out of shifting, cross-cutting lines of affinity that remain grounded in local and national settings. This web takes the form of a patchwork pragmatically assembled and reassembled from disparate and overlapping pieces, rather than a pre-established, neatly laid out and carefully followed plan. (Kurasawa 177)

POSTNATIONAL INTIMACY

'Postnation', as discussed above, is a condition emerging out of a postnational imaginary aimed at a nonterritorial, international allegiance. While recognising the pluralisms of national cultures, 'postnation' promotes a disengagement from nationalist hegemony, and thereby, transforms the state-bound individual identity and augments the geopolitical belonging. It forges a concern for all deterritorialised groups – like the Haitian refugees in Miami or Nicaraguan labourers in Tucson – which eventually gives birth to a cosmopolitan outlook through a translocational intimacy. Leela Gandhi has theorised postnation as a space of 'mutual contagion and subtle intimacies' (129) among the various nations. It is a location where people moving beyond the fixities of the nation-state can arrive at; a juncture (like the 'West Indies' imagined by the cricketers) of no boundaries which entails both the postponement of local identity and its occasional patriotic re-evocation.

Contemporary forms of postnational intimacies include the worldwide forums of social engagements, movements outside the conventional political/institutional frameworks, new forms of postnative art, and 'free enclaves' like temporary autonomous zones (TAZs). The World Social Forum (WSF), representing a multicentric networked intimacy of 'a large number of people, dispersed among most of the nations of the world, who, in contesting the way the world is run, regard each other, most of the time, as allies' (Monbiot 2), is a postnational coordination of civil society activists. As the Forum's 'Charter of Principles' states, it includes people who are 'opposed to neoliberalism and to domination of the world by capital and any form of imperialism, and are committed to building a planetary society directed towards fruitful relationships among Humankind and between it and the Earth' (Web n. p.). ATTAC (Association for the Taxation of Financial Transactions and Aid to Citizens) is another international forum opposed to globalisation, aspiring to create a postnational 'another world' through resistance against 'commercialisation of natural resources', supermarketisation, and 'global economic competition and free markets'. By 'pooling worldwide solidarity and global financing', ATTAC tries to ensure the protection of 'the common goods of humanity (health care, education, water, climate, biodiversity, . . .)' (ATTAC, Web n. p.).

A postnational togetherness can be perceived in various social movements. The many instances include the transnational cooperation among states across the world based on the 2030 Agenda for Sustainable Development, movements around food security such as the 'food sovereignty' movement (nations like Senegal,

Ecuador, Bolivia, Nepal, Mali and Venezuela have constitutionally incorporated this), or 'Slow Food' activism that blends gustatory pleasure with social activism, to spread the message of 'peace, well-being, innovation, tradition, pleasure, happiness, and our desire that Good, Clean, and Fair food be available for everyone' (Petrini, Web n. p.); and various postnational technopolitical movements like #wejustneedtopee, #BringBackOurGirls and other such social media campaigns.

In this context, it is interesting to bring up Žižek's study of the Covid-19 pandemic of 2020. He points out the two major transformations that the pandemic brought out. First, the unrest about the governments' ability to tackle the crisis made one realise that 'being ashamed of one's country, not love of it, may be the true mark of belonging to it' (58). Second, the instances of postnational intimacy. An example of the latter took place when the Israeli Prime Minister Benjamin Netanyahu eagerly offered to help the Palestinian Authority to tackle the pandemic, 'not out of goodness and human consideration, but for the simple fact that it is impossible to separate Jews and Palestinians there—if one group is affected, the other will inevitably also suffer'. Another example of postnational intimacy is the rendering of nationalist claims like 'America (or whosoever else) First' ineffective (14–15). Žižek hopes that there will be a rekindling of 'global solidarity and cooperation' through 'local mobilization of people outside state control' in order to move 'beyond the machinery of single governments' towards an effective postnational 'coordination and collaboration' (67–68).

There is an urgent need to inculcate an effective postnationalism so that globally societies will not become more isolationist in a post–Covid-19 world. We should not displace hyper-globalisation with hyper-nationalism. As Happymon Jacob points out, there is a real danger of a 'new-age racism' emerging through 'state intervention in economic matters and protectionism' (Web n. p.). Contemporary instances, like Cuba assisting Italy to fight the pandemic and the call for the 'progressive international' by Bernie Sanders and Yanis Varoufakis, may, as Noam Chomsky has observed, result in dismantling profit-based globalisation with the realisation that a 'genuine internationalism' based on affective ties among common people in various parts of the world is the only remedy for the 'neoliberal plague' (Rodriguez, Web n. p.). The message of tolerance delivered by the newly elected US President Joe Biden (2021) has renewed the hope for a postnational intimacy: 'It's time to put away the harsh rhetoric, to lower the temperature, to see each other again, to listen to each other again' (Wong, Web n. p.).

Hakim Bey uses the idea of a postnational uprising led by temporary autonomous zones (TAZ), virtual 'gypsies' and 'wanderers with shallow loyalties', replacing the 'technonationalism' of state-sponsored cyber war on enemy states. This postnational uprising is driven by the desire to de-hierarchise the limited accessibility of data by 'counter-Net' activities which include data-piracy, hacking and all sorts of 'clandestine illegal and rebellious use of the Web' (Bey 404). The rave counterculture of 'digital art-religion', based on a combination of music, dance, drugs, trance and travel, is another example of a postnational affinity that, since its beginning during the 1980s, has turned into a revolutionary political movement. This movement is led by neo-nomads from various nation-states who pull themselves together 'in unison', where 'the post-industrial alienated individual sacrifices the self ritually to achieve a spiritual transition into a cyborg-like subjectivity' (Rietveld 55). In the process, they assert 'the will of a significant portion of society to organize and gather for the purposes of creating a new community', to make 'the political statement that we are all equal, and that no matter how different we may think we are, on a more tribal level, we all have the same basic needs as human beings' (Fritz 216–17). Goa, often perceived as 'a melting point for East and West' (D'Andrea 193), for instance, has become a hub of postnational neo-nomads where 'rave' has acquired an overtly religious status: 'Goa trance was mystical music, a rave was a satsang, the DJ was a guru' (Partridge 47).

Art and cinema represent postnation as an alter-identity that prioritises routes over roots without getting completely de-rooted. There are numerous examples like the postnational art of Thai artists Araya Rasdjarmrearnsook and Pinaree Sanpitak. One can also point to the transformation of French 'national' cinema towards becoming postnational since the late 1980s, as reflected in films like *Valmont* (1989), *L'Amant* (The Lover, 1992) and *1492 Christophe Colomb* (1492, Conquest of Paradise, 1992), which consciously downplay their 'Frenchness' (Danan).

CONCLUSION: NATIONALISM IN CONTEMPORARY INDIA AND THE IDEAL OF A PATRIOTIC PLANETARISM

Canadian Prime Minister Justin Trudeau argues that Canada can be regarded as the world's first postnational state, 'There is no core identity, no mainstream in Canada' (Foran). This remark has implications for India where the 'mainstream' majoritarianism is being structured around popular concepts of a 'Hindu Rashtra', strategically propagated by contemporary ultranationalist leaders. This majoritarianism runs counter to India's reverence for the ideal of 'humanity' which was a counterpoint to the European concept of a limited 'national identity'. This reverence for the ideal of humanity comes across clearly in the non-sectarian humanist/modernist positions embraced by Indian postnationalist thinkers like Nehru, Iqbal, Tagore and Gandhi.

Having discovered India's uniqueness – 'the continuity of a cultural tradition through five thousand years of history, of invasion and upheaval, a tradition which was widespread among the masses and powerfully influenced them' (52) – Nehru asserted that '[w]e shall have to put an end to the national state and devise a collectivism which neither degrades nor enslaves' (543). Beck has described Nehru's uncompleted 'politics of postnationalism' where 'the cosmopolitan project contradicts and replaces the nation-state project' (14).

Iqbal's postnationalism is ambivalently conveyed in his elaboration of the notion of selfhood (*khudi*): 'In the higher Sufism of Islam unitive experience is not the finite ego effacing its own identity by some sort of absorption into the Infinite Ego; it is rather the Infinite passing into the loving embrace of the finite' (Iqbal, *The Reconstruction of Religious Thought in Islam* 88). His description in *Javid Nama* – where at the dawn of creation 'everywhere out of the rapture and yearning [*zauq va shauq*] for the seizing of selfhood [*khud-gari*] / arose the cry I am another [*digaram*] and you are yet another [*digari*]' (13) – affirms that Iqbal was obliquely postnational, despite his contradictions.

Tagore approached the 'national' in multiple ways – '*deshabhiman*', '*swadeshprem*', '*deshbhakti*', '*swadeshchetana*' – during his early life. Eventually, based on his '*visvovod*' – or 'Vision of Non-National Neo-Universalism' (Quayum) – Tagore evolved himself into an ardent postnational critic of nationalism:

> The hungry self of the Nation shall burst,
> in a violence of fury from its own shameless feeding
> For it has made the world its food. ('The Sunset of the Century' qtd. in *Nationalism* 80–81)

Tagore's postnationalism emerges from his realisation that 'the Nation is the greatest evil for the Nation, that all its precautions are against it, and any new birth of its fellow in the world is always followed in its mind by the dread of a new peril' (*Nationalism* 17–18).

Contemporary India has witnessed the gradual transformation of the modern state into a biopolitical machinery regulating the lives of the inhabitants in terms of, as Foucault has described in another context, 'value and utility' (Foucault, *The History of Sexuality* 144). This is sanctioned by the state, and is often in contradiction with the notions of worth and usefulness as perceived by the people. As Foucault points out in *Society Must Be Defended*, nationalism has proved to be a viable means of validating 'a "biopolitics" of the human race' (243) where the 'value and utility' of the state, if projected strategically as a prerequisite for protecting the 'national' concern and propagated profitably in provoking hypernational sentiments of the countrymen, seems to effectively derive a majoritarian support from the nation. As Agamben has shown, oppressive nationalism strips people of 'every political status' and reduces them to a 'bare life' (*Homo Sacer* 171). Agamben also introduces the idea of the 'state of exception'. The oppressive state builds camps or creates a camp-like condition in an entire region, where 'everything is possible' (170), which gradually turns into a prolonged, undeviating condition in the name of national security: 'the declaration of the state of exception has gradually been replaced by an unprecedented generalization of the paradigm of security as the normal technique of government' (Agamben, *State of Exception* 14). One may argue that contemporary India has witnessed many instances – such as the state's response to people displaced by the Sardar Sarovar Dam, the widespread euphoria of hypernationalism witnessed in various parts of the country, the state's implementation of National Register of Citizens (NRC) in Assam, the conditions in post–Article-370 Kashmir, and cases of mobocracy – of the emergence of a 'camp nationalism'. In a 'camp nationalism', 'citizens can be said . . . to appear virtually as *homines sacri* [those reduced to a state of bare life]' (*Homo Sacer* 111).

It is in this context that one might want to recall, and return to, Tagore's and Gandhi's notions and ideals of nationalism. The postnational in Tagore can be easily discerned in his ideas of '*jiban-debota*' and '*mukti*''. The notion of '*jiban-debota*' implies a life where living itself becomes worship when it is directed at the search for that part of God, contained in Man, which is guided by the principle of love – for 'we have our greatest delight when we realize ourselves in others, and this is the definition of love' (Das 102). The idea of '*mukti*' implies freedom from all sorts of practices which erect immutable and immovable walls between people. The principle of 'hospitality' – as opposed to hostility – which dominates all his writings on '*Visva-Bharati*' and '*Visva-Sahitya*' (world literature) pleads for the demise of nation-states, which may pave way for a postnational global order based on a deep sense of sympathy, sacrifice and mutual understanding. Tagore envisions a morally and politically enlightened principle of reciprocal recognitions and harmony of adjustments for an intimate multicultural 'unity within diversity . . . the underlying unity that federate all apparent differences without undermining the external differences' (Tagore, *Itihas* 10).

In Mahatma Gandhi too one can perceive, in Appadurai's words, a 'postnational patriotism' (Appadurai, *Modernity at Large*): 'Our patriotism is so conceived that we want our freedom not to injure the freedom of any other country or any single individual. We believe . . . in the greatest good of all, including the meanest of creatures amongst all God's creation' (Gandhi, *Collected Works* Vol. 53 349). Guided by his inner spiritual domain (*adhyatma*), Gandhi's patriotic discourse of *swaraj* (self-rule) allows him to aspire for *sarvodaya* (welfare for all), through compassion (*karuna*), non-violence (*ahimsa*), and a postnational capacity to sacrifice for the others' sake (*tapas*). Gandhi's patriotic ideal of *swaraj*, and his postnational ideal of universal welfare enunciated by *sarvodaya* (Bondurant 156), can be correlated with various perspectives related to posthumanism – particularly Peter-Paul Verbeek's post-anthropological shift to connect the 'human' with 'non-human', and the notion of 'panhumanity' (Franklin, Lury and Stacey 26) that upholds a sense of interconnected interdependence between humans and the non-human planetary ambiance. Such a perspective inspires one to argue that from postnationalism, we are heading towards a quest for harmony through a patriotic planetarism.

As Guha points out, in India, 'anti-patriotism . . . cronyism . . . and the global rise of nativism and fundamentalism have acted as a spur . . . a provocation to the rise of jingoism' (Web n. p.). It is in this context that one needs to derive inspiration from Bloch, from his idea of 'the *Not* as *Not Yet*' which 'passes straight through Becoming and beyond it' (37). Bloch's idea and ideal raises the prospect of multiple, evolving and endless affiliations across space, time, races and ethnicities. To exemplify this with a catalogue of affiliations – it is this 'principle of hope' that inspires the patriotic planetarism of a Bengali queer living in Darjeeling to forge a vernacular nationalistic bond with Bengalis living in Bengaluru; participate in an intercultural exchange with Limbu ethnic groups based on a constitutional nationalism; share a cross-border nationalist bond with Bangladeshi citizens; remain a transnational 'non-indigenous ally' of Dalit movements, or a 'honorary Dalit'; be a global human rights activist associated, virtually, with environmental campaigns; retain a cosmonational intimacy with the global Sindhi diaspora or the Tibetans in exile; inculcate a cosmopolitan love for world music; share a posthuman intimacy with the adopted red panda in the Darjeeling zoo; be involved with the queer postnation across the globe; and provide, out of patriotism, occasional donations to the Prime Minister's Relief Fund. Hence, the ideal of the patriotic planetarist is based on such endless affiliations that accumulate in the course of an eternal expansion of a patriot's shifting associations with every aspect of the planet.

REFERENCES

Agamben, Giorgio. *Homo Sacer: Sovereign Power and Bare Life*. Tr. D. Heller-Roazen. Stanford: Stanford UP, 1998. Print.

---. *State of Exception*. Tr. K. Attell. Chicago: U of Chicago P, 2005. Print.

Appadurai, Arjun. 'Dead Certainty: Ethnic Violence in the Era of Globalization'. *Development and Change* 29 (1998): 905–25. Print.

---. *Modernity at Large: Cultural Dimensions of Globalization*. Minneapolis: U of Minnesota P, 1996. Print.

Appiah, Kwame Anthony. 'Cosmopolitan Patriots'. *Critical Inquiry* 23.3 (1997): 617–39. Print.

ATTAC. 'An Organization for Another World'. 1998. Web. 6 November 2020. <https://www.attac.org/en/overview>.

Beck, Ulrich. 'Sociology in the Second Age of Modernity'. *Conceiving Cosmopolitanism*. Ed. Robin Cohen, and Steven Vertovec. Oxford: Oxford UP, 2002. Print.

Bey, Hakim. 'The Temporary Autonomous Zone'. *Crypto Anarchy, Cyberstates, and Pirate Utopias*. Ed. Peter Ludlow. Cambridge: MIT Press, 2001. 401–34. Print.

Bhabha, Homi. *The Location of Culture*. London: Routledge, 1994. Print.

---. 'The Vernacular Cosmopolitan'. *Voices of the Crossing: The Impact of Britain on Writers from Asia, the Caribbean, and Africa*. Ed. Ferdinand Dennis, and Naseem Khan. London: Serpent's Tail, 2000. 133–42. Print.

Bloch, Ernest. *The Principle of Hope. Vol. I*. Trans. Francoise Wuilmart. Paris: Gallimard, 1976. Print.

Bondurant, Joan V. *Conquest of Violence: The Gandhian Philosophy of Conflict*. Princeton: Princeton UP, 1958. Print.

Bonikowski, Bart. 'Varieties of Popular Nationalism in Modern Democracies: An Inductive Approach to Comparative Research on Political Culture.' WCFIA Working Paper (2013). Weathered Center for International Affairs, Harvard University, Cambridge, MA. Print.

Bosniak, Linda S. 'The State of Citizenship: Citizenship Denationalized'. *Indiana Journal of Global Legal Studies* 7.2: 447–510. Print.

Brah, Avtar. *Cartographies of Diaspora: Contesting Identities*. London: Routledge, 1996. Print.

Braidotti, Rosi, Patrick Hanafin, and Bolette Blaagaard, eds. *After Cosmopolitanism*. New York: Routledge, 2013. Print.

Buttle, Nicholas. 'Critical Nationalism: A Liberal Prescription?'. *Nations and Nationalism* 6.1 (2000): 111–27. Print.

Cederlof, Gunnel, and Kalyanakrishnan Sivaramakrishnan, ed. *Ecological Nationalisms: Nature, Livelihoods, and Identifies in South Asia*. Seattle: U of Washington P, 2006. Print.

Choate, Mark I. *Emigrant Nation: The Making of Italy Abroad.* Cambridge: Harvard UP, 2008. Print.

Cornell, Drucilla. The Ubuntu Project with Stellenbosch University. 2002. Web. 5 November 2020. <https://www.fehe.org/index.php?id=281>.

D'Andrea, Anthony. *Global Nomads: Techno and New Age as Transnational Countercultures in Ibiza and Goa*. New York: Routledge, 2007. Print.

Danan, Martine. 'From a "Prenational" to a "Postnational" French Cinema'. *Film History* 8.1 (1996): 72–84. Print.

Das, Sisir Kumar, ed. *The English Writings of Rabindranath Tagore: Vol. 3*. New Delhi: Sahitya Akademi, 1996. Print.

Derrida, Jacques. *Without Alibi*. Trans. and ed. Peggy Kamuf. California: Stanford UP, 2002. Print.

Duffield, Mark. 'Global Civil War: The Non-Insured, International Containment and Post-Interventionary Society'. *Journal of Refugee Studies* 21 (2008): 145–65. Print.

Foran, Charles. 'The Canada experiment: Is This the World's First "Postnational" Country?'. *The Guardian*, 4 January 2017. Print.

Foucault, Michel. *Society Must Be Defended: Lectures at the Collège de France, 1975–76*. Tr. D. Macey. Ed. M. Bertani, and A. I. Davidson. London: Penguin, 2003. Print.

---. *The History of Sexuality, Volume 1: An Introduction*. Tr. R. Hurley. London: Penguin, 1990. Print.

Franklin, Sarah, Celia Lury, and Jackie Stacey. *Global Nature, Global Culture*. London: Sage, 2000. Print.

Fritz, Jimi. *Rave Culture: An Insider's Overview*. Victoria: Smallfry Press, 1999. Print.

Gandhi, Leela. *Postcolonial Theory: A Critical Introduction*. New South Wales: Allen and Unwin, 1998. Print.

Gandhi, Mohandas K. *Collected Works of Mahatma Gandhi*. 98 vols. New Delhi: Publications Division, 1999. Print.

Gellner, Ernest. *Nationalism*. New York: New York UP, 1998. Print.

Gilroy, Paul. *Against Race: Imaging Political Culture Beyond the Colour Line*. Cambridge: Harvard UP, 2000. Print.

Grewal, Inderpal, and Caren Kaplan, eds. *Scattered Hegemonies: Postmodernity and Transnational Feminist Practices*. Minneapolis: U of Minnesota P, 1994. Print.

Guha, Ramachamdra. 'Patriotism Vs Jingoism'. *Outlook*. 24 January 2018. Web. 9 November 2020. <https://www.outlookindia.com/magazine/story/patriotism-vs-jingoism/299735>.

Habermas, Jurgen. *The Postnational Constellation: Political Essays*. Tr. and ed. Max Pensky. Cambridge: MIT Press, 2001. Print.

Hansen, R. 'The Poverty of Postnationalism: Citizenship, Immigration, and the New Europe'. *Theory and Society* 38.1 (2009): 1–24. Print.

Hiltz, Starr Roxanne, and Murray Turoff. *The Network Nation*. Cambridge: MIT Press, 1993. Print.

Iqbal, Muhammad. *Javid Nama. Kulliyat-e Farsi*. Lahore: Sheikh Ghulam & Sons, 1985. Print.

---. *The Reconstruction of Religious Thought in Islam*. Lahore: Institute of Islamic Culture, 1989. Print.

Jacob, Happymon. 'COVID-19 and the Crumbling World Order'. *The Hindu*. 13 April 2020. Web. 8 November 2020. <https://www.thehindu.com/opinion/op-ed/covid-19-and-the-crumbling-world-order/article31324259.ece>.

James, C. L. R. *Mariners, Renegades and Castaways: The Story of Herman Melville and the World We Live In*. Ed. Donald E. Pease. Hanover, NH: Dartmouth College Press, 2001. Print.

Kastoryano, Riva. *Vers un nationalisme transnational: Redéfinir la nation, le nationalsime et le territoire* ['Towards a Transnational Nationalism: Redefining the Nation, the Nationalism and the Territory']. *Revue Française de Science Politique* 56.4 (2006): 533–53. Print.

Kim, Jaeeun. 'The Making and Unmaking of a "Transborder Nation": South Korea During and After the Cold War'. *Theory and Society* 38.2 (2009): 133–64. Print.

Kristeva, Julia. *Nations Without Nationalism*. Trans. Leon S. Roudiez. New York: Columbia UP, 1993. Print.

Kurasawa, Fuyuki. *The Work of Global Justice: Human Rights as Practices*. Cambridge: Cambridge UP, 2007. Print.

Laguerre, Michel S. *The Multisite Nation: Crossborder Organizations, Transfrontier Infrastructure, and Global Digital Public Sphere*. Berkeley: Palgrave Macmillan, 2016. Print.

Lee, Benjamin. 'Critical Internationalism'. *Public Culture* 7.3 (1995): 559-92. Print.

Levine, Donald N. 'Reconfiguring the Ethiopian Nation in a Global Era'. *Analise Sociale* 41.2 (2011): 311–27. Print.

Lloyd, Genevieve. *Spinoza and the Ethics*. London: Routledge, 1996. Print.

Mbembe, Achille. 'Necropolitics'. *Public Culture* 15.1 (2003): 11–40. Print.

Monbiot, George. *Manifesto for a New World Order*. New York: The New Press, 2003. Print.

Nehru, Jawaharlal. *The Discovery of India*. New York: John Day, 1946. Print.

Nussbaum, Martha. 'Climate Change: Why Theories of Justice Matter'. *Chicago Journal of International Law* 13 (2013): 469–85. Print.

---. 'Toward a Globally Sensitive Patriotism'. *Daedalus* 137.3 (2008): 78–93. Print.

Parisi, Luciana. *Abstract Sex: Philosophy, Biotechnology, and the Mutation of Desire*. London: Continuum Press, 2004. Print.

Parry, Benita. 'The Contradictions of Cultural Studies'. *Transition* 53 (1991): 37–45. Print.

Partridge, Christopher. 'The Spiritual and the Revolutionary: Alternative Spirituality, British Free Festivals, and the Emergence of Rave Culture.' *Culture and Religion* 7.1 (2006): 42–60. Print.

Pavlasek, Michal. 'Cross-Border Nationalism and Religious Fellowship. A Case Study of the Czech Protestant Community in Serbia'. *Cultural Permeations: Anthropological Perspectives*. Ed. Srdjan Radović. Belgrade, 2013. Print.

Petrini, Carlo. 'Taking Back Life: The Earth, the Moon and Abundance'. 2007. Web. 8 November 2020. <https://slowfoodlondon.blogs.com/acta/files/02_visions_and_projects_en.pdf>.

Petryna, Adriana. *Life Exposed: Biological Citizens after Chernobyl*. Princeton: Princeton UP, 2002. Print.

Pogge, Thomas. 'Cosmopolitanism and Sovereignty'. *Ethics* 103.1 (1992): 48–75. Print.

Puar, Jasbir. *Terrorist Assemblages: Homonationalism in Queer Times*. Durham: Duke UP, 2007. Print.

Quayum, Mohammad A. 'Paradisiacal Imagination: Rabindranath Tagore's *Visvovod* or Vision of Non-National Neo-Universalism'. *Quodlibet: The Australian Journal of Trans-national Writing* 1 (2005): Web. 9 December 2020. <https://fhrc.flinders.edu.au/ejournals/quodlibet/vol1/downloads/Tagore.pdf>.

Rietveld, Hillegonda C. 'Ephemeral Spirit: Sacrificial Cyborg and Communal Soul'. *Rave Culture and Religion*. Ed. Graham St. John. London: Routledge, 2004. 46–62. Print.

Robinson, William I. 'Social Theory and Globalization: The Rise of a Transnational State'. *Theory and Society* 30.2 (2001): 157–200. Print.

Rodriguez, Jared. 'Chomsky and Pollin: To Heal From COVID-19, We Must Imagine a Different World'. *Truthout*. Web. 8 November 2020. <https://truthout.org/articles/chomsky-and-pollin-to-heal-from-covid-19-we-must-imagine-a-different-world/>.

Sarmela, Matti. 'Postnationalism'. *The Wiley Blackwell Encyclopedia of Race, Ethnicity, and Nationalism*. Ed. John Stone et al. New Jersey: Wiley, 2016. 1671–81. Print.

Sassen, Saskia. 'The Need to Distinguish Denationalized and Postnational'. *Indiana Journal of Global Legal Studies* 7.2 (2000): 575–84. Print.

Schiller, Nina Glick. 'Transnational Nation-states and their Citizens: The Asian Experience'. *Globalization and the Asia-Pacific: Contested Territories*. Ed. Peter Dicken et al. New York: Routledge, 1999. Print.

Schiller, Nina Glick, and Georges Fouron. 'Transnational Lives and National Identities: The Identity Politics of Haitian Immigrants'. *Transnationalism from Below*. Ed. Michael P. Smith, and Louis E. Guarnizo. New Brunswick: Transaction Publishers, 1998. 130–61. Print.

Sharma, Mukul. *Green and Saffron: Hindu Nationalism and Indian Environmental Politics*. Ranikhet: Permanent Black, 2012. Print.

Shiva, Vandana. *Biopiracy: The Plunder of Nature and Knowledge*. Boston: South End Press, 1997. Print.

Soysal, Yasemin Nohuglu. 'Changing Parameters of Citizenship and Claims-Making: Organized Islam in European Public Spheres'. *Theory and Society* 26.4 (1997): 509–27. Print.

---. *Limits of Citizenship: Migrants and Postnational Membership in Europe*. Chicago: U of Chicago P, 1994. Print.

Tagore, Rabindranath. *Itihas* [History]. Visva-bharati: Kolkata, 1946. Print.

---. *Nationalism*. Madras: Macmillan India, 1976. Print.

Tololyan, Khachig. 'The American Model of Diasporic Discourse'. *Diasporas and Ethnic Migrants*. Ed. Rainer Munz, and Rainer Ohliger. London: Frank Cass, 2003. Print.

Touraine, Alain. *Can We Live Together?: Equality and Difference*. Trans. David Macey. Stanford: Stanford UP, 2000. Print.

Verbeek, Peter-Paul. *Moralizing Technology: Understanding and Designing the Morality of Things*. Chicago: U of Chicago P, 2011. Print.

Virilio, Paul. *Desert Screen: War at the Speed of Light*. London: Continuum, 2002. Print.

Wang, Horng-luen. 'Mind the Gap: On Post-National Idea(l)s and the Nationalist Reality'. *Social Analysis: The International Journal of Social and Cultural Practice* 46.2 (2002): 139–47. Print.

Weinbaum, Alys Eve, and Brent Hayes Edwards. 'On Critical Globality'. *Ariel: A Review of International English Literature* 31.1 and 2 (2000): 255–74. Print.

West, Cornell. *Prophetic Thought in Postmodern Times*. Monroe: Common Courage Press, 1994. Print.

Wong, Julia Carrie. 'Unity Amid Diversity: Key Takeaways from Biden's and Harris's Speeches'. *The Guardian*. Web. 9 December 2020. <https://www.theguardian.com/us-news/2020/nov/07/joe-biden-kamala-harris-victory-speeches-key-takeaways>.

World Social Forum (WSF). 'World Social Forum Charter of Principles'. 2002. Web. 6 November 2020. <https://fsm2016.org/en/sinformer/a-propos-du-forum-social-mondial/>.

Žižek, Slavoj. *Pandemic! Covid-19 Shakes the World.* New York and London: OR Books, 2020. Print.

Glossary of Select Terms

Biopolitics: Coined by Rudolf Kjellén, 'biopolitics' may be regarded as an intersectional study of political science and biology. Kjellén used the term to describe how the state as a quasi-biological organism deals with the 'civil war' between various communities that comprise the state. According to Michel Foucault, the term denotes the mechanism by which the government, through the deployment of political and state machineries, regulates each and every aspect of the public life in the state.

Cosmopolitanism: The term is derived from the Greek '*kosmopolites*', meaning 'citizens of the world'. Cosmopolitanism, as a socio-political philosophy, advocates that irrespective of the differences in their origins and political affiliations, all human beings are to be considered as part of a single universal community of global citizens. The primary objective of cosmopolitanism is to foster a global commitment among people of diverse nations to promote human rights, justice and multiculturalism, and to minimise international economic inequalities.

Ecoglobalism: Inspired by contemporary risk research, ecocriticism and globalisation, ecoglobalism addresses issues related to environmental risks, worldwide. Its foundation is the realisation that the entire world faces the risk of various environmental crises (such as climate change, acid rain, etc.), and that the global environmental crisis is intimately connected with local environmental anxieties. Proponents of ecoglobalism try to address issues of environmental concerns on a planetary scale, as a shared risk experience of the global community.

Governmentality: Michel Foucault defined the term as the technique using which the state, in order to curtail its role as a centralised apparatus for imposing power from above, turns the general public into self-regulated beings. This is achieved through the masses internalising ideologies that are sanctioned by the state and propagated by the government. Certain forms of knowledge are produced and effectively disseminated through institutions such as schools, asylums, hospitals and prisons, so that individuals are auto-corrected as per the desires of the government and, thereby, turned into auto-regulated agents of the state.

Green/Eco nationalism: It is a communitarian outlook aimed at minimising the nation's dependency for energy and fuel on foreign sources, by promoting alternative resources available within the territorial boundaries of the nation-state. It also promotes conservation of endangered species and indigenous ecologies. As an extreme form of national pride, green/eco nationalism might result in an isolationist agenda, and treat all other nations as possible threats to the ecology of one's own territory.

Hypernationalism: This refers to the belief that one's own nation-state is superior over all others. Hypernationalism, also known as ultranationalism, emerges out of an extreme form of divisive, national jingoism, which often brands anyone who is critical of the state machineries as 'anti-national'.

Multinationalism: This refers to the various concerns related to the impact of, and challenges and transformations that emerge from, the cultural diversities among communities within a sovereign territory. These diversities may be based on ethnic, linguistic or religious differences. Multiculturalism – as opposed to the 'melting pot' notion of minority communities getting coopted within majoritarian ethos – aims to safeguard the uniqueness of the various 'little traditions' within the nation-state. It treats minority groups – as well as immigrants who want to be a part of the plural society – as equals.

Neocolonialism: Neocolonialism is used in two different senses. First, to refer to the authoritarian intrusion of powerful nations in influencing the economies, cultures and politics of developing nations. This is not carried out directly through armed invasions, but achieved under the guise of providing 'assistance'. Second, to provide a counter-narrative to the argument that colonialism ended when foreign rulers were ousted from the colonies. In this sense, neocolonialism underscores that postcolonial governments continue to replicate colonial oppression, resulting in the internal colonisation of various marginalised people and communities.

Neoliberalism: This refers to the twentieth-century phenomenon of reviving nineteenth-century notions related to the liberalisation of state-governed economies through encouraging competitive free-market policies. In sociopolitical domain, neoliberalism refers to a paradigm shift in focus – from strengthening human collectivities (for example, trade unions, family, etc.) to promoting human beings as 'individuals'. Ultimately, like the pro-market policies which are framed around finance capitalism and profit–loss calculations, human existence too comes to be valued in terms of consumption and self-gratification, widening social, political and cultural inequalities.

Official nationalism: Official nationalism signifies an officially generated nationalism, or a 'nationalism from above' (unlike the 'popular' nationalism or the 'nationalism from below' that spontaneously evolves from a mass awakening). Official nationalism is imposed on the masses by the elite ruling class, through continuous circulation and manipulation, with the help of various instruments of state propaganda.

Planetarity: The term was coined by Gayatri Chakraborty Spivak to counter the homogenising tendency of globalisation, through a Utopian vision of the economic ascendancy of the Global South and refers to the impossibility of representing the planet in a uniform manner. Nowadays, the term is used to imply the significance of understanding the relationality of the planetary condition. It explores the world of relations, not only among human beings but also among the human and the non-human elements of the planet.

Quasi-state: This refers to a state that is yet to be created formally but has been demanded by a secessionist or a home-rule movement. A quasi-state represents the desires of a people who feel that they represent a separate nation (proto-nation) within the nation-state where they have their 'official' citizenship. Therefore, they demand a separate nation-state of their own. Many of them like Croatia, Macedonia, Bosnia and Herzegovina, Serbia, Slovenia and Montenegro, within the former Yugoslavia, have attained complete statehood. Some others like QwaQwa which was granted self-government in 1974 but was re-integrated with

South Africa in 1994, have remained as quasi-states. Other examples of quasi-states include the Federal Republic of Ambazonia in Cameroon.

Self-determination: This refers to the process through which a group of people, who imagine themselves as a separate nation and inculcate some degree of national consciousness, strive to form their own sovereign state and form their own government. The right to self-determination is considered to be one of the central principles of international law.

Subnationalism: Subnationalism implies a decentralised concern and anxiety among a particular group of citizens to assert their identity around specific issues. Subnationalist groups believe that their concerns are not properly represented or addressed by the nation-state, and suffer from a sense of being excluded. Subnationalism, thus, may arise out of demands (not necessarily secessionist) of groups of citizens for sufficient provisions to overcome their sense of depravation. This sense of being excluded from the mainstream is often related to a specific regional/linguistic/ethnic identity, or any other identity which remains unacknowledged within the nation-state.

Transnationalism: Transnationalism represents a hybrid cross-civilisational consciousness of interconnection among countries and continents. It is a result of rapid cross-border economic and sociocultural exchanges created by migration and diasporic communities. Transnationalism manifests in the formation of supranational associations, non-governmental organisations, networked/cyber communities, and 'people-led' civil society movements.

Texts for Further Reading

Billig, Michael. *Banal Nationalism*. London: Sage, 1995. Print.

Breen, Keith, and Shane O'Neill, eds. *After the Nation? Critical Reflections on Nationalism and Postnationalism*. London: Palgrave Macmillan, 2010. Print.

Cohen, Joshua, ed. *For Love of Country: Debating the Limits of Patriotism*. By Martha Nussbaum and respondents. Boston: Beacon Press, 1996. Print.

Dieckoff, Alain, ed. *The Politics of Belonging: Nationalism, Liberalism, and Pluralism*. Lanham: Lexington, 2004. Print.

Gans, Chaim. *The Limits of Nationalism*. Cambridge: Cambridge UP, 2003. Print.

Gellner, Ernest. *Nations and Nationalism*. Oxford: Blackwell, 1983. Print.

Hazony, Yoram. *The Virtue of Nationalism*. New York: Basic Books, 2018. Print.

Herb, Guntram H., and David H. Kaplan, eds. *Nations and Nationalism: A Global Historical Overview*. 4 Vols. Santa Barbara: ABC Clio, 2008. Print.

Hobsbawm, Eric. *Nations and Nationalism since 1780: Programme, Myth, Reality*. Cambridge: Cambridge UP, 1990. Print.

Hogan, Jackie. *Gender, Race and National Identity: Nations of Flesh and Blood*. London: Routledge, 2009. Print.

Joppke, Christian. *Neoliberal Nationalism: Immigration and the Rise of the Populist Right*. Cambridge: Cambridge UP, 2020. Print.

Kymlicka, Will, ed. *The Rights of Minority Cultures*. Oxford: Oxford UP, 1995. Print.

Miller, David. *On Nationality*. Oxford: Oxford UP, 1995. Print.

Miscevic, Nenad, ed. *Nationalism and Ethnic Conflict: Philosophical Perspectives*. La Salle: Open Court, 2000. Print.

Motyl, Alexander, ed. *Encyclopedia of Nationalism*. Vols. I and II. New York: Academic Press, 2001. Print.

Özkirimli, Umut. *Theories of Nationalism: A Critical Introduction*. London: Palgrave Macmillan, 2017. Print.

Smith, Anthony D. *National Identity*. Harmondsworth: Penguin, 1991. Print.

Spencer, Philip, and Howard Wollman. *Nationalism: A Critical Introduction*. London: Sage, 2002. Print.

Tagore, Rabindranath. *Nationalism*. New Delhi: Penguin Books India, 2009. Print.

Tamir, Yael. *Why Nationalism?* Princeton: Princeton UP, 2019. Print.

Thapar, Romila, A. G. Noorani, and Sadanand Menon. *On Nationalism*. New Delhi: Aleph Book Company, 2016. Print.